Aggression, Crime and International Security

Aggression, Crime and International Security examines the concept of aggression in international relations and how it has been dealt with by international law and collective security organisations.

This book analyses the evolution of the concept of aggression in international relations from World War I to the post-Rome Statute era. It charts the emergence of two competing visions of this notion: on the one hand, as a triggering mechanism for collective security enforcement among states, and, on the other, as an international crime giving rise to individual responsibility. The author argues that despite certain contemporary international trends suggesting a shift away from traditional, state-centric power structures towards a more cosmopolitan, globalised polity, the history of the concept of aggression demonstrates just how far away this is in reality. By examining aggression in theory and practice at the League of Nations, the Nuremberg and Tokyo Trials, the United Nations, the conference establishing the Rome Statute, and beyond, the book reveals the recurring moral, political and legal challenges this concept poses – challenges which continue to be at the forefront of thinking about international relations today.

This book will be of great interest to students of International Law, War Crimes, International Relations and Security Studies.

Page Wilson is a Senior Lecturer in the Department of International Affairs at the Royal Military Academy Sandhurst, UK. She has a PhD in International Relations from the London School of Economics and qualified as a solicitor in Melbourne, Australia.

Contemporary security studies
Series Editors: James Gow and Rachel Kerr
King's College London

This series focuses on new research across the spectrum of international peace and security, in an era where each year throws up multiple examples of conflicts that present new security challenges in the world around them.

NATO's Secret Armies
Operation Gladio and terrorism in Western Europe
Daniele Ganser

The US, NATO and Military Burden-sharing
Peter Kent Forster and Stephen J. Cimbala

Russian Governance in the Twenty-first Century
Geo-strategy, geopolitics and new governance
Irina Isakova

The Foreign Office and Finland 1938–1940
Diplomatic sideshow
Craig Gerrard

Rethinking the Nature of War
Edited by Isabelle Duyvesteyn and Jan Angstrom

Perception and Reality in the Modern Yugoslav Conflict
Myth, falsehood and deceit 1991–1995
Brendan O'Shea

The Political Economy of Peacebuilding in Post-Dayton Bosnia
Tim Donais

The Distracted Eagle
The rift between America and old Europe
Peter H. Merkl

The Iraq War
European perspectives on politics, strategy, and operations
Edited by Jan Hallenberg and Håkan Karlsson

Strategic Contest
Weapons proliferation and war in the greater Middle East
Richard L. Russell

Propaganda, the Press and Conflict
The Gulf War and Kosovo
David R. Willcox

Missile Defence
International, regional and national implications
Edited by Bertel Heurlin and Sten Rynning

The Political Road to War with Iraq
Bush, 9/11 and the drive to overthrow Saddam
Nick Ritchie and Paul Rogers

Bosnian Security after Dayton
New perspectives
Edited by Michael A. Innes

Kennedy, Johnson and NATO
Britain, America and the Dynamics of Alliance, 1962–68
Andrew Priest

Small Arms and Security
New emerging international norms
Denise Garcia

The United States and Europe
Beyond the neo-conservative divide?
Edited by John Baylis and Jon Roper

Russia, NATO and Cooperative Security
Bridging the gap
Lionel Ponsard

International Law and International Relations
Bridging theory and practice
Edited by Tom Biersteker, Peter Spiro, Chandra Lekha Sriram and Veronica Raffo

Deterring International Terrorism and Rogue States
US national security policy after 9/11
James H. Lebovic

Vietnam in Iraq
Tactics, lessons, legacies and ghosts
Edited by John Dumbrell and David Ryan

Understanding Victory and Defeat in Contemporary War
Edited by Jan Angstrom and Isabelle Duyvesteyn

Propaganda and Information Warfare in the Twenty-first Century
Altered images and deception operations
Scot Macdonald

Governance in Post-conflict Societies
Rebuilding fragile states
Edited by Derick W. Brinkerhoff

European Security in the Twenty-first Century
The challenge of multipolarity
Adrian Hyde-Price

Ethics, Technology and the American Way of War
Cruise missiles and US security policy
Reuben E. Brigety II

International Law and the Use of Armed Force
The UN charter and the major powers
Joel H. Westra

Disease and Security
Natural plagues and biological weapons in East Asia
Christian Enermark

Explaining War and Peace
Case studies and necessary condition counterfactuals
Jack Levy and Gary Goertz

War, Image and Legitimacy
Viewing contemporary conflict
James Gow and Milena Michalski

Security Strategies and American World Order
Lost power
Birthe Hansen, Peter Toft and Anders Wivel

War, Torture and Terrorism
Rethinking the rules of international security
Edited by Anthony F. Lang, Jr. and Amanda Russell Beattie

America and Iraq
Policy making, intervention and regional politics
Edited by David Ryan and Patrick Kiely

European Security in a Global Context
Internal and external dynamics
Edited by Thierry Tardy

Women and Political Violence
Female combatants in ethno-national conflict
Miranda H. Alison

Justice, Intervention and Force in International Relations
Reassessing just war theory in the 21st century
Kimberley A. Hudson

Clinton's Foreign Policy
Between the Bushes, 1992–2000
John Dumbrell

Aggression, Crime and International Security
Moral, political and legal dimensions of international relations
Page Wilson

Aggression, Crime and International Security

Moral, political and legal dimensions of international relations

Page Wilson

Routledge
Taylor & Francis Group

LONDON AND NEW YORK

First published 2009
by Routledge
2 Park Square, Milton Park, Abingdon, Oxon OX14 4RN

Simultaneously published in the USA and Canada
by Routledge
711 Third Avenue, New York, NY 10017

Routledge is an imprint of the Taylor & Francis Group, an informa business

First issued in paperback 2012

© 2009 Page Wilson

Typeset in Times by Wearset Ltd, Boldon, Tyne and Wear

British Library Cataloguing in Publication Data
A catalogue record for this book is available from the British Library

Library of Congress Cataloging in Publication Data
A catalog record for this book has been requested

ISBN13: 978-0-415-48524-1 (hbk)
ISBN13: 978-0-415-69156-7 (pbk)
ISBN13: 978-0-203-87737-1 (ebk)

Contents

Acknowledgements

There are many people I would like to thank for their contribution to the writing of this book. I am grateful to my PhD supervisor, Chris Brown, for his invaluable guidance through the doctoral process, for his insights into international relations as a field of academic inquiry, and, of course, for his helpful comments on my work to date. In addition, Peter Wilson provided useful feedback on a previous version of my chapter concerning the League of Nations. Early meetings with Gerry Simpson and Chris Greenwood assisted me in clarifying and strengthening the legal aspects of my planned scheme of work. Derek McDougall, who offered me the opportunity to teach at the University of Melbourne from 1999 to 2000, provided the catalyst for thinking seriously about undertaking doctoral studies, and since this time he has regularly and generously acted as a sounding-board for all matters academic and intellectual.

In 2004, I was fortunate to meet with Ben Ferencz, a former Nuremberg prosecutor and long-time advocate of strengthening resistance to aggression through law; I am grateful to him for providing a comprehensive explanation of the many difficult issues in this area, responding patiently to my questions, and offering access to many hard-to-find documents. I am appreciative of the support of the University of London's Central Research Fund towards my trip to New York for this purpose.

On a more personal note, I would like to thank Arnaud and his family for their ongoing support, kindness and understanding, particularly during my last doctoral year. Finally, I would like to extend an extra special thank you to my grandmother Rae, and my mother Mary-Louise, for being there throughout the many, many years of study which have culminated in this book. Their contribution has been my greatest source of strength throughout the doctoral process and indeed throughout my life.

PW
March 2009

Abbreviations

GA Res	General Assembly Resolution
HRW	Human Rights Watch
ICC	International Criminal Court
ICJ	International Court of Justice
ICTR	International Criminal Tribunal for Rwanda
ICTY	International Criminal Tribunal for Former Yugoslavia
ILC	International Law Commission
IMT	International Military Tribunal (Nuremberg)
IMTFE	International Military Tribunal for the Far East (Tokyo)
IST	Iraqi Special Tribunal, 2004–
P5	Permanent Five member states of the UN Security Council: China, France, Russia, United Kingdom, United States
SCAP	Supreme Commander of the Allied Powers
SC Res	Security Council Resolution
UK	United Kingdom
UN	United Nations
UNCIO	United Nations Conference on International Organisation
UNWCC	United Nations War Crimes Commission
US	United States
WGCA	Working Group on the Crime of Aggression

1 The concept of aggression in international relations

In the post-Cold War era, the role played by standards or rules regulating conduct both between and among states and individuals has received increased scrutiny. This is due, at least in part, to the proliferation of such rules resulting from the end of the superpower conflict and generally higher levels of cooperation among states that have marked this period. At the same time, growing interdependence among states – especially in the economic sphere – as part of broader globalisation processes has enmeshed many states in a web of diverse obligations covering an ever-flourishing range of activity. Thus, today, as a result of its membership of various international organisations, a state may find itself simultaneously obliged by a European Union directive to change its own domestic social legislation, prevailed upon by NATO to provide military assistance to a peacekeeping mission, the subject of a trade ruling by the WTO and under pressure to comply with a ruling of the UN Human Rights Committee – to name but a few examples. While it is true that membership of such organisations is voluntary – and therefore, formally, states are free to withdraw from or reject membership – in practice rejection is more and more difficult as issue areas become increasingly interlinked. Consequently, burgeoning interdependence means relations between states become more frequent and sustained, and the number of occasions upon which, for instance, state A is prepared to accept political concessions in one area on the condition that state B accepts economic concessions in another, also grows. Where interdependence among states is both deep and wide, the follow-on costs of rejecting a particular obligation are likely to be higher.

Like states, individuals have also found themselves subject to an expanding range of rules in recent years. While domestic standards for individual conduct are nothing new, these are now supplemented by a variety of regional and international rules. Thus, Europeans are bound by a whole host of EU technical standards governing areas such as construction, food supplements and health and safety. Under the ICC Statute, an individual may be prosecuted for genocide, war crimes and/or crimes against humanity where either their state of nationality or the state where the alleged crimes occurred is a state party to the Statute and is 'unwilling or incapable genuinely to carry out the investigation or prosecution'.[1] Even the highest national office-holders cannot automatically escape personal individual criminal responsibility: the House of Lords' decision in *Pinochet*[2] recognised that the principle of sovereign immunity is not without limits. The conduct of individuals as employees is also subject to constraint, as non-state actors such as corporations sign up to international standards regulating areas including financial reporting and labour conditions.[3] Online interactions also bring individuals within the remit of foreign and international norms as never before. As a consequence, a growing number of individuals find themselves at the centre of diverse regimes of obligation, with little guidance on how to reconcile different obligations, and where reconciliation is not possible, which can and should take priority.

This proliferation of obligations regulating the conduct of states and individuals has given rise to growing interest in the nature and *locus* of binding authority in international affairs. Drawing on the above examples, the pertinent questions thus become: What type of obligation (if any?) is being created when a corporation endorses a voluntary international standard, and how does this rule differ from a state's obligation to contribute under the terms of a military alliance? Is the former a moral obligation only and the latter a political and legal obligation? Or does each type of obligation contain within it moral, political and legal elements? Most significantly, who has competence to decide these questions, and what are the distinctions between political, legal and moral obligations in terms of consequences? These questions of authority, or ultimate decision-making or enforcement power in international affairs, are at the heart of the debate between two schools of thought in particular: cosmopolitanism and communitarianism. Generally speaking, cosmopolitans argue that universal standards applicable to humankind should take priority in international affairs, and that examples such as the current international human rights regime demonstrate a move in that direction. By contrast, communitarians contend that the 'community' is the main source of obligations, and that a plurality of communities exist worldwide. The cosmopolitan–communitarian debate will be discussed in greater detail below; it suffices at this point simply to acknowledge that while rules for states and individuals have multiplied exponentially in the current era, fundamental questions about the rule-makers, the nature of the obligations that are created and the basis of rule-making authority remain.

These key questions about rule-making in the international arena have emerged time and again in the context of efforts over the last ninety years to entrench and develop a rule prohibiting aggression. In order to achieve the goal of outlawing aggression, diplomats, lawyers and politicians alike have had to grapple first with the primary substantive issues raised by this concept – such as what aggression actually *is*, who is capable of committing it, and against whom it is committed. In the process of discussing these matters, however, secondary questions – including which body or bodies are the most appropriate for ruling that an aggression has occurred on a specific occasion, what the consequences of such a ruling are (related closely to the question of what the *purpose* of a rule banning aggression is), and the procedure for making such a ruling – have inevitably come to the fore. A reconsideration of the concept of aggression's role in international relations can therefore be expected to shed fresh light on the current theoretical revival of these latter normative questions.

Such reconsideration is also timely in light of the first review conference of the statute establishing the International Criminal Court, due to be held in 2010. Unlike genocide, war crimes and crimes against humanity, the crime of aggression occupies an uneasy position within the 1998 ICC Statute. Under article 5(2), the exercise of ICC jurisdiction over aggression was deferred until 'a provision is adopted ... defining the crime and setting out the conditions under which the Court shall exercise jurisdiction ...'.[4] The 2010 review conference will be the first opportunity for state parties to the Statute to reopen discussion of its provisions, and it is anticipated that the status of the crime of aggression will be one of the top review items. A renewed account of the long history of attempts to proscribe aggression will thus provide the necessary background against which these upcoming efforts may be contextualised and evaluated.

It is argued here that the role played by the concept of aggression in international relations demonstrates the ongoing significance of the state and the perennial constraints of cosmopolitan thought. While aspirational, ideal thinking has shaped and informed events at key moments of international affairs, it is also important to recognise the limitations of the cosmopolitan 'project' to date and to consider how a long-term lack of progress on vital issues threatens to undermine further those achievements that have been made. Thus, the concept of aggression provides an important case study of the tensions between cosmopolitan and communitarian thought in the practice of international relations and acts as a reminder of the significant challenges confronting cosmopolitans.

Before making this argument, however, it is first important to set out what we mean by the concept of aggression. As shall be demonstrated, much time and effort has been devoted to completing this task, with little success; nevertheless, it is possible to outline those features of the concept of aggression which are least controversial in order to reveal the parameters of this study and the assumptions upon which it is based. Following this, the cosmopolitan and communitarian schools of thought will be discussed, and how these schools underpin particular theories of aggression will be examined. This chapter will conclude by summarising the themes which will be developed throughout the book.

The concept of aggression: basic features

While the history of the concept of aggression in international relations – as revealed in the following pages – indicates just how highly contested the meaning of 'aggression' is, some fundamental characteristics of the notion can be identified which provide a general point of departure for this inquiry.

First and foremost, aggression is the ultimate universal negative value. Virtually all actors on the international stage agree that aggression is behaviour that is bad or wrong. This is demonstrated by the fact that no actors, in any circumstances, seek to identify themselves as an aggressor or champion their conduct in the name of aggression. Actors justify all sorts of acts – whether military, diplomatic, economic, or political, from threat of boycott to full-scale war – on diverse bases, including self-determination, humanitarian grounds, a miserable human rights record, national security and even receipt of some perceived insult, but never on account of their own aggression. In fact, essentially the only occasions upon which the concept of aggression makes headlines outside UN circles is by reference to the acts of *others*. Recent examples include Israeli actions in Gaza being described by the Hamas leadership as aggression,[5] North Korean nuclear posturing being justified as an attempt to deter the 'US threat of aggression',[6] and the UK Foreign Secretary declaring that 'Russia Will Not Benefit From its Aggression',[7] in relation to the crisis with Georgia of summer 2008. From this usage, it may be concluded that aggression is something that 'other' actors do, not 'us', whoever 'we' may be. The concept of aggression, at its crux, therefore assumes that a distinction between good and bad conduct is possible in international affairs, and on the basis of this assumption actors compete to ensure their conduct is viewed as being on the right side of this divide.

Distinguishing aggression from good or rightful conduct raises the question of the *purpose* of such distinction. Classifying behaviour as bad or wrong suggests an obligation to do something about it; otherwise it is not evident why one would bother with classification at all. However, the nature of the obligation created by a declaration that aggression has occurred is unclear – is it intended to trigger global law enforcement action against the aggressor? Is it intended to justify punishment of the aggressor and create a deterrent for others? Perhaps all of the above? While the concept of aggression seems to imply some duty to act in response, the type of response and the appropriate respondent are subject to significant contention.

A third point that can be made about the concept of aggression is that it must be committed by an aggressor, since 'behaviour' implies agency. In other words, aggression is the product of an agent's acts; the agent must *know* the behaviour contemplated is bad or wrong and must *intend* to do it. A mere international event leading to bad consequences – such as a tsunami – is not sufficient to amount to an aggression, because no agent capable of knowledge or forming an intention initiated it. Similarly, the act of funding a peaceful political opposition group that decides subsequently to divert this funding to paramilitaries, thereby triggering an interstate or civil war, cannot be categorised as an aggression, since there is nothing inherently bad or wrong in funding opposition groups, and the actor providing the funds could not have known what later decisions would be made. Of course, in circumstances where evidence suggests the funding provider did in fact know of the group's paramilitary associations, and the final destination of the funding, the answer might be different.

This third observation raises a related question: Who or what is the agent of aggression? The conventional answer to this question has been the state. However, the conviction of various individuals at the post-World War II Nuremberg and Tokyo trials for aggression, reference to the crime of aggression within the ICC Statute – the remit of which extends to individuals only[8] – as well as occasional statements made in UN Security Council resolutions[9] suggest that non-state groups and individuals are also capable of committing aggression.

Despite some expansion beyond the state in the range of actors capable of committing aggression, on the associated issue of who or what may be the target of aggression, the answer still seems to be the state only. The cited, recent instances above where 'aggression' has been named all claim a state – or, in the case of Gaza, a pseudo-state authority – as a target. Similarly, all individuals convicted of the crime of aggression at Nuremberg and Tokyo were prosecuted in relation to their contribution to the invasion, occupation, or annexation of one or more foreign states. While in theory it may be possible to commit an aggression against some other non-state collective entity, it seems necessary that any target of aggression enjoy some form of recognition and personality in its own right. Without such recognition and personality of the collective entity, it is difficult to see how aggression can be distinguished from acts committed against individuals such as genocide, crimes against humanity or war crimes, albeit on a massive scale. Given that traditionally, states have enjoyed the exclusive rights to international recognition and personality, it is unsurprising that they have been characterised as the victims of aggression to date. The concept of aggression therefore assumes that the damage caused by aggression is directed at, and borne by, the state or state-like authority, and is more than simply the sum of the ills resulting from that damage that are suffered by individuals of the victim state. Consequently, committing an aggression amounts to an attack upon the state and thus represents a particular type of political act which other conduct – as reprehensible as it may be – is not.

The final point that can be made about the concept of aggression concerns its substance. At minimum, aggression involves an international use of armed force, though it will be demonstrated that attempts have been made to extend the notion to encompass 'economic aggression' and, especially during the Cold War, 'ideological aggression'. It is the use of armed force across state frontiers which distinguishes aggression from domestic, political attacks upon the state, such as sedition, insurrection or a *coup d'état*. As regards the form an international use of armed force might take to qualify as aggression, this remains a highly controversial topic – beyond an overt war of conquest, where a state's leadership publicly declares its intentions to conquer a particular territory, and then sets about doing so,[10] there is very little consensus. In terms of the gravity of the international use of armed force required, the most severe and/or large-scale uses are most likely to be considered as aggression, while less serious instances, such as limited border clashes, may or may not be so considered. It seems that the very strong consensus surrounding aggression as a negative value breaks down quickly when considering in detail its constitutive elements.

Moving beyond this outline is fraught with challenges. However, the general picture created provides a framework through which the relevant literature may be compared and assessed. We shall now discuss how cosmopolitans and communitarians think about the nature of international obligations – such as those implied by the concept of aggression – and how these inform different theories of aggression.

The cosmopolitan 'project' and aggression

Before looking at cosmopolitan thought in detail, a caveat is necessary. Labelling various theorists as 'cosmopolitan' or 'communitarian' is a convenient classification system for the purposes of comparison. However, like most classification devices, the boundaries of each category are not set in stone, and variations within each exist. While generalisations are difficult, broad themes uniting each school can be identified, and it is to these that we now turn.

The rise of international organisations, non-state actors and their very active rule-making role in recent years has provided significant encouragement to cosmopolitans, who argue that every individual is of equal moral value and that this 'basic constitutive principle'[11] is, or should be, the cornerstone of global governance. Thus, cosmopolitans point to current developments such as the emergence of transnational civil society groups, the success of the EU, as well as the worldwide spread of human rights discourse, democracy and international law as evidence of a nascent global public sphere within which universal rights and universal justice prevail over other competing values reflecting particular cultural, religious, social, historical, ethnic, or economic perspectives. It is important to note that cosmopolitans are not by definition anti-state; most contemporary cosmopolitans view the state as a part – albeit a subordinate one – of a much broader movement towards an inclusive world of free and equal individuals, whose ability to participate in global decision-making processes is not determined simply by the relative power wielded by their state of nationality, but is channelled through multi-layered governance mechanisms.[12] Nevertheless, the main units of analysis with which cosmopolitans are primarily concerned are the individual on the one hand and global humankind on the other. These twin emphases in cosmopolitan thought clearly bear some relation to those of liberal political philosophy, and the former's focus on universal humanity resonates with the natural law tradition and may be traced back at least as far as Francisco de Vitoria and Francisco Suarez.[13] While cosmopolitan works have become increasingly prominent, two writers in particular will be highlighted here in order to further elaborate the cosmopolitan cause.

In his 2004 article, Daniele Archibugi identified and discussed a number of assumptions underpinning the 'cosmopolitan democracy project',[14] which provides more profound insight into some of the central concerns of cosmopolitanism:

1 Democracy should be conceived as a process, not a set of norms or procedures.
2 Democracy within states is hindered by a system of states in conflict.
3 Democratic states prefer peace, but domestic democracy does not necessarily generate a 'virtuous foreign policy'.[15]
4 Global democracy is more than the accomplishment of domestic democracy in every state.
5 The political independence of states is undermined by globalisation – as a consequence, state-based democracy is made less efficacious.
6 As regards an increasing and significant number of issue areas, the relevant 'stakeholders' communities'[16] do not by necessity correspond with territorial

divisions into states. Examples include environmental issues which are described as 'authentically global',[17] or transnational matters of importance to more limited communities, such as the impact of strategic decisions by a corporation on its global workforce.

7   Globalisation produces new social movements concerned with issues impacting upon other individuals and communities. These issues may be very remote in geographical and cultural terms from the movement's own political community.[18]

Examining the degree to which these assumptions reflect international affairs to date, Archibugi concludes that although some important successes towards democratisation at the intra-state level have been achieved, democratisation of the global system has been less successful. In particular, the absence of one institution crucial to global democracy is noted: a world parliament, which is described as 'an ancient and utopian proposition which has repeatedly re-emerged ... and which should today be at the core of global movements' campaigns'.[19] This observation builds towards a more general point about cosmopolitan democracy theory '[needing] to be more boldly integrated into a realistic transformation of society':[20]

> There is an increasing recognition of the political role of international public opinion ... and this in turn needs to be backed with a more solid theoretical background ... I would welcome campaigns that pursue realistic and limited objectives, but with a view to the desirable long-term world order.[21]

While acknowledging the current limitations of cosmopolitan democracy theory, however, Archibugi remains upbeat about achieving global democratisation that has proven elusive thus far:

> I do not expect to see the creation of a global democratic system as a result of a unique and massive transformation; quite the opposite. It is more feasible to take little steps forward yielding tangible results. Cosmopolitan democracy ... suggests a journey along which humanity could be brought closer together and whose final destination we can only guess.... *But I wish to point out that each step towards a cosmopolitan democracy is in itself a desirable objective.* For the first time in history, states with democratic regimes are concentrating an amount of economic, technological, military, ideological and political resources sufficient to ensure control over the entire world. Despite this, military force once again rules international politics. Cosmopolitan democracy will be nothing more than a miserable consolation if it proves incapable of restraining the consolidation of this increasingly hegemonic power.[22]

According to David Held, Archibugi's 'little steps' towards a cosmopolitan order have already taken place. Held cites developments such as the social chapter contained within the EU's Maastricht Treaty, the activism of transnational civil society groups at meetings including the Rio Conference on the Environment and the Beijing Conference on Women, as well as the diverse scope of UN activities to support the view that changes are taking place which 'point in the direction of establishing new modes of holding transnational power systems to account'.[23] As with Archibugi, for Held, globalisation creates 'circumstances of cosmopolitanism' which make necessary a shared framework of law and regulation. The existing, large bodies of EU law and international treaty law on topics such as human rights and the environment demonstrate that cosmopolitanism is not a utopian dream but is 'embedded in rule systems and institutions that have already transformed state sovereignty in many ways'.[24]

Held argues that a shift is discernible from a classical model of sovereignty in which ultimate decision-making and enforcement authority resides with the state to a liberal international model of sovereignty where the legitimacy of a state's authority is contingent upon its democratic credentials and human rights record.[25] Whereas states were the sole subjects of international law under the classical model, states now share this status with individuals and minority groups in the liberal international model of sovereignty. While various achievements are associated with this shift, the liberal international model of sovereignty also suffers from a number of weaknesses – among them the challenge of accomplishing global transparency, accountability and democracy, as well as the inadequacy of limited, intergovernmental institutions for resolving issues of global importance. It is in response to these deficiencies that Held envisages a cosmopolitan world order based on seven universally shared principles which lay the foundation for 'the protection and nurturing of each person's equal interest in the determination of the institutions that govern his or her life':

1   equal worth and dignity;
2   active agency;
3   personal responsibility and accountability;
4   consent;
5   reflexive deliberation and collective decision-making through voting procedures;
6   inclusiveness and subsidiarity;
7   avoidance of serious harm and the amelioration of urgent need.[26]

Of these, principles 1 to 3 are identified as 'constituting principles' establishing the basic organisational characteristics of a cosmopolitan world, and principles 4 to 6 represent the 'legitimating principles' which aim to transform individual or private acts into collective, public decisions and regimes. Importantly, the seventh guideline is classed as a prioritising principle creating 'a moral framework for focusing public policy on those who are most vulnerable',[27] though evidently this principle falls very far short of a decision-making procedure for resolving all political conflicts of priority. Held further acknowledges that there is no objective, set meaning for the seven principles he sets down but rather the specific meaning of these cosmopolitan universal principles is made manifest in 'situated discussions'.[28] He labels this process of application of principle and interpretation 'layered' cosmopolitanism.[29] Like Archibugi, Held recognises the need for 'the entrenchment of democratic public realms'[30] if cosmopolitan principles are to be institutionalised, and he goes on to identify the institutional requirements of cosmopolitanism from the legal, political, economic and cultural perspectives. These include:

1   An interconnected global legal framework, incorporating aspects of criminal, commercial and civil law.
2   'The entrenchment of cosmopolitan democratic law'.[31]
3   Submission to ICJ and ICC jurisdiction.
4   The creation of 'an effective, accountable, international military force for last-resort use of coercive power in defence of cosmopolitan law.[32]
5   'The celebration of difference, diversity and hybridity while learning how to "reason from the point of view of others" and mediate traditions'.[33]

Thus, cosmopolitans emphasise events which, according to them, are rewriting conventional, state-based rules about political participation and legal regulation, and advocate the worldwide spread of universal moral values reflecting human worth – such as global democracy.

Aggression as a trigger for collective security

It has already been suggested that aggression is the ultimate universal negative value. For this reason, its role in international relations makes a good test for cosmopolitan claims about the progress of their project. Certainly, cosmopolitan principles informed the writings of interwar lawyers such as Quincy Wright, who sought to make the concept of aggression operational as a trigger for collective security measures.

As self-help and the balance of power left many states unable to obtain even average levels of security 'at least without costs which will seriously impair their economic and social progress',[34] Wright argued for a system whereby the decision that aggression had taken place and the identification of the aggressor/s created a formal, legal basis for suppressing the wrongful action. In such a system, the nature and scope of the response made would be entirely at the discretion of the relevant authoritative decision-maker. Thus, the main purpose of this legal decision-making process was the timely initiation of international peace enforcement measures and the restoration of international order. For this to work, a rapid identification procedure for aggression was crucial, in light of the ability of most modern military forces to cause enormous destruction very quickly. This requirement also seemed to support the drafting of clear international guidelines as to what constituted an aggression, so that, where necessary, a fast international military response in protection of international order was made possible.

From the mid-1930s onward, Wright focused on producing these guidelines and devising a legal procedure for determining the existence of aggression. Wright insisted that a 'definition of aggression is clearly vital to this objective of eliminating war, both legally and materially'.[35] For him, therefore, aggression was as much a legal problem as a political one. On this basis, Wright defined aggression as a lack of compliance by a state with an international dispute settlement procedure:

> an aggressor is a state which is under an obligation not to resort to force, which is employing force against another state, and which refuses to accept an armistice proposed in accordance with a procedure which it has accepted to implement its no-force obligation.[36]

By relying on the 'observation of present facts',[37] rather than on an inquiry into the substance of the conflict and how, when and by whom hostilities commenced, Wright considered his own test of aggression as superior. However, there was a caveat: Wright's test must be applied quickly in order to ensure 'substantial justice'[38] is done between the parties. Hence, Wright concludes:

> 'A technical and automatic definition' of aggression, such as that here proposed, is 'necessary' and is not 'contrary to justice or impracticable', but it may appear to be so unless applied rapidly.... While it is believed the test of aggression here proposed conforms to the standards of practicability and justice, it cannot be applied satisfactorily without discretion. While it is as automatic as may be in the varied conditions of international relations, a test applicable with mechanical precision cannot be expected.[39]

Clearly, Wright's procedural approach, which avoids any adjudication of the merits of a conflict, assumes the universal, positive value of the international order violated by the conflict. However, unlike some present-day cosmopolitans, he rejected attempts to widen notions of international justice beyond this narrow frame. For him, aggression remained a rule of order, not a principle of justice, and:

> The effort to identify aggression with 'unjust war' ... is quite contrary to the conception of aggression used in League of Nations and United Nations discussions. It would mark the abandonment of the efforts to prevent hostilities by law....[40]

Subsequently, other lawyers have also turned their attention to the legal obligations and consequences of aggression, although most have demonstrated greater regard for the significant political challenges underpinning efforts to outlaw aggression than Wright ever did. Nevertheless, these lawyers support the aspirational element inherent to the cosmopolitan project and therefore also fall within this broad category.

For instance, in 1968 Bengt Broms took up Wright's self-imposed task of 'defining' aggression, producing a book outlining his own definition prescriptions, while deftly avoiding the preliminary political issue – namely, the purpose of, or rationale for, a definition of aggression.[41] However, as regards his prescriptions,

Broms does acknowledge to some extent the importance of political factors. Thus, for example, he noted that the main prerequisite of any definition of aggression was acceptance of it by the permanent members of the Security Council (P5). This justified a definition which strongly reflected the wishes of these states.[42] As a consequence, Broms advocated the limitation of the definition of aggression to armed activities, in light of substantial Anglo-American resistance to anything broader in scope at the time of writing. Despite this political restriction, Broms remained committed to the task of defining aggression:

> So much work has already been done by the various organs and suborgans of the United Nations, not to mention the organs and suborgans of the League of Nations, that to abandon this question now, when there is apparently a slightly better understanding among the members of the United Nations and especially among the permanent members of the Security Council, would be a great pity.[43]

Benjamin Ferencz, too, endorses efforts towards cosmopolitan aims, while recognising the political difficulties of achieving those aims. Aware of the significant pitfalls of Wright's approach, Ferencz cautions that 'unless change [to a particular international order] by non-violent means is made possible, change by violent means will be made inevitable'.[44] Until this time, 'defining' aggression is a hortatory, not legal, victory – on the condition that such a definition is followed by a broader movement towards the goals of social justice, peace and security. If, on the other hand, a definition of aggression was used exclusively by the great powers to entrench the status quo, it would be, at most, 'a very fragile shield'.[45] Thus, for Ferencz, the value of the General Assembly's Definition of Aggression[46] emanated less from its actual content and more as a symbol of a broad-based, international consensus not to accept passively ongoing warmongering. The fact that this definition emerged from the General Assembly, with its worldwide state representation and equality of voting, imbued it with a high level of legitimacy, hence further highlighting the strength of this consensus. Consequently, while Ferencz is quick to recognise the weaknesses inherent within GA Res 3314, he argues that it represented:

> a visible reaffirmation of the indomitable hope and determination that there must be legal limits to the use of armed force, and that the existing international anarchy must be brought to an end.[47]

Aggression as an international crime giving rise to individual responsibility

The grave and large-scale consequences of aggression, and the resulting strong and widespread perception of aggression as a negative value, suggest that peace enforcement measures are simply not sufficient to combat this event: measures designed to punish the aggressor and deter others from committing future aggressions are also needed. Given that aggression, if it is to mean something more than the total number of wrongs done to individuals in the course of an international use of armed force, must comprise an act against a state or state-like entity, it is at the international level that the issue of punishment arises. Whether it is states, individuals and/or non-state groups which are bound by the universal negative value of aggression is an important question for deciding who are the appropriate subjects of punishment. While punishment of aggressor states remained a topic of discussion into the UN period,[48] it is only in the context of individual responsibility of high-ranking state officials that the crime of aggression has ever been prosecuted. Individuals, rather than states, being held criminally responsible for breaches of universal standards reflects cosmopolitan principles, and the current revival in cosmopolitan thinking has helped keep the crime of aggression, conceived as an offence committed by individuals, a live issue today. Once again, it is international lawyers who have contributed the most to these efforts.

For the purposes of individual criminal responsibility, Ferencz argues that no further legal work 'defining' aggression is necessary. The Nuremberg Charter's statement establishing the 'planning, preparation, initiation and waging of a war of aggression' as a crime was applied appropriately by the members of the International Military Tribunal (IMT), and remains an appropriate statement of individual criminal responsibility for aggression today. However, Ferencz notes that it is no longer possible to assume that the Nuremberg approach to aggression attracts widespread international support, in light of the serious disagreements that emerged at the 1998 Rome Conference in response to the recommendations of the International Law Commission (ILC), which also argued that greater precision than that contained in the Nuremberg statement was unnecessary.[49]

Yoram Dinstein also upholds the Nuremberg statement as the foundation for prosecuting the crime of aggression, and makes the case in favour of individual responsibility for aggression most strongly:

> the criminality of aggressive war has entrenched itself in an impregnable position in contemporary international law. It is true that the full consequences of this criminality are not always agreed upon.... But it cannot be denied that responsibility for international crimes, as distinct from responsibility for ordinary breaches of international law, entails the punishment of individuals.[50]

As a practical matter, Dinstein contends that elements of the Nuremberg statement would be difficult to pinpoint as separate stages in a given set of facts, and thus prosecution would be unlikely where no war in fact resulted.[51] 'Participation in a common plan or conspiracy', also within article 6 of the Nuremberg Charter, would need to be proximate in terms of time to the allegedly criminal conduct, and for this reason it is similarly improbable that a conspiracy not leading to actual war would be prosecuted.

Dinstein relies on the principle from the *High Command* case[52] to assert that all 'individuals at the policy-making level' are possible perpetrators of the crime of aggression, and that the relevant test examines the actual power exercised at the time by the individual. While military figures might be the most likely perpetrators, cabinet members, other officials or even 'an influential person in public affairs or in the economy' might also be found guilty.[53] As a crime against peace is an ongoing offence, latecoming participants are as guilty as those who initiated the crime, and what follows the crime against peace in terms of military strategies or other acts makes no difference to the fact that a crime of peace has occurred. For a guilty verdict, it must be proven that the accused had the intention to commit a crime against peace.

Defences available to alleged perpetrators of a crime against peace include mistake of law, mistake of fact, duress and insanity; but claims of obedience to national law, superior orders,[54] or act of state will be held inadmissible. Finally, Dinstein notes how unsatisfactory it is that currently, individuals can only be prosecuted for a crime against peace by domestic judicial organs, given that the nature of the crime means domestic proceedings invariably lead to allegations of bias against the prosecuting body, resulting in impressions of 'victors' justice'. Like Held, Dinstein calls for the implementation of effective international legal enforcement measures to address this problem.

Communitarianism and aggression

Certain critics of cosmopolitanism argue that its focus on the individual on the one hand, and all humanity on the other, ignores the crucial role that diverse communities play in creating and upholding values. On this view, it is the precise mixture of social, cultural, religious, ethnic and other factors within a particular community that operates to make meaningful notions of authority, rights and justice. Indeed, some communitarians hold that 'no values can exist independently of communal identification'.[55] As a result, communitarians are sceptical about universal claims and emphasise cooperation among a plurality of communities in lieu of a global public sphere ripe for 'governance'.

If the 'community' is central to communitarian claims, then what is meant by this term? As communitarianism tends to be a label assigned to certain theorists rather than a category of self-identification, generalisations about communitarian thinking are difficult. Within the realm of normative international relations theory, the relevant value-creating community is usually equated with the state. However, this is not the case for communitarians within the field of political philosophy.[56] For instance, Charles Taylor's work suggests a form of community that is not synonymous with the state.[57] On the other hand, Michael Walzer's *Just and Unjust Wars* has been criticised for its strong statist qualities, though the author himself has acknowledged that he does not view the state by necessity as concomitant with the community.[58] Others argue that a more careful reading of the full range of Walzer's work indicates a clear division between the state and the community.[59] Walzer's writings are especially relevant in the context of this study; thus it is his work and the communitarian themes it develops which shall be emphasised here.

In *Just and Unjust Wars*, Walzer developed his own theory of aggression, based upon the following six assumptions:

1   The existence of an international society of autonomous states.
2   The international society's law creates membership rights, with priority given to the rights of 'territorial integrity and political sovereignty'.
3   Aggression comprises any use of force, or imminent threat thereof, by a state against the territorial integrity or political sovereignty of another, and represents criminal conduct.
4   Two types of combative response are justified by aggression: a war of self-defence by the victim state and law enforcement action by the victim state and any other member of international society.
5   War is justified exclusively by aggression.
6   After the aggressor has been repelled, it can also be subjected to punishment.[60]

Thus, according to Walzer, the concept of aggression rests upon foundations that are inherently communitarian: the lack of a world state ensures that territorial integrity and political sovereignty are the supreme rights within international society. However, at the same time, he suggests that these rights are themselves derived from the 'right of men and women to build a common life and risk their individual lives only when they freely choose to do so'[61] – a universal claim. In a similar nod to particularist and universal tensions in international affairs, he accepts that the rights of individuals can be acknowledged within international society – for instance, through state-endorsed UN agreements to this effect – yet they cannot be upheld without challenging the basic tenets of that society, namely the continued survival of the distinct, independent states.[62]

The universal and particular aspects of international values and the relationship between them are developed further in Walzer's 1994 work.[63] Here, Walzer argues that a community's cultural, political, religious and historical traditions create the conditions for the emergence of a detailed and profound 'moral maximalism', or a 'thick' understanding of values, rights and justice. From the diverse iterations of 'moral maximalism' worldwide reflecting each community's unique set of culturally, politically, religiously and historically located circumstances, a universal, 'moral minimalism' may be drawn, which amounts to a 'thin' understanding of what is meant by values, rights and justice. It is this 'thin' universal notion which enables individuals across various communities – despite very different life circumstances – to comprehend each other when they make normative demands.

As an example, Walzer uses the 1989 Czech 'Velvet Revolution', where people were marching with placards bearing the terms 'Truth' and 'Justice'. The resonance around the world generated by this event, and the support it attracted from others outside the immediate community – with their own, 'thick' understandings of what 'truth' and 'justice' meant – represented a 'universal moment', or an occasion upon which a 'thin' understanding of these terms is widely recognised and promoted. A 'universal moment' is described by Walzer as the 'product of historical conjuncture', and requires a trigger sufficiently powerful that the concerns of others outside the community take centre stage over local issues, if only for an instant. Such a trigger may be 'a personal or social crisis, or a political confrontation';[64] or it may be that '[w]hat unites us [across communities] at such a time is more the sense of a common enemy than the commitment to a common culture'.[65] If the latter is true, Walzer's 'universal moment' may not actually be universal at all, raising doubts as to whether his 'thin' moral framework can ever take priority over particular, 'thick' ones.[66]

The communitarian emphasis on the state or community as the most important source of values for individuals clearly dovetails with realism in international relations theory, which has criticised the 'legalistic–moralistic' approach that often accompanies cosmopolitan thought generally and underpins notions of aggression specifically. While Morgenthau recognised that a form of international morality had existed historically, he contended that the shift from aristocratic government towards democracy transformed international morality 'from a reality to a mere figure of speech'.[67] This transformation, in conjunction with the advent of nationalism, had the effect of 'weaken[ing], to the point of ineffectiveness, the universal, supranational moral rules of conduct, which before the age of nationalism had imposed a system – however precarious and wide-meshed – of limitations upon the foreign policies of individual nations'.[68] Democracy and nationalism had also 'greatly strengthened the tendency of individual nations to endow their particular national systems of ethics with universal validity'.[69] Thus, Morgenthau questioned the very foundations inherent to any notion of aggression: 'to know that nations are subject to the moral law is one thing, while to pretend to know with certainty what is good and evil in the relations among nations is quite another.'[70]

Picking up this theme, Julius Stone claimed that the concept of aggression acts simply as a tool of political warfare among states.[71] Although a lawyer himself, he flatly denied the 'need' for a definition of aggression for the purpose of maintaining international order effectively, and countered that, in fact, a definition of aggression is unviable, unacceptable to states and in any case undesirable, for a great number of reasons.

According to Stone, while each state continues to pursue its own vested interests, it will seek to protect these interests by branding as 'aggression' conduct which threatens them. The heterogeneity of states ensures that differences in both the substance and priority of their vested interests emerge. Thus, disagreement ensues as to what conduct constitutes aggression, as each state seeks to assert, and attract support for, a universally recognised concept which reflects its own preferences, in order to gain and maintain advantage over other states. As a result, the international debates about aggression directly reflect the rivalry between the most and least powerful states in international politics; they are not genuine attempts to reach by consensus an internationally authoritative definition of aggression to act as the triggering mechanism in a fully functional collective security system. Consequently, in Stone's view, the real standards used by states to evaluate the various draft definitions of aggression are:

1   whether the proposed definition would stigmatise as aggression, action which that state may in some yet unforeseen but not unforeseeable future circumstances feel justified and even compelled to take;
2   whether the indirect effect of the definition is such as to grant an excessive licence for illegal and predatory activities by other states, by condemning as 'aggression' the only kind of vindication of violated rights that may in fact be available.[72]

The relatively high level of uncertainty in the international arena over the longer term means that states have a strong incentive to safeguard their freedom of action by ensuring maximum flexibility for themselves in any internationally recognised definition of aggression. As a result, draft 'definitions' of aggression merely preserve within their own terms differences of views among states. This allows sufficient ambiguity of language that political arguments about aggression can continue to be fought under the cloak of legal conflicts of interpretation. Thus, states remain free to unilaterally accuse each other of aggression, which they usually do in an attempt to harness the emotive value of this term[73] and gain political support for their cause both domestically and abroad. Just as Morgenthau had dismissed modern references to international morality as a 'figure of speech', Stone described GA Res 3314 as a 'verbal tour de force', rather than 'a miraculous conversion of strategic political and economic conflicts into a harmonious consensus'.[74]

In support of his argument, Stone also noted the institutional limitations of international law: 'the international community lacks any collective means of vindication of violated legal rights, as well as any collective means of legislative adjustment of new conflicting claims, or even of existing legal rights.'[75] Without addressing these constraints, Stone stressed that an internationally endorsed definition of aggression would protect indefinitely existing injustices from redress. Such a definition could not be expected to perform tasks normally undertaken at the domestic level by comprehensive and sophisticated bodies of constitutional and criminal law, simply because these have not sufficiently developed in the international sphere.[76] In addition, Stone remained sceptical about aggression as an international crime.[77]

Further developing Stone's argument in relation to the crime of aggression, Jovan Babic contends that the crime of aggression amounts to a crime against defeat, and thus its nature is political, not legal or moral.[78] To him, the cost of incorporating the concept of aggression into international law is the loss of the concept of war, which is unwarranted in the absence of a world state.[79] In Babic's view, the concept of aggression reduces war to a type of police measure, with the moral correctness or incorrectness of each side already decided before military action takes place; Babic refers to this as the 'right of victory'.[80] By contrast, the traditional rules of warfare dictate that adversaries entering war must accept the outcome as just. The only basis in support of a 'right of victory' is naked power, and thus the subjective and prior determination of which side is entitled to the right of victory – necessarily assumed by the introduction of the concept of aggression into international law – ensures that crimes against peace remain a political tool used by the powerful, without moral or legal resonance.[81]

Similarly, Constantine Antonopoulos argues that 'aggression' – conceived as something more than just a synonym for unlawful use of force – is without foundation. While agreeing with Ferencz and Dinstein that, for the purposes of international criminal law, the Nuremberg statement of the crime of aggression is sufficient, Antonopoulos limits the usefulness of 'aggression' to a basic classification device only, not as a separate notion in and of itself:

> What really matters is the unlawfulness of the use of force and its magnitude, not by reference to an abstract concept of aggression, but to fact and legal evaluation on the basis of the current state of the law regarding the use of force by states. This is possible only if aggression is viewed as a generic term connoting unlawful use of force, and not as an abstract concept having a life of its own, which presupposes by definition the unlawfulness of a use of force as if every controversy surrounding the use of force by states has been resolved.[82]

Like Ferencz, Antonopoulos recognises however that states continue to pursue a 'definition' of aggression in an international criminal law context – as confirmed by the wording of article 5(2) of the Rome Statute. He explains that this preoccupation with defining aggression delays further the possibility of future prosecution of the crime of aggression, and serves the purpose of obscuring from superficial view the very real hesitancy of states to subject to judicial inquiry their resorts to interstate force.[83] Therefore, according to Antonopoulos, the crucial requirement for the purpose of prosecuting an alleged crime of aggression is a decision as to whether or not the use of force in question is lawful, not a definition of aggression beyond that which appears in the Nuremberg Charter. Unfortunately, however, there are some serious difficulties with this line of argument.[84]

Conclusion – aggression: moral anathema, political problem, legal solution?

Recent globalising trends, such as the rise of non-state actors, have led to fresh consideration of the basis and sources of authority and rule-making in international relations, which has brought into question the ongoing significance of the state. The cosmopolitan–communitarian debate which has emerged in international theory reveals two different ways of approaching these issues. On the one hand, cosmopolitans argue that such trends are proof of an emergent global political sphere founded on the universal, moral equality of all individuals where the state is just one among many actors on the world stage. On the other, communitarians contend that the state – to the extent that it qualifies as a 'community' – remains prominent, as it is only through the particular cultural, ethnic, religious and historical orientations of the community in question that values can be made meaningful for individual members of that community. In particular, there are two key issues raised by the cosmopolitan and communitarian theorists discussed here which are worth noting. The first concerns the significance of current trends collectively referred to as 'globalisation': is the cosmopolitan camp correct in asserting that these developments represent positive progress towards a world polity characterised by global democracy, or are we simply experiencing a Walzerian 'universal moment'? The second issue concerns the importance of truly global institutions – such as a world parliament, effective law enforcement mechanisms and a compulsory judicial process. Is Archibugi's claim about the positive value per se of 'each step towards a cosmopolitan democracy' correct, or are communitarians right to prioritise the impact of the absence of these institutions – namely, the unavailability of worldwide, authoritative mechanisms for peaceful change – as a major limiting factor on cosmopolitan goals?

As perhaps the most universally negative value in international relations, the concept of aggression is a topic well suited to testing out these claims. The argument was introduced that this study of the concept of aggression reveals both cosmopolitan and communitarian impulses, though ultimately it highlights the significant, long-term obstacles challenging further cosmopolitan progress. Having identified the basic features of aggression, various theories of aggression were then discussed and compared. Approaches to the concept of aggression diverged according to purpose. Thus, in relation to aggression as a collective security trigger, we saw that lawyers Wright and Broms framed the issue squarely in terms of 'defining' aggression, with very limited recognition of the major, unresolved political issues of international organisation outlined above that such a task assumed. While Ferencz, also a lawyer, acknowledged more openly the political issues raised by the concept of aggression yet upheld its moral contribution, it is Walzer and Stone who more fully developed the view that it is the politics, not the law, of aggression which poses the overwhelming hurdle to the concept of aggression playing a greater role in peace enforcement.

In terms of aggression as an international crime, both Ferencz and Dinstein argued in favour of using the Nuremberg statement of aggression; fixation at the 1998 Rome Conference on 'defining' aggression further was considered by both to be superfluous. Antonopoulos explained this fixation by reference to political preferences, noting states' reluctance to submit their uses of interstate force to judicial consideration. For him, aggression was the same name as an unlawful use of force. By contrast, Dinstein insisted on the 'impregnable position' of the crime of aggression in international law, while Babic argued that it comprised a crime against defeat and was therefore simply a political tool for the most powerful to wield in pursuit of their own interests. It is these battles among the purpose, significance and consequences of the concept of aggression which shall be analysed in the following pages with a view to revealing new insight into the nature of rules and rule-making in present-day international relations.

2 Aggression in the post-World War I settlement

The disaster of World War I led initially to profound disenchantment with traditional means of international organisation based on balance-of-power considerations. Alternative methods for managing international affairs were now sought, and it was this impetus which motivated the emergence of cosmopolitan thinking in this field, founded chiefly upon the value of equality and the existence of universal moral principles. During this period of cosmopolitan popularity, new ideas were promoted explicitly and unapologetically by reference to moral arguments; the worlds of politics and law were considered secondary, and only relevant to the extent that they were the means through which the identified moral aims would be achieved. On this view, the experience of World War I had proven that approaches to the problems of international organisation which began from the political and legal standpoint did not work, and that some other, higher foundation was required. It was on the basis of this cosmopolitan mandate that Woodrow Wilson crafted his Fourteen Points for international order in 1918, and that ideas such as self-determination, global disarmament and aggression started to gain currency.

In this chapter, it will be demonstrated that Wilson's charismatic leadership and the support he enjoyed from international public opinion for his cosmopolitan dream of establishing a global collective security system underpinned by universal moral values were important influences in shaping the post-World War I settlement. However, it will also be argued that this vision was not shared by some within the Wilson administration; by foreign governments, which were still smarting from their own experience of World War I; or by the US Senate. The impact of this opposition in the drafting and ratification of the League Covenant, article 231 of the Treaty of Versailles concerning reparations, and articles 227–230 concerning punishment of the Kaiser and other German nationals overwhelmed Wilson's original goal of a security organisation incorporating a positive, mutual, cast-iron obligation among signatories to defend each other against aggression. Instead, aggression played a dual role in the post-World War I settlement – on the one hand, forming the central triggering mechanism for the new collective security system, while at the same time justifying punitive measures against Germany imposed according to old-style rules of power politics. The result was the creation and operation of a post-World War I international security system which reflected the narrow self-interest of the major European powers to a far greater extent than Wilson's cosmopolitan aspirations.

Aggression and the League of Nations: article 10 of the Covenant

Pre-Paris drafts: 1914–1918

The concept of aggression originated at the US presidential level in relation to efforts to organise international politics in the post-World War I period according to a collective security model. In December 1914, Colonel House, confidant of President Wilson, approached him with a proposal for an agreement between the US and the states of South America, the substance of which was summarised by the President as follows:

> 1st. Mutual guarantees of political independence under republican form of government and mutual guarantees of territorial integrity.
>
> 2nd. Mutual agreements that the Government of each of the contracting parties acquire complete control within its jurisdiction of the manufacture and sale of munitions of war.[1]

House argued that, if successful, this type of accord could also act as a model for the nations of Europe once the war ended. In a precursor to the present-day cosmopolitan tendency to extrapolate from Europe to the world, Wilson quickly saw the potential of House's proposal for securing not just a European peace but a global one. During his re-election campaign of 1916, Wilson announced that 'the world has a right to be free from every disturbance of its peace that has its origins in aggression and disregard of the rights of peoples and nations'.[2] In January 1918, Wilson publicised his plan for postwar settlement: the Fourteen Points. It was the last of these points which captured Wilson's vision of postwar international security:

> 14. The formation of a general association of nations under specific covenants for the purpose of affording mutual guarantees of political independence and territorial integrity for large and small states alike.[3]

Thus, with states committing themselves to act jointly in defence of one another's political independence and territorial integrity, war could be averted and the old *realpolitik* system overcome. This approach rested on the assumption that all participants accepted peace – and the particular distribution of power upon which it was made manifest – as a moral value. This shared moral outlook meant that challenges to peace would be readily identifiable by all participants, who would collectively mount a full, final and punitive response. Of course, for a security system in which peace was ascribed moral value to work, some method of peaceful change would have to be thought of and agreed upon. Having established the basic moral obligation underpinning his collective security system, it was the peaceful change mechanism which Wilson then focused upon in the lead-up to the Paris Peace Conference.

However, Wilson's desire for a collective security system was not universally embraced among his American advisers. From his Fourteen Points speech up until his arrival in Paris almost a year later, Wilson's own, verbose version of what was to become article 10 of the League Covenant – the crux of the new collective security system – had not changed:

> The Contracting Powers unite in guaranteeing to each other political independence and territorial integrity; but it is understood between them that such territorial readjustments, if any, as may in the future become necessary by reason of changes in present racial conditions and aspirations or present social and political relationships, pursuant to the principle of self-determination, and also such territorial readjustments as may in the judgment of three-fourths of the Delegates be demanded by the welfare and manifest interest of the peoples concerned, may be effected if agreeable to those peoples; and that territorial changes may in equity involve material compensation. The Contracting Powers accept without reservation the principle that the peace of the world is superior in importance to every question of political jurisdiction or boundary.[4]

The many difficulties raised by such a detailed and unconventional provision establishing not only the positive obligation of states to act in particular circumstances, but also incorporating the seeds of a peaceful change mechanism, were not lost on some of those within Wilson's government. Robert Lansing, Secretary of State, urged Wilson on 7 January 1919 to adopt a negative form of guarantee, arguing that most states favoured an agreement of 'self-denying character'[5] rather than binding themselves to a vague but obligatory duty to act in the future. He also noted that anti-League interests would exploit a positive guarantee, especially in the US, by questioning its consistency with the US Constitution's allocation of war-making powers, the Monroe Doctrine and the traditional American foreign policy of isolationism, thus helping to undermine American support for the League. David Hunter Miller, Legal Advisor to the American Peace Commission, initially backed Lansing's view, but became more apathetic as time passed, probably in response to Wilson's insistence on positive guarantees.[6]

It was against this background of discussions that by 20 January 1919, Wilson had incorporated the words 'as against external aggression' into the second line of his draft article, after the words 'territorial integrity', on the suggestion of General Tasker Bliss. From Bliss' military perspective, it was important to clarify the nature of the guarantees being entered into, and more specifically to stipulate that member obligations extended to aggression from non-domestic sources only. Wilson himself also recognised the necessity of preserving the rights of each people within a state to revolt against their own government,[7] and hence he included the Bliss amendment.

It is important to note that Wilson's focus was to create a living institution with the scope to address all international threats to peace; he placed little value on the consideration of legal technicalities, and therefore concerns about the ambiguity of the meaning of 'aggression' or the very wide scope of the obligations being created were of little consequence to him.[8] From Wilson's perspective, an international system that recognised the moral value of peace would have no difficulty recognising aggression in practice, and unlike narrower terms such as 'armed attack' or 'armed hostilities', 'aggression' was sufficiently flexible to move with the times, capturing innovative ways of destroying a state's political independence or territorial integrity. As a Covenant term, 'aggression' had the added advantage of currency in everyday language, important to Wilson for a number of reasons. First, it reflected his high level of popularity among peoples worldwide, and Wilson's eagerness to achieve a 'people's peace'.[9] Second, its incorporation at the heart of the Covenant helped to communicate reassurance to the public that its hopes for a new international security system to prevent another world war had been accomplished. Third, identifying 'aggression' as the main target of League action acted as an invitation to the public to participate in world affairs: it brought the burgeoning, political watchdog power exercised by public opinion to bear upon one of the most prized and jealously guarded decision-making powers traditionally reserved to a tiny minority within the realm of high politics.[10]

Since the Fourteen Points speech, Britain too had been drafting plans for implementing Wilson's goal. The Phillimore Plan of March 1918,[11] the Smuts Plan of December 1918[12] and the Cecil Plan of 14 January 1919[13] all reflected the British preference for a negatively framed guarantee: namely, a promise by League members *not* to start a war: (1) without first submitting the dispute to the prescribed settlement procedure, and (2) against any member that complied with the result of this procedure. Only in the event that a member breached this undertaking did the other states accept the active obligation to take all measures appropriate for restraining that member. The situation where the procedure produced no result was left open, and thus presumably the path to war also. This approach was a significant departure from the Wilsonian preference for a system founded upon positive obligations, and remained a source of tension between the British and American delegations from the commencement of negotiations in Paris onward.

In the face of Wilson's insistence that a positive duty to tackle aggression form the crux of the League system, it is not surprising that Britain eventually changed strategy and released a new proposal, replacing Wilson's guarantees with the undertaking:

> to respect the territorial integrity of all States members of the League, and to protect them from foreign aggression, and they agree to prevent any attempts by other States forcibly to alter the territorial settlement existing at the date of, or established by, the present treaties of peace.[14]

A few days later, Miller was sent to meet with Cecil in order to agree to a joint Anglo-American draft, which produced in its first sentence virtually the first part of what became article 10: 'The High Contracting Powers undertake to respect and preserve as against external aggression the territorial integrity and existing political independence of all States members of the League.'[15] The rest of the provision from this draft, which attempted to reconcile with this duty the issues of self-determination and peaceful change, was later abandoned.[16] This sentence from the Cecil–Miller draft was later incorporated into the Hurst[17]–Miller draft of 1 February 1919, which was subsequently chosen as the basis upon which discussions of the League of Nations Commission would occur.[18] Hence, prior to Paris, Wilson's vision of states solemnly undertaking positive, moral obligations to combat aggression remained largely intact.

The Paris peace negotiations, 18 January 1919 to 1921 January 1920

British unease with the radical Wilsonian vision of combating every aggression affecting the territorial integrity or political independence of League members did not wane at Paris. Although Cecil's own draft of 20 January referred to 'aggression', it is evident that its meaning continued to worry him deeply throughout the Commission's discussions. Miller reported that Cecil believed that the article 10 obligation extended to war 'if it means anything', and 'that things are being put in [to article 10] which cannot be carried out literally and in all respects'.[19] In fact, according to Miller, Cecil still opposed creating positive obligations in principle, and wished article 10 as drafted to be struck out entirely.[20] Britain was supported in this view by Canada and Australia, both of which feared greatly being dragged into another European war.[21]

However, knowing that complete abolition of the article was a political impossibility, Cecil settled for proposing, on behalf of Britain, the omission of 'and preserve as against external aggression' from the text, in an attempt to limit the scope of the obligation being undertaken. To abide by the minimal, vague requirement to *respect* the political independence and territorial integrity of members was one thing; to agree to *preserve* these *against external aggression* – an explicit, active, open-ended duty – was quite another. In light of Britain's status as a great power, it was aware that the cost of any collective anti-aggression response would fall disproportionately on its shoulders, and hence it was loath to commit itself to a broad-ranging obligation to act in uncertain and potentially unforeseeable future conditions. When it became evident that Britain would not achieve its proposed amendment, Cecil later sought to further qualify article 10 by suggesting the addition of a clause permitting the intermittent revision of treaties – an attempt to address the thorny issue of peaceful change. However, Cecil later conceded that this would not only undermine the duty to preserve, but also the basic 'respect' obligation; hence the peaceful change provision was incorporated elsewhere in the Covenant.[22]

By contrast, France proposed to widen the obligation of state parties to act in relation to *all* external aggression by omitting article 10's reference to territorial integrity and existing political independence. The development of article 10 thus far was viewed by France as much too weak, and it fought hard for a more powerful League. According to the French view, this League would include an international general staff to consider military and naval questions, with a rapid reaction force at its disposal comprising the armed forces of members. In light of France's experience of World War I, it sought from the Covenant the very strongest and most extensive guarantees possible, especially if the League was meant to supersede alliances as the traditional means of regulating the balance of power, in accordance with Wilsonian views. Failing the achievement of ironclad security guarantees in the League Covenant, France would have preferred to abandon the League altogether and return to conventional security measures employed at the conclusion of wars: namely, the imposition of a punitive peace on the vanquished, and a new round of alliance-building.[23]

The American position was predictable. Wilson strongly supported collective security, maintaining the importance of article 10 on the basis that 'there must be a provision that we mean business and not only discussion. This idea, not necessarily these words, is the key to the whole Covenant.'[24] He wanted to ensure that the League, from its commencement, was 'more than an influential debating society'.[25] To overcome the divergence between the expansive French approach to the League and the conservative British approach, Wilson suggested the addition of the second part of article 10: 'In case of any such aggression the Executive Council shall advise the plan and the means by which this obligation shall be fulfilled.' This reassured the British that the Council – on which Britain would hold a permanent seat – would in practice control League responses to any alleged aggression, thus qualifying to a significant extent the broad, abstract and positive undertaking Wilson required. This addition also carried implications of the institutionalisation of international military decision-making and cooperation which the French favoured, and for these reasons the suggestion was acceptable to both Britain and France, and thus was adopted.[26]

The remaining drafting changes were largely cosmetic. Thus, by 14 February 1919, the day Wilson left Europe to consult members of the legislative bodies in the US about the Covenant, article 10 read:

> The High Contracting Parties undertake to respect and preserve as against external aggression the territorial integrity and existing political independence of all States members of the League. In case of any such aggression or in case of any threat or danger of such aggression the Executive Council shall advise upon the means by which this obligation shall be fulfilled.[27]

Although discussions about article 10 continued on Wilson's return to Europe on 14 March, it is largely this text which was finally adopted into the Treaty of Versailles and agreed by the Allied and Associated Powers and Germany on 28 June 1919. Although the wording of this provision reveals a strong cosmopolitan influence, it is also evident that throughout the Paris negotiations the drafting of the 'guarantee' against aggression provoked significant resistance, derived from calculations of individual self-interest by the major European states, having regard to their own historical, cultural and political preferences in the aftermath of devastating conflict.

Wilson, article 10 and the fight for ratification

The significance and operation of article 10 were central in the battle to secure US ratification of the Treaty of Versailles. Confusion reigned over the article; however, once the status of the Monroe Doctrine with respect to the Covenant had been clarified,[28] two issues remained: (1) the interrelationship between the Covenant and the war-making power of Congress; and (2) the degree to which article 10 froze the 1919 political and territorial status quo, endorsing it with uniform legitimacy worldwide.

In response to the first concern, Wilson emphasised the 'new role and ... new responsibility'[29] of the US created out of World War I, and the moral character of article 10. 'All the ideals of American history'[30] militated against the US continuing in its isolationist foreign policy. Wilson reaffirmed to the Senate Foreign Relations Committee on 19 August 1919 that in the event of an external aggression, the US retained veto power over any decision by the Council to advise members as to their obligations. Thus, article 10 was significant for reasons of morality: it formed 'a very grave and solemn moral obligation', but not a legal one, and hence was 'binding in conscience only, not in law'.[31] On questioning, Wilson reiterated that the article represented 'an attitude of comradeship and protection among the members of the League, which in its very nature is moral and not legal'.[32] According to Wilson, if an obvious breach of article 10 occurred, such as an uncontested invasion, the only legal duty which would arise on the part of a member would be to apply the 'automatic punishments of the Covenant'.[33] There would be no immediate legal obligation to wage war, though Wilson conceded, depending on the circumstances, there might be 'a very strong moral obligation'.[34] Wilson's efforts to focus on the moral value of article 10 and play down its legal effect did not impress the Committee on Foreign Relations, which stipulated in its report to the Senate:

> Under no circumstances must there be any legal or moral obligation upon the United States to enter into war or to send its army and navy abroad or without the unfettered action of Congress to impose economic boycotts on other countries ... nor can any opportunity of charging the United States with bad faith be permitted....[35]

In relation to the reverse situation – the power of the League to curb unilateral US action – Wilson was more realistic: the League would, to a certain extent, infringe the sovereignty of the US, but the requirement that League decisions be unanimous meant the US could prevent any action being taken against itself. In any case, the Council only had the power to advise; it was up to individual states to decide whether or how to implement Council decisions. Thus, US actions would in all likelihood remain free from interference. However, the mere possibility of interference from non-American sources in US foreign affairs was seized upon by staunch opponents of the League, such as Senator Henry Cabot Lodge, and exploited to great effect.[36]

The second concern also generated much public debate. Some viewed article 10 as cementing for all time the mistakes contained in the peace treaty, thereby requiring the US to guarantee indefinitely an unjust and unstable settlement.[37] Certain commentators also pointed out the inconsistency between the new rules accepted as the *modus operandi* of the League, and the way in which the post-World War I peace settlement itself had been achieved via recourse to old-style diplomacy.[38] In defence of the article, Wilson noted the protection it offered to small states, and the restraints it placed on the more powerful. Without article 10,

> we have guaranteed that any imperialistic enterprise may revive, we have guaranteed that there is no barrier to the ambition of nations [including the United States] that have the power to dominate, we have abdicated the whole position of right and substituted the principle of might.[39]

Wilson's responses to the concerns raised in relation to article 10 did nothing to assuage his detractors. Article 10 remained their main target of criticism, and played a leading role in the Senate's rejection of the Covenant, and consequently also the Treaty of Versailles, on 19 November 1919.[40] Thus, despite the incorporation into the Covenant of concessions to narrowly framed self-interest on the part of the European powers – which had already circumscribed Wilson's much broader moral aims – the US Senate remained suspicious of the political and legal consequences flowing from the codification of supposed moral duties supported on cosmopolitan grounds. Even this more modest version of cosmopolitanism was too much for the US Senate, and as a result, the League was robbed of its most powerful potential ally.

Aggression and the end of World War I: article 231 of the Treaty of Versailles

Tensions between a collective security model invoking apparently moral principles and what 'security' meant to different states individually were especially evident in the reparations provisions of the Treaty of Versailles. That Germany had to pay something to fix the damage resulting from four years of industrialised warfare was beyond question, even to the Germans themselves. However, the divergence in Allied views on what this liability entailed in practical terms was so profound that it threatened to destroy altogether Allied cooperation in the peacemaking process. Despite Wilson's warning to delegates at the Peace Conference 'that it was impossible with one foot in the Old Order and the other in the New to arrive anywhere', this conflict remained.[41] It was in these circumstances that a compromise was brokered, with the concept of aggression being used to justify the wholesale assignment of moral responsibility for World

War I to Germany, and consequently, an accompanying degree of economic responsibility.

Possibly the most intense argument among the Allies concerned whether Germany should be compelled to pay reparations for civilian damage, or an indemnity, which would include reparations and a portion of the Allies' war costs. Informed by both legal advice and League aspirations, the American view favoured reparations only: the US interpretation of the pre-armistice agreement of 5 November 1918 signed between the Allies and Germany precluded compensation for anything other than civilian damage. Indeed, Wilson argued in response to the inclusion of war costs that it 'is clearly inconsistent with what we deliberately led the enemy to expect and cannot now honorably alter simply because we have the power'.[42]

However, Britain, France and their associated allies had other ideas, which reflected their own bitter experiences of World War I and their desire to 'make Germany pay'. This was evident from the pre-Armistice agreement onward, when Britain suggested that reference to German 'invasion' should be replaced by 'aggression', so that Britain, as an uninvaded ally, might secure its own compensation claim, as well as that of its Dominions.[43] Despite the terms of this earlier agreement limiting German liability to civilian damage, Britain, and every other non-American delegation to the Peace Conference, promptly submitted a claim for the reimbursement of all their war costs.[44] Britain was under particular pressure to do so: the Prime Minister, David Lloyd George, had just been re-elected on a platform which had exploited very successfully the desire of the British public and some newspaper owners to enforce a punitive settlement on Germany.[45] In addition, the inflammatory remarks of Australian Prime Minister Billy Hughes, who insisted upon an indemnity, added to the pressure on Lloyd George to push for the recompense of war costs in full. Once Lloyd George adopted this view at the Conference, public expectations in Britain were raised even higher, placing the Prime Minister in a very difficult position when it became clear that Britain would receive nowhere near her entire war costs in repayment, which exceeded those of France.[46]

Only France was more adamant than Britain that Germany must repay on the basis of an indemnity policy. Having experienced the most direct damage during the war,[47] and still feeling vulnerable, the French had an obvious interest in ensuring that the payment of reparations was sufficiently onerous to keep Germany economically weak for some time. It was also convenient for France to support the maximum reimbursement, even in the knowledge that Germany would not be able to pay it, in the hope of forcing the other Allies to shoulder some of the burden. France favoured the continuation of economic cooperation among the Allies in peacetime and saw this strategy as a way of getting its wish.[48]

By the time of Wilson's departure from Europe on 14 February 1919, it was evident that no consensus as to the final figure Germany should pay would be reached among the great powers. Whereas the US suggested the total sum should be £4.4 billion, Britain argued for £24 billion and France preferred £44 billion.[49] Of course, further exacerbating the difficulty of determining an amount was the fact that at the time of these negotiations, there was simply no way of knowing accurately (1) the extent and value of the damage caused by Germany; and (2) the capacity of Germany to pay for it.[50] The fear of potential consequences if the figure set for repayment by Germany was either too low or too high also played on the minds of the Allies, and influenced their numbers accordingly.

The solution to this impasse was crafted by John Foster Dulles of the American delegation. His idea was to draft a provision stating Germany's responsibility in theory for the whole cost of the war, but reducing its actual liability to an amount that it was able to pay. Thus, similarly to the way in which Wilson would later seek to convince the US Senate of the distinction between moral and legal obligations created in article 10 of the Covenant, in relation to the reparations provision, Germany's obligations were also neatly separated into moral and legal categories. Dulles' proposal was readily supported by Lloyd George, and article 231 was drawn up and subsequently approved on 7 April as follows:

> Article 231. The Allied and Associated Governments affirm and Germany accepts the responsibility of Germany and her allies for causing all the damage to which the Allied and Associated Governments and their nationals have been subjected as a consequence of the war imposed upon them by the aggression of Germany and her allies.[51]

Thus, it was the labelling of Germany's conduct in World War I as aggression – the same term used to describe the target conduct and triggering mechanism of the new League system – that justified the punitive measures imposed on Germany by the Allies as part of the peace agreement. While this move overcame the immediate diplomatic bottleneck among the Allies, the topic of reparations remained difficult over the longer term.[52]

German reaction to the Treaty of Versailles' reparations provisions was very hostile. Having accepted in principle its financial obligations to compensate for some damage – namely that inflicted upon France and Belgium[53] – Germany now found itself lumbered with the entire moral blame for the war. Worse, no final payment figure had been included in the Treaty, and the Germans consequently complained of being forced to sign a 'blank cheque'.[54] Nevertheless, Germany had little choice but to accept the Treaty terms as proposed, not least because the complex series of interwoven Allied compromises embodied in the draft left limited scope for German input, without destroying altogether the Conference's hard-won achievements.[55] The fact that Germany was kept out of the League system until 1926 also ensured that it could not, in the interim, appeal directly to this body to seek variation of the Treaty's terms. Wilson's warning about the effect of keeping 'one foot in the Old Order' seemed to be coming true.

When 1921 came, the Commission set the total amount at £6.6 billion, but in practice, clever drafting and finance arrangements ensured that Germany was bound to pay under half this sum.[56] Although Germany received credit for payments already made, and its payment schedule was revised in its favour a number of times, it continued to oppose bitterly the reparations scheme, and frequently defaulted on payments. That German 'aggression' was not merely a political mistake but also somehow morally aberrant behaviour in a way that the previous war-mongering of other powers had not been was a proposition rejected outright by German opinion. This opposition was masterfully exploited by Hitler and contributed greatly to Nazism's initial rise to power.[57] Other developments also raised doubts about Germany's identification in the Treaty of Versailles as sole aggressor responsible for World War I, such as the publication of Keynes' work[58] and of previously classified documents which pointed to the responsibility of the prior governments of Russia and Austria-Hungary, arms manufacturers or capitalism.[59] Thus although, by 1932, Germany may have paid only about £1.1 billion reparations in total, events impacting on international political conditions meant that none of the Allies was willing any longer to exercise its enforcement powers under the Treaty in order to compel Germany to pay more. Changing perceptions of the reparations clauses, and the emergence of more pressing political priorities, such as the rise of fascism in Italy and Germany and bolshevism in Russia, overtook the ongoing implementation of the reparations provisions, which were concerned with assigning moral and legal responsibility for political events now long since past.[60]

Aggression and articles 227–230 of the Treaty of Versailles

Attempts to impose punishment were not limited to the German state. As part of the punitive measures set down by the Treaty of Versailles, the Allies stated their intention to try Kaiser Wilhelm, the German head of state during World War I, for 'a supreme offence against international morality and the sanctity of treaties'.[61] The tribunal established for this purpose would be 'guided by the highest motives of international policy, with a view to vindicating the solemn obligations of international undertakings and the validity of international morality'.[62] Further provisions in the Treaty of Versailles compelled Germany: (1) to accept the right of the Allies to prosecute in military tribunals German nationals alleged to have violated the laws and customs of war or to have committed crimes against Allied nationals;[63] (2) to surrender German nationals requested by the Allies;[64] and (3) to provide all necessary documentation in these matters.[65]

Article 227 was included in the Treaty of Versailles as a result of the findings of the Commission on Responsibilities, a fifteen-member panel established in January 1919 by the Paris Peace Conference to enquire into the origins of World War I. The Commission concluded that the German government assisted Austria-Hungary to initiate war against Serbia, and that Kaiser Wilhelm acted either as the leader of the German government at the relevant time, or as the government itself. It further concluded that through Germany's breach of Belgian neutrality, Germany had provoked Britain to enter into World War I.[66] Once again, it was Britain and France that were most in favour of punishing Germany by trying Kaiser Wilhelm. As cosmopolitan as Wilson's approach to maintaining international peace and security was, even he rejected efforts to punish the Kaiser in relation to his involvement in World War I, and Wilson was supported in this view by US members of the Commission and Japan.[67] Despite Wilson's opposition, and demonstrating his desire to uphold moral and legal distinctions in the peace settlement, he attempted a draft of article 227 which included an explicit statement that the offence Kaiser Wilhelm was being charged with was not criminal. However, this was later excluded, probably on the suggestion of Lloyd George, Britain's Prime Minister.[68]

Just how 'thin' the notion of international morality was at this time was confirmed when the Allied Powers took steps to enforce article 227. Kaiser Wilhelm had already escaped to the Netherlands, a neutral state not party to the Treaty of Versailles, by the time the latter was signed; thus, in January 1920, the Supreme Council issued to the Netherlands a formal demand for Kaiser Wilhelm. Insisting that its demand be fulfilled on moral grounds and spurning any potential legal counter-arguments, the Supreme Council implored the Dutch Government to observe its:

> duty to insure the execution of Article 227 without allowing themselves to be stopped by arguments, because it is not a question of a public accusation with juridical character as regards its basis, but an act of high international policy imposed by the universal conscience, in which legal forms have been provided solely to assure to the accused such guarantees as were never before recognized in public law.[69]

In response, the Dutch government refused to surrender Kaiser Wilhelm, arguing that it was bound by no international duty to do so, and that Dutch tradition 'has made this country always a ground of refuge for the vanquished in international conflicts'.[70] Further correspondence between the Dutch authorities and the twenty-six-member Council of Ambassadors, which was charged with implementing the terms of the Treaty of Versailles, took place in February and March 1920 without resolution, and Kaiser Wilhelm enjoyed the protection afforded to him by the Dutch government for the rest of his life.[71] Thus, the universality of the 'international morality' upon which the Allies sought to rely in order to gain custody of Kaiser Wilhelm was strongly rejected.

The enforcement of articles 228–230 of the Treaty of Versailles experienced only slightly more success. At the beginning of February 1920, the Council of Ambassadors identified 900 Germany nationals it wished to prosecute, and presented their names to the president of the German peace delegation in Paris.[72] However, Germany later advised that on political and economic grounds it could not surrender these nationals in accordance with Allied demands, but would be willing to prosecute the 900 before a German court at Leipzig. The Allies accepted this proposal, on the proviso that if they felt that justice had not been served by the Leipzig court they could establish their own tribunals for trying the German nationals. In the end, only a tiny fraction of the 900 were tried by a German high court, and these were either acquitted or only very lightly punished.[73]

Conclusion

Aggression's role within the post-World War I peace settlement reveals a number of fresh insights into the broad themes introduced in the last chapter. While the impact of cosmopolitan thinking was evident from Wilson's staunch approach to international organisation and the popularity of this approach with the people of the world, his vision of collective security was undermined by understandings of 'security' on the part of the European Allies which more narrowly reflected their own, individual historical experiences, economic needs and political priorities. Far from being resolved, these tensions were simply preserved within the text of the Treaty of Versailles itself, as demonstrated by the two-part role played by the concept of aggression in this document. Aggression was simultaneously the heart of the new League security system and justification of a peace settlement brokered according to old rules of international security, an irreconcilable paradox. Even the diluted version of the central League obligation to preserve members from aggression – which left fulfilment of that obligation in the hands of the Executive Council and therefore subject to the will of the major powers – was considered too restrictive by the US Senate, which ultimately voted the Covenant down and left the League without its most important backer. From this, it is clear in practice how narrowly self-interested states can be, and how easily cosmopolitan aspirations can be made subject to compromises and qualifications reflecting the narrow self-interests of particular states. This suggests that the pro-cosmopolitan tendencies immediately following the tragedy of World War I are better described as a type of 'universal moment' quickly overtaken by the usual range of state-based concerns, rather than marking a fundamental, progressive change towards cosmopolitan objectives.

Wilson's approach to the issue of aggression also demonstrated the limits of his cosmopolitan framework. For the purposes of international peace and security, he actively promoted the promulgation by states of the mutually binding moral duty to combat aggression in international affairs, as revealed in his representations about the League Covenant to the US Senate. By emphasising the moral nature of this obligation, he sought to overcome concerns about its legal consequences. Wilson's aim of achieving a 'people's peace' and his public statements also suggest that he recognised moral principles that were binding on all individuals, and that this latter form of morality also had some role to play in international affairs. However, it is equally clear that Wilson viewed aggression ultimately as a moral problem among *states*. His various attempts to draft and include a mechanism for peaceful change in the Covenant showed an understanding of how crucial such a mechanism would be to a fully functional, state-based collective security system committed to preserving members from aggression. If states were to fulfil their moral obligations under the Covenant, alternative means of adjusting the status quo without recourse to aggression would need to be adopted and applied.

Consistent with this state-based view, Wilson saw 'aggression' for the purposes of punishment and deterrence as essentially an interstate matter. This is supported by his opposition to prosecuting Kaiser Wilhelm for his role in World War I. Thus, for Wilson, aggression was a question of state responsibility, not individual responsibility – it was for states to decide on the punitive measures to be applied against an aggressor *state*. Wilson's conservative approach to the issue of German reparations suggests that he appreciated the difficulties of resolving questions of justice on the international stage, and in any case saw these as subordinate to issues concerning international peace and security. The political challenges presented by Allied efforts to enforce either state or individual responsibility for German aggression and the effect of these on international security were also discussed in this chapter. Thus, Wilson's valiant attempt to get states to recognise a binding moral obligation to preserve each other against external aggression may be contrasted with later, more ambitious cosmopolitan efforts to address questions of international peace and security as well as uphold universal notions of justice by imposing individual responsibility for international acts.

3   State aggression at the League, 1920 to 1940

In the last chapter we saw that the concept of aggression was incorporated inconsistently into the Treaty of Versailles, revealing tensions between Wilson's collective security model and more conventional approaches based on the narrow self-interest of the major powers in the aftermath of devastating conflict. In this chapter it will be further demonstrated how the latter tendency eroded to a significant extent the League system, as some states sought to clarify the meaning and consequences of League obligations, while others circumvented or undermined League procedures as situations affecting international security arose. Nevertheless, on certain occasions the moral duty contained in article 10 of the Covenant was invoked and conflicts were contained. Thus, although the concept of aggression failed to prevent the outbreak of World War II, it did contribute to the resolution of small-scale disputes.

Canadian attempts to amend article 10

In the early interwar years, it became quickly apparent that the crux of the League system – namely the obligation to combat aggression – was not only viewed warily by the United States; certain League members themselves were also worried by it. In particular, Canada was deeply concerned about the endurance of article 10 despite its protests during the peace negotiations, and proposed the provision be struck out altogether during the first and second assemblies of the League. Canadian opposition revisited criticisms raised during the US ratification debate, and directly attacked what Canada saw as the underlying assumptions of article 10. For Canada, the obligation incorporated into article 10 took for granted that: (1) all existing territorial boundaries were just and expedient; (2) these boundaries would continue permanently to be just and expedient; and (3) the Signatories to the Covenant held themselves responsible for these boundaries.[1] In light of the dynamism of international conditions, Canada argued that it was not possible to determine if a given frontier would always conform with the needs of justice, and consequently Canada did not wish to be called upon to defend a potentially unjust state of affairs. Canada also claimed that, if Wilson had been correct and League members were legally free to ignore the advice of the Council as to how to fulfil the obligations created by article 10, the provision was worthless in reality anyway. This was considered sufficient reason for members seeking to rely upon article 10 for protection, as well as for members providing that protection, to complain.[2]

In response to these concerns, the First Committee of the League drafted a report reiterating that article 10 does not cement the existing territorial status quo for all time, but merely delegitimises acts of external aggression as a way of changing territorial integrity and political independence.[3] Other members favouring a strong League insisted that article 10 was the foundation of the Covenant, and they simply would not entertain the possibility of its exclusion.

However, this did not satisfy Canada, which was still anxious to avoid any commitments that might oblige it to participate in another world war.[4] By the fourth League Assembly of 1923, accepting that its chances of getting article 10 severed from the Covenant were slim, Canada altered course, suggesting an 'interpretive resolution' in order to clarify the scope of article 10. The two main points Canada wished to make explicit were: (1) that the Council, when advising the application of military measures under article 10, would be bound to consider the 'geographical situation and the special conditions of each State';[5] and (2) that each member retained the power to determine to what extent it must use its armed forces in conformity with this obligation. Although, as Walters argues, each of these conditions were implicit in the drafting of article 10 anyway, on political grounds it had been convenient not to acknowledge them expressly, in order to reassure those states most in need of international security guarantees.[6] In the final result, the interpretive resolution was not adopted as a consequence of the single negative vote of Persia, though the resolution attracted support from twenty-eight other powers excluding Canada.[7] The Canadian insistence on precision as regards the article 10 moral obligation had brought the attention of League members and public opinion to its weaknesses in practice. Despite the formal failure of the interpretive resolution, its terms remained the implicit understanding of how League procedures would work.

The widespread awareness produced by the Canadian campaign that each League member was ultimately free to decide how to respond to the advice of the Council in the event of an external aggression, reinforced just how far traditional approaches to international security based on states' narrow self-interest had infiltrated the idea of collective security at the crux of the League systems. The realisation that the moral obligation created in relation to aggression under article 10 would crucially depend on members' willingness to implement it, and therefore was not as iron-clad as it first appeared, led to a reconsideration of other Covenant provisions. Through this process, another weakness of the Covenant was identified.

The 'gap' in the Covenant

Certain League members now noted publicly that even if articles 11 to 16 of the Covenant were strictly adhered to, war was still a possibility.[8] The questions were raised: how was this 'gap' reconcilable with the undertaking in article 10, and what measures could be taken to eradicate the 'gap'?

In an effort to strengthen international security against these perceived flaws, efforts were made both inside and outside the League, once again reflecting the tension between attempts to keep the vision of collective security alive and reliance on states' own, individual security priorities. Within the League, the Treaty of Mutual Guarantee and Geneva Protocol never made it past the draft stage. It was against this backdrop that League attention shifted back to the Covenant, and the issue of defining aggression arose.[9] Noting the great difficulty of gaining unanimous support for any definition of aggression, the League's Committee on Arbitration and Security concluded in 1928 that 'any attempt to lay down rigid or absolute criteria in advance for determining an aggressor would be unlikely in existing circumstances to lead to any practical result'.[10] Nevertheless, the report of the second session of the Committee identified certain acts, drawn from earlier agreements, which could be classified as acts of aggression in certain circumstances.[11] Two suggestions about *how* to decide whether or not aggression had taken place were also made by the Committee: (1) determination by unanimous vote of the Council, not counting the votes of the belligerent parties, as per the Locarno Treaty system;[12] and (2) determination as per the Geneval Protocol system, which presumed that any state engaged in hostilities was an aggressor. However, the Committee also acknowledged serious objections to both of these approaches.[13] The failure of League attempts to broker new international security assurances and the dead-end it reached in relation to defining aggression led to the abandonment in 1928 of efforts to bridge the 'gap' in the Covenant. The League's narrow focus on 'defining' aggression implicitly confirmed the failure of collective security in practice – aggression was no longer a moral trigger for action upon which the maintenance of international security could be assured; it now apparently required legal-style 'definition' to achieve its purpose more effectively. Wilson's exhortation that it was the notion behind article 10 – namely that there exists a moral obligation among member states to preserve each other against external aggression – 'not necessarily these words, [which were] the key to the whole Covenant'[14] had long been forgotten.

The 1933 Soviet Draft Definition of the Aggressor

Efforts to define aggression were revived in 1933, with the submission by the Soviet Union of a Draft Definition of the Aggressor. The Soviet Definition listed five acts, the initial commission of which would make any state the aggressor.[15] It expressly rejected any form of political, strategic and economic justifications for the five aggressive acts listed, and it also reiterated the right of a threatened state to resort to 'diplomatic or other means' for the solution of the conflict, including military measures short of crossing international boundaries. Consideration of this draft definition, along with a Belgian proposal concerning the fact-finding process in the case of aggression, was delegated to the Committee on Security Questions, which produced the Politis Report of May 1933. Ultimately, despite amendments to the Soviet draft, it did not attract sufficient support and was therefore not finalised.[16]

This is not surprising, as by 1933 political conditions had shifted once again. By this date, the unwillingness of important League members to address many serious conflicts was very evident from experience,[17] and it was equally clear that no definition of aggression – even if consensus around a definition was possible – would overcome this problem on its own. In fact, the Soviet Union's Draft Definition of the Aggressor is better interpreted not as an altruistic, last-ditch attempt to make collective security a reality for all, but more as an individual reaction to these changed political circumstances of the 1930s. In particular, the departure of Germany and Japan from the League in 1933 motivated the Soviet Union to join the League and submit its Draft Definition of the Aggressor, so that it could have a basis upon which to call for assistance, however unassured, in the event of German or Japanese attack.[18]

International security agreements made outside the League

Furthermore, the signing of security treaties outside the League merely underscored the high level of scepticism among members with regard to the League's central moral obligation to preserve each other against aggression. The 1925 signing of the Locarno Pacts between Germany, France, Belgium, Britain, Italy, Poland and Czechoslovakia was a significant example. According to this treaty, Germany, France and Belgium agreed to view existing boundaries and the demilitarised Rhineland zone as inviolable, and to not attack, invade or resort to war against one another in any circumstance. Britain and Italy, as guarantors of the agreement, were to help any victim state at once in the event of breach. Four arbitration conventions were included in the pacts, and any party which refused to surrender to arbitration, or to abide by the arbitral award recommended in accordance with these procedures, would be considered the aggressor.

The Locarno Pacts undermined League procedures greatly by providing an alternative international forum for discussion and dispute settlement among the important Locarno states. These states no longer had much incentive to use the League, which could only operate with the agreement of a much larger group of nations. Locarno also provided its signatories with a good cover for meeting exclusively and privately to discuss matters of concern, the scope of which extended in practice to include issues properly within the League's jurisdiction. Hence, as early as five years after its establishment, the League had in practice been downgraded to the 'influential debating society'[19] Wilson had feared; the damaging effect of these private 'Locarno Tea Parties'[20] is revealed in the following section.

Aggression and League practice

As situations impacting on international security arose during the interwar years, the limitations of the League system became even more evident. No authority existed to compel commitment to League procedures by members, so certain situations were addressed outside the League altogether by agreement of the affected states. On other occasions, League procedures were manipulated in the self-interest of the major powers, leading to intensified conflict without resolution. Despite these failings, article 10 was applied successfully in certain circumstances. Even the moral foundation of article 10 was invoked successfully on one occasion, in circumstances where reliance on a strict interpretation of the provision would have provided no recourse. The following examples illustrate the nature and extent of the contribution to the maintenance of international security made by the concept of aggression.

Successful applications of article 10

Greece–Bulgaria Dispute, 1925

Article 10 was first applied successfully in 1925 to a dispute occurring along the frontier between Greece and Bulgaria. In October of that year, following the Greek invasion of Bulgaria, the latter requested on the basis of articles 10 and 11 that the Secretary-General convene immediately a meeting of the Council. Greece denied any aggressive intent, claiming it was compelled to act in defence of its border populations, which were constantly under threat from Bulgarian gangs.[21] The following day, the Acting President of the Council issued a telegram to the Greek and Bulgarian governments reminding them of their obligations under article 12 of the Covenant to submit their dispute to arbitration or inquiry by the council, and urging them to refrain from any further military actions and to return to their respective frontiers pending Council consideration. Three days later, the Council met and placed a time limit of sixty hours on both of the parties to bring effect to the Acting President's suggested actions. The Council also requested that France, Britain and Italy send representatives to the area to observe and report once these actions had been completed. By 29 October, the Council was informed that both sides had complied with the Acting President's request, and the Council then appointed a Commission of Inquiry to visit the site of the incident and investigate its causes. The Commission later concluded in December 1925 that responsibility for the initial incident was shared, and it recommended that Greece pay Bulgaria £45,000 for its losses, a figure which took into account the death of a Greek officer during the skirmish. Once again Greece and Bulgaria complied promptly with the Commission's findings and the dispute was settled.

A more obvious, textbook example of collective security in practice is difficult to imagine. The crossing of a border by armed forces without the prior consent of the relevant state typified 'external aggression' under article 10. Thus, immediate Council response was the obvious requirement, the complication of considering the Greek defence argument being unnecessary at this stage. Once the situation had stabilised, then the Commission of Inquiry turned to consider the merits of each side's claims, which is evident in its final conclusion that both states were responsible.

Crucially, rapid and effective League action in this case was made possible because the vital interests of the great powers were not involved; there were no powerful political factors constraining the League in the performance of its functions. In the absence of such obstacles, the unhindered Council performed its duties efficiently, and Greece and Bulgaria followed the Council's recommendations.

Ethiopia vs. British–Italian Agreement, 1926

Perhaps the most unique situation in which the League was approached on the basis of article 10 concerned an agreement between Italy and Britain to support each other in their efforts to promote their economic interests in Ethiopia. Prior to the agreement, Britain had attempted to negotiate directly with Ethiopia for permission to build a dam in Lake Tsana, but these negotiations had not been concluded. In exchange for Italian backing of this objective, Britain agreed to assist Italy to obtain its own concessions from Ethiopia, which included the grant to Italy of a zone of exclusive economic influence in the west of Ethiopia.[22]

In June 1926, both Italy and Britain communicated these terms to the Regent of Ethiopia, who promptly forwarded the correspondence and his own letter of protest to the Secretary-General and requested that all documents be circulated to League members for their consideration.[23] The Regent interpreted the agreement as a bilateral pact to exert pressure upon Ethiopia in the event that it denied the economic concessions sought, and claimed that this comprised an indirect threat to Ethiopia's territorial integrity and political independence, thus breaching article 10.

Before the Regent had an opportunity to respond to the Secretary-General's inquiry as to whether Ethiopia wished to place the issue on the agenda of the next Council meeting, Britain and Italy sent letters to the Secretary-General disavowing any ill-intentions on their part, maintaining that the agreement was only binding between themselves, and upholding the freedom of Ethiopia to make its own decisions. The issue was thus resolved through the good offices of the League before it reached the Council stage.

What is striking about the Ethiopian–British–Italian case is that the Regent of Ethiopia sought to classify as aggression conduct differing greatly from that originally intended by Covenant drafters. Here, no armed hostilities had broken out, nor did there seem to be any imminent prospect that they would. The aggression complained of was conceived in purely economic and political, not military, terms: the coordination of the strategies of two great powers in their own best interests in order to influence the foreign policies of a weaker power. Why did Britain and Italy back down from their original position before the Ethiopian situation ever made it on to the Council agenda? Ultimately, the political cost to Britain and Italy in terms of embarrassment, damage to reputation and the potential loss of public support for any League system at all in the event of obvious great power bullying outweighed the marginal benefits conferred by the agreement, and thus it was shelved – at least publicly. On this occasion, it was more prudent for Britain and Italy to support the League system in which they enjoyed prominent positions by distancing themselves from an agreement which was inconsistent with League values, than to insist on their own immediate, narrowly framed self-interest, which might irreparably damage that system.

This scenario revealed how the Covenant's central moral obligation could be used by smaller powers to defend their own interests against major powers. Although the conduct of Britain and Italy did not fall within the scope of behaviour conventionally referred to as 'aggression', it was contrary to the spirit of state equality and cooperation upon which the League was established. Given it was the major powers themselves that had had the greatest input into the shape and operation of the League, proof that two of these powers did not consider themselves bound to act in accordance with values underpinning their own international security system was a serious public embarrassment. If left unaddressed, such an issue could undermine dramatically confidence in the League system as a whole, thus generating a descent into anarchy. With little to gain from upholding the agreement, Britain and Italy publicly sought to explain their actions in terms consistent with League principles. Ethiopia had successfully used article 10 and the League system to raise awareness of its plight and exert moral pressure on Britain and Italy to back down. Had the article 10 obligation targeted acts more specifically, referring to 'armed attack', 'invasion' or 'occupation' instead of 'aggression', it is unlikely that Ethiopia would have been successful. Although successful on this occasion, there would be other occasions when invocation of the article 10 obligation would be less successful.

Unsuccessful applications of article 10

Manchuria 1931–1933

In September 1931, Japanese forces left their posts along the Southern Manchurian railway zone and occupied the Chinese cities of Mukden, Antung and other locations. China was quick to denounce Japanese actions as aggressive, and formally invoked article 11 of the Covenant in its appeal to the League. Japan argued that the Chinese army had attacked the railway zone, and that Japanese measures were merely by way of response to ensure the safety of the lives and property of Japanese nationals. Although the Council adopted a resolution requesting Japan to withdraw and China to assume responsibility for the safety of the Japanese during this process, a Commission of Inquiry was not sent at this stage. Despite support for a commission from the UK and China, the US viewed direct negotiation between Japan and China as the preferred method of settling the dispute. Hence, in an effort not to isolate the US after the advent of its more cooperative approach to the League since 1928, the Council refrained from sending a commission.

By early October, Japan had bombed the city of Chinchow and there appeared to be few signs that Japan would comply with the Council's September resolution. At the following Council meeting, the US sent a representative, but their role was limited to listening to the Council's discussions as they related to the provisions of the Kellogg–Briand Pact.[24] A second resolution was instigated at the end of October requesting the completion of the Japanese withdrawal within three weeks, followed by the resumption of direct negotiations, but Japan voted against this resolution, and because of the unanimity rule concerning article 11, the resolution was of no legal effect.[25] Although the major powers were in a position to refute this legal interpretation, each was preoccupied with problems closer to home,[26] and the smaller powers were left impotent without major power leadership.

During November and December 1931 the situation deteriorated further, while the League struggled to harness the collective political will necessary to address the situation and keep apace of events: by the end of February 1932, Japan had three provinces of China under direct Japanese control. Out of desperation, and following the expansion of fighting to Shanghai, on 29 January, China requested the application of article 10 to the dispute.[27] Japan contended that aggression under article 10 occurred only when a member 'intends to occupy the territory of another Power with the determination to remain there ... when there is permanent occupation with clearly indicated territorial designs'.[28] Japan sought to argue on the basis of necessity that her actions did not amount to aggression: once the safety of Japanese nationals had been ensured and the possibility of Chinese attack of the railway zone thwarted, Japan would withdraw.

In an attempt to circumvent the paralysis of the Council, the dispute was referred to the Assembly. It was in this forum that public opinion in favour of China began to mobilise, which was China's primary aim in seeking Assembly involvement. By September 1932, the report of a Commission of Inquiry largely vindicated the Chinese version of events, and the Assembly adopted a series of recommendations for settling the dispute in accordance with this report. Moreover, the US endorsed the Assembly's conclusions. In the face of such opposition, Japan chose to withdraw from the League in March 1933. By May of that year, both sides had signed a truce which kept the peace between them until 1937.

However, in July 1937, a new outbreak of hostilities near Beijing reignited the Sino-Japanese conflict. China initially approached the signatories of the nine-power Treaty of 1922, which laid down the principle of respect for the status quo in China, but a conference of the parties did not result in any action. Thus, in 1938, China appealed to the League for sanctions to be applied against Japan in accordance with article 16. Although the Council determined that members were entitled to apply the measures stipulated under article 16, in practice this had little effect. By this time, inconsistent application of the obligations under the Covenant was commonplace: Germany and Italy had already been successful in Spain[29] and Czechoslovakia, and the most powerful League members were even less prepared to fulfil the duty of combating Japan. Hence, the great powers' preoccupation with their own, individual priorities shaped the way in which League procedures were applied from the start of the dispute, and as a result the League failed to uphold the article 10 obligation owed to China in response to Japanese aggression.[30]

Italo-Ethiopian Dispute 1935–1936

Lessons for potential aggressors from the Sino-Japanese dispute were not lost on Italy. An incident between Italian and Ethiopian armed forces broke out on

5 December 1934 at Wal-Wal, which Ethiopia requested the Secretary-General bring to the Council's attention. By 15 January 1935 Ethiopia had put in a formal request for the dispute to be included on the Council's agenda. However, Italy convinced the Council and Ethiopia to accept postponement of League discussion in relation to the dispute on the basis that Italy would settle it in accordance with an existing agreement between the two states.[31] Despite consistent appeals by Ethiopia to the Council to take up the dispute in the months that followed, it was not until September 1935, when Ethiopia exhorted the Council to exercise its powers under articles 10 and 15, that the Council included the dispute on its agenda.

During the intervening period, Italy had ample opportunity to maximise the delay of League procedures so that its preparations for war could progress. Its main strategy for achieving this was to appear to pursue peaceful options via diplomatic channels outside the League. Britain and France cooperated with Italy in this endeavour because they were relying on Italian support to assist them in combating the increasing threat posed by Nazism. In addition, as a consequence of the intimacy and conviviality of the Locarno power meetings, it seemed appropriate to Britain, France and Italy to arrive at a solution among themselves, seeking League endorsement for this solution after the fact, rather than using the League exclusively and from the outset.[32] Thus, at the Stresa Conference, Britain and France agreed not to promote the Ethiopian request within the League, leaving the issue of Italy's African aims undiscussed, in exchange for Italian backing of Anglo-French ideas for peace in Europe and the continuing obligations of the Locarno Treaty.[33] Britain and France made further attempts themselves to resolve Italy's territorial designs in Africa, but to no avail.

By September, Italy had changed tactics: it now argued that Ethiopia was not entitled to be considered a member of the League at all on the basis of its behaviour and features of its internal regime. It was now too late for Italy to withdraw from its plans, and for the Council to prevent the imminent conflict. On 3 October, Italy invaded Ethiopia; four days later, the Council concluded that Italy had resorted to war in violation of article 12, and sanctions were applied under article 16 on 18 November.

However, the ongoing Anglo-French priority of keeping potential allies close in the face of rising Nazism meant that the proposals put forward by Britain and France to the League's Sanctions Committee were designed not to provoke from Italy serious retaliatory measures. For this reason also, France indulged Italian bullying by securing a two-week postponement of the Sanctions Committee, which provided Italy with some much needed respite. When the Sanctions Committee finally met on 12 December, the proposal of Britain and France offered Italy an exchange of territories, a zone of economic expansion and settlement in resolution of the dispute with Ethiopia. This proposal was strongly rejected by public opinion in the UK, USA and smaller states; but as a new peace initiative requiring consideration by Italy and Ethiopia, it prevented further discussion in the Sanctions Committee of the extension of sanctions to crucial commodities such as oil.

In the early months of 1936 Italy continued its invasion, until it agreed with Ethiopia on 3 March to reopen negotiations at the request of the Council. However,

Hitler's rejection of the Locarno Treaty and remilitarisation of the Rhineland on 7 March provided Britain and France with even greater reason to be lenient towards Italy. From the Anglo-French perspective, it was now more important than ever to retain Italian goodwill, in order to encourage Italy to enforce the Locarno obligations against Germany. Italy used its membership of the League as a vehicle for wooing Anglo-French support and to secure further delays until its armed forces were victorious and officially annexed Ethiopia on 9 May. The League eventually abandoned its failed sanctions the following month, and passed a resolution requesting members to forward to the organisation their conclusions from this situation with the aim of improving the application of the Covenant's provisions.

Throughout this episode, and up until the Italian withdrawal from the League in December 1937, the approaching European conflict with Hitler preoccupied Britain and France and, given their status as important League members, influenced the way in which League procedures were applied against Italy. League obligations, therefore, proved useless in terms of maintaining international security in circumstances where they conflicted with the narrowly self-interested calculations of security by the major powers. On these occasions, regardless of the outcry of public opinion in some of these states, the extent to which League procedures became a vehicle for the perpetuation of power-balancing among the major states, instead of the means by which great power aggrandisement against smaller states could be prevented, is apparent.

Disputes where article 10 was not applied by the League

In addition, there were a number of conflicts either dealt with by the League in a piecemeal way, or not addressed under League provisions at all, again as a result of the priority allocated by the great powers to their own narrow self-interest. For instance, when Poland seized the traditional Lithuanian capital of Vilna in 1920, the Council called on the former to cease breaching her obligations under the Covenant, and recommended that the Vilna residents themselves should decide whether to be part of Poland or Lithuania. Despite the agreement to preliminary peace terms, fighting continued, and it was not until seven years later that the Council succeeded in terminating the state of war. The special relationship with France enjoyed by Poland worked to the latter's advantage by blocking any possible Council military action in response to the occupation of Vilna.[34]

Similarly, when Turkey invaded Armenia in the same year, the lack of interest on the part of League members, especially Britain and France, in committing military assistance to the conflict meant that the League had to decline the Supreme Council of the Allied Power's request to accept a mandate over Armenia.[35] Although the Assembly brokered an agreement reducing arms to the area, by the time any assistance was able to be given, Armenia no longer existed. Armenia's location along the Soviet Union's border and the preoccupation of the stronger members of the League with the challenges posed by the immediate post-World War I settlement resulted in the loss of Armenia to the Soviet Union.

In addition, the 1923 French seizure of mines and factories in the Ruhr region of Germany as a form of guarantee for the payment of reparations may also have been pursued under article 10. In fact, Council intervention was desired by a broad base of members, but was scuppered by France's resolute will to have its way on this issue. Thus, in this case the determination of just one great power was sufficient to prevent a security issue of critical importance to all from being considered by the Council.

Finland did not even bother to refer to article 10 in its 1939 appeal to the League about an unexpected attack by the Soviet Union, citing articles 11 and 15 instead. Nevertheless, by resolution, the Assembly declared that:

> by the aggression which it has committed against Finland, the Union of Soviet Socialist Republics has failed to observe not only its special political agreements with Finland but also article 12 of the Covenant of the League of Nations and the Pact of Paris.[36]

As a result, the League formally excluded the Soviet Union from its membership under article 16. This was the strongest and most significant response the League made against aggression, though in terms of both the broader strategic context and the League's international status it was a case of too little, too late.

Perhaps the greatest example highlighting the degree to which balance-of-power considerations remained predominant in the security calculations of the major powers, reducing the League to a vehicle for pursuing these broader aims, was the reaction to growing German aggression from 1933 onward. Having withdrawn Germany from the League during this year, Hitler pursued rearmament at an alarming pace, culminating initially in the remilitarisation of the Rhineland in breach of the Locarno Pacts, and followed by the annexation of Austria in March 1938. No action was taken in response to these serious violations of the League Covenant; it was only when Hitler's demands for Czechoslovakia became increasingly insistent that Britain, France, Italy and Germany met in September 1938 and agreed to partition the Sudeten area in Germany's favour. However, this meeting did not take place at the League, but rather at Munich, behind closed doors, during which time the League and its other members were reduced to the role of mere spectators. War was looming, and in light of the failure of these negotiations and the mixed track record of the League, more and more League members affirmed publicly their absolute freedom to decide how to respond to international military conflict.[37] Despite the Munich agreement, in March 1939, Germany occupied Bohemia, and by September of that year, when Germany attacked Poland, the stage was set for the onset of World War II.

Conclusion

This chapter has demonstrated that concerns about the specific consequences of the moral obligation to combat aggression – which had kept the US out of the League – continued to spread among League members during the interwar years.

The drive to make precise what League members had signed up for exposed the fragility of the League system, which led to internal and external efforts to bolster international security. As part of this process, League members started to consider how to 'define' aggression, an initiative which marked the final abandonment of attempts to make work a state-based, morally binding international security regime in favour of more legalistic approaches. As will be demonstrated, this move towards framing aggression as a legal problem in need of 'definition' outlasted the League and continues to attract some support to the present day.

This chapter also highlighted the vulnerabilities of a morally based international security regime when unaccompanied by effective mechanisms for peaceful change. Article 19 of the Covenant, which established a discretionary power on the part of the Assembly to reconsider intermittently treaties and 'international conditions whose continuance might endanger the peace of the world', provided inadequate reassurance to members such as Canada that just change could and would be accommodated by the League. To make peaceful and just change a regular reality in international affairs, what was needed was more than simply a Covenant provision permitting it; a procedure for achieving peaceful and just change needed to be formulated, agreed upon among members states and, crucially, enforced. These much greater challenges were left unaddressed by the post-World War I settlement, but remained nonetheless essential for a functioning collective security system. Consequently, when disputes among states did emerge, the weakness of peaceful change mechanisms meant that these disputes often evolved into hostile conflict, and, as we saw in the case of Manchuria (1931–1933) and Ethiopia (1935–1936), the League's role was not only diminished but what small part it did play reflected the underlying, individual security priorities among competing great powers. The League's lack of enforcement measures also meant that states were free to address security matters among themselves without League involvement. We saw that on various occasions article 10 was not invoked at all, and outcomes once again reflected major power priorities.

However, we also saw that where great power priorities were not immediately affected, or where issues arose which primarily threatened the reputation or status of great powers, the moral obligation underpinning the Covenant could be activated successfully. For instance, the 1925 dispute between smaller powers Greece and Bulgaria was resolved successfully through the rapid and impartial application of League procedures. In addition, Ethiopia's successful characterisation of British and Italian economic diplomacy as inconsistent with the article 10 obligation forced a great power backdown on moral grounds, in circumstances very different from those in relation to which the collective security provision of the Covenant was meant to be applied. This case confirmed that the League was capable of exerting moral pressure on members, including the great powers. Thus, while the Covenant's article 10 moral obligation to preserve against aggression did play a role in international relations during the interwar years, this role was constrained significantly by both the priorities of the most powerful individual states, and the weakness of international mechanisms for peaceful and just change.

4 Aggression and individual criminal responsibility at Nuremberg and subsequent trials

The concept of aggression re-emerged internationally in the closing days of World War II as the Allies considered what to do with the growing number of captured German elites. Proposals discussed within the US administration reflected both communitarian and cosmopolitan thinking. The former was evident in the proposal of the US Secretary of Treasury, who argued in terms of the narrow self-interest of the USA: what was required was another punitive peace, this time leaving Germany utterly unable to initiate future conflict. On this view, top German leaders would be summarily executed as they were captured. Reflecting a more cosmopolitan outlook, the Secretary of War – supported by military leaders – preferred a less harsh peace settlement, arguing in favour of a fair trial process. Going even further than the unsuccessful attempt to prosecute Kaiser Wilhelm on supposedly universal moral grounds at the conclusion of World War I, the latter group eventually endorsed a *criminal* trial of *individual* German leaders, with aggression as the central charge. This proposal was adopted by the USA, and with few political alternatives available, Allied agreement was achieved, though the UK, France and the Soviet Union remained uneasy about the shaky legal basis and prospective implications of the American plan.

Thus, the way in which the Nuremberg Charter was negotiated – like the Treaty of Versailles before it – reflected cosmopolitan tendencies on the part of the USA in tension with the European allies' individual, localised understandings of the relationship between politics, law and morality in international affairs. Thus, the final terms of the document reflect this tension, and those issues in relation to which no agreement could be made among the Allies were simply left out of the document. The inclusion of the crime of aggression in the Nuremberg Charter made it possible to link top-level Nuremberg defendants to particular wartime activities on the ground, and hence they were of crucial significance on this occasion.

The strong, cosmopolitan thinking that underpinned the political decision to prosecute German elites for the crime of aggression – and the expansive charges it provoked on the part of the prosecution – can be contrasted with the conservative approach to this crime adopted by the majority of Nuremberg judges themselves. In rejecting many of the arguments of the prosecution, the judges limited significantly the scope of the crime of aggression, therefore addressing to a great extent various 'victors' justice' criticisms of the trial. The outcome of the trial also demonstrated an appreciation of the complexities of evaluating and adjudicating upon an individual's motives and actions at the international level. While in this case the cosmopolitan impetus of the US was tempered by both the individual preferences of the European allies and judicial conservatism to achieve the articulation of a restricted but balanced individual crime of aggression, the same cannot be said in the context of the Tokyo trial, as the next chapter will demonstrate.

The end of World War II in Europe and the problem of the top-ranking Nazis

In 1944 to 1945, the issue of working out what to do with the surviving members of the Nazi leadership regime was gaining priority within US policy-making circles as concerns mounted over the possibility that, as World War II came to an end, Nazi leaders might flee Germany and seek political asylum in a neutral state.[1] Ways of resolving this issue strongly reflected the respective preferences of different actors within the US administration for the type of peace to be pursued in Germany, both as part of the strategy for ending World War II and for the post-war settlement. Two divergent schools of thought emerged.

One school, led by US Secretary of Treasury Henry Morgenthau Jr, supported the idea of using approaching military units to execute summarily top Nazi officials. On this view, any of the Allied powers would be entitled, on meeting any member of a prearranged list of high-ranking Nazis and on confirmation of their identity, to kill them immediately. Ultimate decision-making authority in relation to this task would rest with individual, Allied military commanders; they would retain full discretion as to the means of identity confirmation, as well as the timing and method of execution in accordance with the military practices of their own particular state. This approach, which emerged in September 1944, was promoted as part of a programme which aimed to destroy completely Germany's future ability to wage war, and to establish a general international deterrent via the imposition of a harsh punishment. Other components of this programme included a rigorous agenda of German deindustrialisation and pasturalisation, with the intention of leaving that state economically powerless; the purging of Nazis from German institutions; and the use of extensive detention powers to apprehend all members of organisations such as the SS and others in business, law and education.[2] The Morgenthau Plan was so thorough and severe that it even contemplated the removal from Germany of Hitler Youth members and other children exposed to Nazism.[3] Morgenthau thought a more lenient occupation policy than his would not only be unjust, but might also enable Germany to instigate another phase of expansionism and atrocities.[4]

A second view, developed by Secretary of War Henry Stimson, later emerged, urging on political and moral grounds a fair trial for those within the Nazi leadership. To Stimson, depriving Germany of the means of achieving economic prosperity 'would be just such a crime as the Germans themselves hoped to perpetuate upon their victims – it would be a crime against civilisation itself'.[5] Worse, Stimson believed the strongly punitive economic basis of the Morgenthau Plan would cripple the German economy at a time of already great disruption to European markets generally, thus generating a catalyst for future war.[6] Stimson's call for a more moderate Allied reaction appealed to military leaders, who knew that a successful, final advance would crucially depend on the maintenance of stability and order in the territory already overrun by the Allies – a condition that would be entirely undermined by arrests on a massive scale and destruction of economic capacity.[7] In Stimson's view, only great power support for the rule of law buttressed by the force of concerned public opinion could reduce or end aggression for good. A trial of the leading Nazis would not only provide a mechanism by which convicted Nazi elites could be punished, but would also create an important educational record from which future generations could learn, thus making possible the avoidance of subsequent large-scale international conflicts.[8] Eventually, the Stimson view prevailed and became official US policy, with President Truman coming out strongly in favour of an international trial procedure following his appointment to office in April 1945.

However, Allied support for a trial of the top Nazis was by no means assured. In fact, Churchill and Roosevelt had already accepted a summary of the Morgenthau Plan's recommendations in Quebec on 15 September 1944.[9] Complicating the matter further, a third view had emerged: the British Lord Chancellor, Lord Simon, cognisant of the political and legal difficulties presented by the proposed trial of the top Nazis, had instead promoted a 'political' execution of these men along similar lines to those used by the British government against Napoleon in 1815. According to this approach, decision-making authority concerning the fate of German elites resided with the Allied political leaders collectively, with usual diplomatic practices of negotiation and consensus-building being used to determine the nature of the decision taken. Simon had been promoting this view for more than two years, and Churchill himself had been supporting this position in cabinet for over a year.

British opposition to a trial remained steadfast, despite a failed attempt to come to an Anglo-American compromise – namely a perfunctory 'arraignment' procedure, which would see the leading Nazis indicted before an Allied tribunal, a quick ruling on the charges made, and an appropriate punishment decided. Even this modest proposal attracted savage criticism within the British camp. Critics argued that a pseudo-trial along these lines would please no one, and through the blurring of 'political and judicial jurisdiction' Britain would be on the receiving end of 'the worst of both worlds'.[10] On this basis, British cabinet members rejected the proposal, formally communicating to the USA on 12 April 1945 that Britain would not accept a trial or hearing for Hitler and his colleagues, favouring a 'political disposition' instead.[11]

In light of British opposition to a trial, Stalin's pro-trial stance provided the American proposal with welcome support. At the meeting of the USA, UK and Soviet Union at Yalta in February 1945, Stalin had repeated his view that 'the grand criminals should be tried before being shot'.[12] Although far from what the USA had in mind in terms of how the trial procedure would function, at least this statement indicated backing in principle for some sort of judicial process to be incorporated into Allied plans for the top Nazis. When it became known to the USA in April that France was also in favour of a trial procedure,[13] it was clear that staunch British opposition to the use of legal mechanisms for dealing with the top Nazis could be routed by the USA, and that a trial could proceed. Hence, general agreement among the foreign ministers of the UK, Soviet Union and France to a trial by international military tribunal of the top Nazis was secured by the USA in May 1945, at the United Nations Conference on International Organisation (UNCIO) held at San Francisco.[14] The American vision of a moderate peace settlement incorporating the rule of law had won its first major victory.

Prosecuting the Nazi elite: political and legal challenges

How to bring together the realities of Nazi warmongering, the substance of relevant international law on the topic of armed conflict and the wish to prosecute individuals criminally for the excesses of Nazism was a preoccupation of pro-trial policy advisers from the outset. Worldwide horror at the systematic slaughter carried out by the Nazis produced an overwhelming sense that violation of some moral code had occurred, but beyond this instinctive response there were no easy answers. While 'aggression' in abstract terms might have been recognised by League members in 1919 as a wrong committed against any one of them in relation to which they agreed to come to each other's aid, the League record itself had demonstrated that in practice, collective measures to counteract aggression were unreliable. For this reason, difficult political questions might re-emerge if the Allies sought to prosecute German conduct as 'aggression'. Legally, this course of action also presented problems, resting on the twin assumptions that: (1) aggression amounted to an international crime pre-World War II; and (2) aggression was an international crime giving rise to individual criminal responsibility. The role of these two assumptions at the cornerstone of the American case against the top Nazis generated much debate within the US administration and later among the Allies.

The USA and the crime of aggression

In November 1944, it was an ongoing consideration within the United Nations War Crimes Commission (UNWCC)[15] of whether or not aggressive war was a crime that accelerated decisions at the higher tiers of the US government about which crimes would be prosecuted at the International Military Tribunal. The State and War Departments were still debating these topics when the American member of the Commission approached Stimson for instructions in relation to a proposal tabled at the Commission which urged a United Nations declaration as to the criminality of aggressive war.[16] Critics of the proposal to prosecute aggressive war as a crime demolished this idea on legal grounds; however, they failed to provide any adequate solution to the underlying political problem: namely, how to reconcile public expectations of a strong and united Allied stance against the Nazi regime with no apparent political, legal or moral foundation upon which to distinguish Allied conduct from German conduct in World War II.

On this point, the contributing role played by the Allies in the failure of the League system to counteract German aggression was difficult to escape. The fact remained that no action was taken by any of the World War II Allied powers in response to Germany's remilitarisation of the Rhineland in 1933 – although a breach of the Locarno Pacts – or in relation to the 1938 Anschluss. When finally compelled to act, appeasement in the form of the Munich Agreement rather than resistance was the initial chosen policy of the UK and France. This publicly known history prevented the Allies from arguing the high moral ground in support of the claim that the prohibition of aggression was taken very seriously after World War I. Moreover, legal argument about Germany acting in breach of Covenant obligations was shaky at best, given that Germany had withdrawn from the League in 1933 before many of her worst excesses took place. Lieutenant Freeman, one of the Department of War's top legal advisers, summed up the difficulty best when he indicated that if the UNWCC supported the idea that aggressive war was criminal, it would damage its reputation within the legal community; yet if international public opinion learned that the Allies failed to hold the top Nazis criminally responsible for the war, it would be outraged.[17]

The intransigence of this problem provided some leeway for Stimson and his supporters to further endorse the criminal prosecution of aggressive war through legal innovation. However, deadlock continued, and it appeared towards the end of 1944 that, as a result of this thorny challenge, the Nuremberg trial plan in its entirety would have to be abandoned. It was only further outrage within US policy-making circles at the killing of seventy American prisoners near Malmedy, Belgium, on 17 December, which provided the necessary political and moral impetus to promote consensus around a trial, founded upon the premise that aggressive war was a crime.[18]

By 3 January 1945, and in response to pressure from the American UNWCC representative for some clear instructions, Roosevelt personally indicated that he favoured charging the top Nazis with 'waging aggressive and unprovoked warfare in violation of the Kellogg Pact',[19] and that this might be used in combination with a conspiracy charge. In late January, a draft memorandum endorsed by the War, State and Justice Departments was forwarded to the President, in which conventional war crimes took centre stage and the charge of waging a war of aggression was only mentioned in passing.[20] However, with the advent of the Truman presidency, and the subsequent choice of Robert Jackson as chief US war crimes prosecutor in May 1945, aggression became the key charge. Jackson's position, combined with his deep conviction that the charge of aggression was the heart of the case against the leading members of the Nazi regime, ensured that the prominence of this charge was resurrected and reiterated in virtually every Allied public pronouncement on war crimes policy produced from May 1945 until the close of the Nuremberg trial in 1946.[21] For Jackson, all

Nazi crimes derived first and foremost from the crime of aggression, and thus its inclusion and definition within the document establishing the IMT was vital.

The other allied powers and the crime of aggression

However, Jackson's preference for the criminal prosecution of aggressive war was not immediately supported by the other allies. At meetings of the London Conference which ran from 26 June 1945, the UK, Soviet Union and France raised many of the same objections to the criminality of aggression which had been played out earlier within US bureaucratic circles. Thus, although Britain had finally accepted in principle the US draft proposal concerning the trial of the top Nazis, Britain continued to refer to the lack of established sanction for the crime of aggression as a major setback.[22] In addition, though the French conceded that the crime of aggression was 'morally and politically desirable',[23] they rejected its legality. France reiterated with approval a statement by Professor Trainin, one of the Soviet Union's leading legal scholars present at the Conference: 'the effort to make war of aggression a crime is still tentative'.[24]

In an attempt to overcome these objections, at a meeting of the London Conference on 19 July, 1945, the USA tabled a proposal defining aggression which it suggested be included in what was to become the Nuremberg Charter. It was in relation to this proposal that major great power differences over the purposes of a trial process for the top Nazis really came to a head. The US proposal drew heavily on the 1933 draft definition proposed by the Soviet Union under League auspices and the treaties of non-aggression between the Soviet Union and her neighbours agreed in 1931 to 1932.[25] The USA did not wish to 'litigate the cause of the war'[26] and in its view the incorporation of a definition of aggression into the Nuremberg Charter would help to avoid this outcome. From the American perspective,

> We either have to define [aggression] now, in which case it will end argument at the trial, or define it at the trial, in which case it will be the subject of an argument in which the Germans will participate; and it seems to me that it is much better that we face it now and preclude all of that argument.[27]

The UK backed the American proposal to include a definition of aggression in the Nuremberg Charter, on the basis that without one, 'we are rather opening the door for trouble'.[28] The British explained that the Conference had only three options where the Nuremberg Charter was concerned: (1) to omit aggression altogether from the charges, which was unappealing 'because it is the essence of our complaint against the Germans'[29]; (2) to include aggression undefined, which would mean enduring political debate at the trial about what is aggression; or (3) to define aggression.

By contrast, the Soviet Union argued that neither the London Conference nor the IMT was competent to define aggression, and that instead this was a task falling within the remit of the UN organisation. The purpose of the IMT was only to 'determine the measure of guilt of each particular person and mete out the necessary punishment';[30] Allied statements during World War II such as the Moscow and Yalta Declarations[31] had already established that Nazi leaders were criminals, and so questions about the causes and motivations for the war would simply not be raised or entertained before the IMT. Even if the London Conference did define aggression, in the Soviet opinion it would not be binding on the top Nazis.[32]

Like the Soviet Union, France did not favour the London Conference defining aggression; it preferred the question of aggression to be left to the judges themselves, relying on prior international documents on aggression to guide their conclusions. France argued that with or without a definition of aggression political controversy would arise, and that public opinion would have difficulty with a Nuremberg Charter definition that had the effect of excluding a potential defence.[33]

In response, the USA held fast to its view that either the London Conference or the IMT would have to define aggression, and sought to distance this task from the general question of defining aggression as a matter of future policy for the UN organisation. In Jackson's view, 'political definition seems to me much more difficult than juridical definition'.[34] Moreover, if the Soviet view was correct, and the criminality of aggression by the Nazi leaders had already been established by previous Allied political decree, Jackson did not see the point of a trial process at all. The meeting adjourned without resolution. The following day, the Soviet delegation pulled out of the agreed plan to visit Nuremberg with the other delegations to assess its suitability as a location for the IMT.

Final consensus on the charge of aggression emerged almost three weeks later, with the signing on 8 August 1945 of the London Agreement creating the International Military Tribunal and incorporating the Nuremberg Charter. From these documents it is evident that little real progress was made towards common agreement about this charge. Ongoing French and Soviet concerns over the uncertainty of international law and the lack of precedent for such a tribunal meant that the Nuremberg Charter omitted any reference to the legal foundations of the charges. Hence, the law on aggressive war, even post-Charter, remained an open question. Despite Anglo-American attempts to include a definition of aggression in the Nuremberg Charter, Franco-Soviet concerns also ensured that this did not occur. The limitation of the charge to 'the European Axis countries' stayed in at Soviet insistence.[35] A further Soviet victory was the renaming of the charge of aggression as a 'Crime Against Peace', a phrase originally used by Professor Trainin. Thus, aggression was to be prosecuted under Charter law according to the following:

> Article 6. (a) Crimes Against Peace: namely, planning, preparation, initiation or waging of a war of aggression, or a war in violation of international treaties, agreements or assurances, or participation in a Common Plan or Conspiracy for the accomplishment of any of the foregoing....[36]

Despite significant misgivings from the other Allied powers, the USA had succeeded in retaining the crime of aggression as the key charge against the top-ranking Nazis.

The crime of aggression at the IMT

With the foundations of the IMT thus laid, the case against the Nuremberg defendants was largely structured by American prosecutors, who sought to prove the existence of a conspiracy to commit aggression, war crimes and crimes against humanity.[37] Adding 'conspiracy' to the crux of the claim against the Nuremberg defendants caused its own problems, because while conspiracy was a reasonably well-developed concept in American law, its meaning in British law was much more limited, and in French and Soviet law it was entirely unknown.[38] This fact helped to determine among the great powers how to divide responsibility for presenting the prosecution's case: at the trial, the USA dealt with the conspiracy charge; the UK handled the aggression charge; France managed war crimes and crimes against humanity in Western Europe; and the Soviet Union was responsible for war crimes and crimes against humanity in Eastern Europe.[39] In practice, American responsibility for the all-encompassing conspiracy charge meant that US prosecutors exercised a high degree of control over how material was presented to the IMT and enjoyed the strategic advantage of introducing this material first, before other Allied prosecutors had an opportunity. Reflecting the significance of the charge of conspiracy in the prosecution's case, all twenty-two defendants were indicted under this head; sixteen were charged with aggression; eighteen were charged with war crimes, and eighteen with crimes against humanity.[40]

The strong American influence over the structure and content of the prosecution's case did not extend to the IMT bench, which proceeded cautiously. In accordance with the strict terms of the Nuremberg Charter, the IMT considered the allegation of conspiracy in relation to the aggression charge only, rejecting the US prosecution's attempt to have conspiracy recognised as an overarching, stand-alone offence incorporating aggression, war crimes and crimes against humanity. The IMT further limited its consideration of the aggression charges by focusing on whether or not the defendants played a role in relation to a war or wars of aggression; the alternative ground of a 'war in violation of international treaties' was left unconsidered.[41]

Having decided that aggression had been committed against twelve states, the IMT then considered very carefully the individual criminal liability of each defendant for this offence. The IMT restricted quite substantially the timing and scope of conduct amounting to the crime of aggression, and as a consequence, four of the sixteen defendants charged with this crime were acquitted of it.[42] Thus, although Schacht and Von Papen had been very active in top Nazi circles from at least 1933 onward, both with roles in the Anschluss, the fact that they began to lose their influence soon after this event was an influential factor in their acquittal.[43] Similarly, Speer's contribution to the German war effort as head of the arms industry from 1942 was not sufficient to prove him guilty of aggression, as Hitler's aggressive wars were already well under way by the time Speer accepted this position, and his contribution in this role only helped Germany 'in the same way that other productive enterprises aid in the waging of war'[44]. In

Von Papen's case, though he committed 'offences against political morality' such as 'intrigue and bullying'[45] to help to achieve the Anschluss, these were not made criminal by the Charter and hence could not establish guilt for a crime of aggression. Finally, the IMT also accepted evidence from the defendants about their activities in opposition to Hitler and his war plans, and about their motivations compelling their participation in Hitler's regime. These factors were also relevant in the acquittal of Schacht and Von Papen.[46]

This conservative approach to the crime of aggression was also reflected in the IMT's sentencing. Of the twelve men out of sixteen convicted of aggression, eight were sentenced to death,[47] three to life imprisonment,[48] one to fifteen years' jail[49] and one to ten years' jail.[50] All twelve men sentenced to death received convictions for war crimes and/or crimes against humanity, thus reflecting the stronger, pre-World War II legal basis underpinning these crimes. This result prevailed, despite the IMT's statement in its judgment that:

> To initiate a war of aggression, therefore, is not only an international crime; it is the supreme international crime differing only from other war crimes in that it contains within itself the accumulated evil of the whole.[51]

In addition, it is apparent that the majority IMT judgment was more than just a judicial rubber-stamp of US political priorities if it is compared with the dissenting IMT judgment entered by the Soviet judge. In accordance with the Soviet political view expressed during Allied negotiations that Nazi leaders had already been declared criminal prior to the Nuremberg Trial, the Soviet judge rejected the acquittals of Schacht, Von Papen and Fritzsche, and argued in favour of the death penalty for Hess. In light of the evidence tendered at trial relating to Schacht and Von Papen's acts of opposition to Nazism, it seems clear that, unlike the majority judges, the Soviet judge was intent on convicting all the Nuremberg defendants without discrimination. Hence, the conservatism inherent in the majority IMT judgment suggests that the way in which the crime of aggression was developed at Nuremberg acted as a restraint on the initial, cosmopolitan-inspired decision to prosecute that crime.

Criticisms of the Nuremberg Trial

The balance struck at Nuremberg between cosmopolitan aspirations promoting the evolution of an international crime of aggression giving rise to individual responsibility and restricted judicial endorsement of this crime has been attacked frequently on the grounds of 'victors' justice'. In the ongoing absence of any global mechanisms for settling questions of justice, however, we are left to consider the justice or injustice of a particular situation in context. It is argued that due consideration of the international political conditions existing at the end of World War II suggest that both the procedure and outcome of Nuremberg achieved substantial justice.

Political criticisms of the Nuremberg Trial

Certain critics justify the rejection of the Nuremberg Trial on policy grounds. They argue that the Nuremberg Trial could become a *political* precedent for victorious powers wishing to prosecute the vanquished. In this way, the Nuremberg Trial could encourage, or at least rationalise, the commission of injustices in the future.

Another political objection questions the wisdom of the Nuremberg Trial from the perspective of international order. Reflecting a very state-centric view, Schick argues that the London Agreement was made by the Allies contrary to state practice and the generally accepted tenets of international law. To him, this indicates a basic lack of understanding for the fact that it is the principles of non-intervention and sovereignty which allow and ensure peaceful coexistence among independent states in the first place.[52] The implication made by Schick is that by creating the IMT, the Allies helped to undermine the constitutive rules of an international society of states as recognised by Walzer.

In relation to these objections, any potential injustice or damage perpetrated by the Nuremberg Trial needs to be assessed in light of historical circumstance. The immediate problem the Allies faced as World War II came to a close was what to do with the top Nazis. The only options available were to: (1) execute them on the spot; (2) gaol them indefinitely without trial; (3) subject them to a trial process; (4) send them into exile or (5) free them. Exile of Napoleon had not prevented him from re-emerging as a political threat to Europe in 1815 and international public opinion combined with the threat of a Nazi resurgence meant Nazi leaders could not be freed. Similarly, gaoling them indefinitely without trial would create further political problems for the Allies by providing inspiration to Nazi revivalists during the Allied occupation of Germany. Hence, in reality, the only actual possibilities were to execute the top Nazis immediately or to hold a trial.[53]

The future possibility of injustice being caused by subsequent Nuremberg-style trials thus needs to be weighed against the very real political risk that the appearance of injustice posed to the Allied occupation and post-war normalisation of Germany. Moreover, from the perspective of the leading Nazis – and keeping in mind that three of them were cleared of all charges at the Nuremberg Trial – it provided a much higher level of fairness than summary justice would have achieved. The full range of procedural guarantees afforded most defendants in modern liberal democratic courts may not have been available to the German defendants, but they had the benefit of many fundamental ones – for instance, the choice of legal counsel, translation of all documents and proceedings, notice periods, even an opportunity at the close of their case to address the Tribunal personally and without challenge from the prosecution.[54]

In addition, while the principles of non-intervention and sovereignty are two of the basic international rules underpinning recognition and cooperation among states, it must be kept in mind that it was flagrant breaches of these principles by the Axis powers which ignited World War II. Axis contravention of these principles compelled the Allies to enter into the war, and, after the war had ended, to punish those responsible for these breaches. Had the Allies not acted in the way they did in response to these obvious, serious and consecutive breaches, the principles of non-intervention and sovereignty may never have regained international acceptance, thus potentially hindering the emergence of any form of state-based international society. In fact, the importance placed by judges on the fundamental rules of international society is apparent from the case of *United States of America* v *Ernst von Weizsacker et al.*[55] In this case, the principle of *pacta sunt servanda*[56] provided the justification for rejecting German claims of self-defence against the punitive provisions of the Treaty of Versailles. The Tribunal concluded that Germany's claim to self-defence was lost when it assured Austria, Czechoslovakia, France and Poland by treaty that it had no territorial claims, and then violated the terms of that agreement. The Tribunal pointed out that strong policy considerations supported this conclusion: if Germany's conduct after these agreements was excused, this would be tantamount to saying that 'no treaty and no assurance by Germany is binding and that the pledged word of Germany is valueless'.[57]

Legal criticisms of the Nuremberg Trial

As foreshadowed in discussions within the US administration and among the Big Four in the lead-up to the Nuremberg Trial, one of the first legal objections raised concerns the status of aggressive war immediately prior to the start of World War II. Even if it is accepted that the Kellogg–Briand Pact of 1928 made aggressive war illegal, it does not necessarily follow that the Pact simultaneously made it criminal. No international agreement criminalising wars of aggression was in force in 1939, and therefore, on the basis of the *nullum crimen sine lege*[58] principle, the Allies were not legally entitled to prosecute the top Nazis for aggression. This argument claims it was unjust to subject Nazi leaders to a legal principle and process which were both so manifestly *ex post facto*.[59]

Developed further, this objection adds that even if the improbable was accepted as true – namely that aggressive war was a crime in 1939 – no law at that time provided for the prosecution of *individuals* accused of its commission. For the establishment of the IMT to confer jurisdiction over the defendants, it would need to be shown that Germany consented to this jurisdiction by treaty, or that this was permitted by customary international law existing in 1939. Neither of these can be demonstrated, and thus no jurisdiction over these defendants could be legally conferred.

In addition, no entity such as the IMT or a permanent international criminal court existed in 1939 which might have prosecuted individuals for crimes against peace. Hence, the decision to go ahead with a criminal trial of the leading Nazis, on the basis of the Allies' view that Germany had resorted to an illegal war, was purely a political decision of the Allies as victors. As long as the right to make these key decisions is reserved to the victorious powers, whatever verdict results 'will constitute a legally problematical and politically hazardous act'.[60]

Further objections cite the procedural aspects of the Nuremberg Charter and Trial to support the conclusion that it amounted to 'victors' justice'. There are an almost infinite number of facts relied upon in support of this contention. For instance, article 3 of the Charter prohibited both prosecuting and defence counsel from challenging the Tribunal or its members. In addition, article 10 permitted individuals to be brought to trial merely on proof of membership of a group or organisation declared criminal by the Tribunal. Despite being called an *International Military Tribunal*, no judges from neutral states, let alone from the Axis powers, were on the bench. The Tribunal's historical interpretation was not impartial, in that it accepted draft, non-binding international documents as good evidence of the principle that aggressive war was considered a crime prior to 1939. Finally, the lack of incorporation of the lessons drawn from Nuremberg in the other constitutive documents of the post-war international order – such as the UN Charter and the Statute of the International Court of Justice – indicate an unwillingness to apply these lessons universally. All of these factors, it is argued, confirm the view that 'victor's justice' prevailed at Nuremberg.

In the context of a sophisticated, highly developed domestic legal order, these criticisms would be serious indeed; however, as raised in the context of the international arena of the 1930s and 1940s, they lack resonance. We have seen how the League system of security faltered in the aftermath of World War I without the accompanying development of worldwide, authoritative mechanisms for peaceful change. In such a highly decentralised international environment, and without innovation, each of the Allies would have dealt with the top Nazis as they saw fit, most likely killing them on capture. Recognising how this outcome could undermine the Allied occupation of Germany and trigger further conflict, it is precisely the absence of any alternative, international method for dealing with the leading Nazis which provoked the predominant political actor, the USA, to push for the establishment of the IMT. In light of the elementary nature of both the content and enforcement of international law at this time, it is counterproductive to attack an innovation designed to address this problem on the basis that it itself does not conform with legal principles more appropriate to a well-established legal system. For instance, the principles of *nullum crimen sine lege, nullum poena sine lege* and the rule against *ex post facto* laws became part of the law of domestic societies at a comparatively late stage of development.[61] Similarly, to expect international defendants to be afforded the same range of procedural guarantees as those enjoyed by defendants in many modern Western liberal democracies is another misapplication of the domestic analogy to international affairs. Hence, these criticisms can be refuted on the basis that the standard by which they measure the legal weaknesses of the Nuremberg Trial ignores the very significant impact of the absence of worldwide mechanisms for peaceful change on the development prospects of international law.

Conclusion

This chapter has demonstrated how cosmopolitan tendencies, supported by favourable political conditions while at the same time reined in by judicial conservatism, can achieve positive results in international relations. The problem of what to do with the Nazi elite in the closing days of World War II and public outcry at Germany's World War II conduct were both strong political factors pushing the Allied powers to come up with a plan which would support Allied occupation policy while at the same time morally condemning Germany's wartime purposes and the means it used to achieve these purposes. Achieving this latter objective would be particularly difficult for the Allies, as there were few grounds upon which to distinguish German means and ends from the conduct of other states – including the Allies – on previous occasions.[62] While in response to this challenge the USA argued in favour of prosecuting the German élites for the crime of aggression, the other Allies were far less enthusiastic, citing the weak legal basis of this approach. Only twenty-five years before, the World War I Allies had failed to persuade the Netherlands of its universal moral obligation to surrender Kaiser Wilhelm. The suggestion therefore that the leading Nazis were now bound individually to uphold international criminal law – itself underpinned by some sense of international morality and a few interwar draft agreements – seemed an even greater stretch.

Nevertheless, once the decision to proceed with prosecution of this crime had been made, differences among the Allies remained with regard to the issue of 'definition' of aggression, which revealed conflicting attitudes towards the international exercise of judicial discretion. While the USA and UK both favoured the inclusion of a definition of aggression in the Charter, France argued that the question of aggression should be left to the judges themselves to sort out, without the constraint of a definition. By contrast, the Soviet Union's position tolerated very little judicial freedom at all, arguing that the judges' role was simply to determine punishment, the guilt of the Nuremberg defendants having already been established by earlier political edict of the Allies themselves. In the end, a general statement outlining the crime of aggression was included in the Charter, which fell short of a very precise definition of acts deemed to comprise aggression, but nevertheless provided some guidance to the judges.

Although the innovation of prosecuting aggression as an individual crime had the potential to impose criminal sanctions against a very wide range of Germans, in practice, liability for this crime was limited to only the most important and central characters in the Hitler regime. In legal terms, the crime of aggression made possible the conviction of Hess, who played a very significant role at the highest echelon of regime leadership, though his individual acts were political rather than military in nature.[63] The restraint demonstrated by the majority of Nuremberg judges acted as an appropriate check where a broader approach may have resulted in the hanging or imprisonment of a large proportion of the population, with the resultant negative political consequences. While both the decision to prosecute the top Nazis and the jurisprudence generated by the Nuremberg Trial have led to many criticisms on 'victors' justice' grounds, these criticisms either fail to provide any satisfactory political alternatives, or apply standards more appropriate to a domestic setting rather than an international sphere characterised by the absence of global, authoritative mechanisms for peaceful change. Thus, the Nuremberg and subsequent trials demonstrate how the interaction of cosmopolitan and more conservative influences can produce a positive outcome – the articulation of an appropriately limited crime within international law – in favourable political conditions.

5 Aggression and individual criminal responsibility at the Tokyo Trial

In the last chapter it was shown how cosmopolitan impulses bolstered by moral outrage at the events of World War II and a lack of political alternatives in relation to the fate of the top Nazis led to their prosecution for the crime of aggression at Nuremberg. However, it was also demonstrated how these largely American impulses were tempered by both the European Allies' diverse views of the role of law in international politics, as well as judicial conservatism on the part of the Nuremberg bench. The combined impact of these influences helped shape the contours of the individual crime of international aggression in such a way as to defeat many of the most strident criticisms of Nuremberg.

The same cannot be said of the trial of Japanese leaders for the crime of aggression held in Tokyo after World War II. In this context, the American push to prosecute this crime was left essentially unfettered by European input. Consequently the pro-prosecution view overran virtually all other factors, including: (1) the legally questionable decision to exclude Emperor Hirohito entirely from the trial; (2) the piecemeal and weak evidence about the conduct of Japanese leaders before and during World War II; and (3) the circumstances of Japanese involvement in World War II. The decision to prosecute the crime of aggression regardless of these considerations militating against such prosecution left the judges with little basis upon which to adjudicate, and therefore the majority view followed closely the initial charges laid against the Japanese defendants. This, and other aspects of the trial, left it open to severe criticism on the grounds of bias, a lack of independence, and injustice, criticism which continues to the present day.[1] Consequently, if Nuremberg demonstrated what positive outcomes cosmopolitan thinking can achieve when grounded by the prevailing political and moral climate as well as judicial caution, Tokyo revealed the negative side of cosmopolitan initiatives which override all else. Before developing these arguments further however, it is necessary first to look more closely at the way in which the Pacific War ended, and how this differed from the final moments of the European War.

The end of World War II in the Asia-Pacific and the establishment of the International Military Tribunal for the Far East (IMTFE)

As in the European theatre, the Allies issued general policy statements during the Pacific War concerning how they planned to deal with Japanese war criminals, leaving the details to be ironed out once surrender and occupation ensued. Hence, the Cairo Declaration of 1 December 1943,[2] issued by the USA, UK and China declared that 'the Three Great Allies are fighting this war to restrain and punish the aggression of Japan'. Similarly, paragraph 10 of the Potsdam Declaration of 26 July 1945[3] indicated that 'stern justice shall be meted out to all war criminals, including those who have visited cruelties upon our prisoners …', and called for Japan's unconditional surrender.

However, the different circumstances surrounding the end of World War II in Europe as compared with World War II in the Asia-Pacific resulted in the prosecution of top elites for war crimes becoming a much more central issue in the Japanese surrender than in its German predecessor. By the date of German surrender on 7 May 1945, the Allies had already taken de facto occupation of much of Germany, Soviet troops had entered Berlin, and Hitler, Germany's dictatorial leader and ultimate mastermind of that country's warmongering, had committed suicide.[4] Others among those who had been part of Hitler's inner circle had either fled, also killed themselves, or joined Admiral Doenitz in the establishment of a new government at Flensburg with the aim of postponing surrender as long as possible so that German military and civilians in the East could be saved from Soviet forces. In short, by this time the German cause had revealed itself as well and truly hopeless, and Doenitz's government had no real choice but to accept the Allies' demand for unconditional surrender.

By contrast, although the outlook was pretty grim for Japan by the time of the Potsdam Declaration, it still had a real choice whether to surrender or to continue to fight. Allied forces had not yet reached Japan – in fact, Japanese forces still controlled Korea and Manchuria, much of China, and virtually the whole of Southeast Asia. Japanese war-making capacity still existed, which included 2.5 million combat-ready troops, 9,000 military aircraft, and ample kamikaze volunteers.[5] Although discussions in the Japanese Supreme Council for the Direction of the War about how to respond to the Potsdam Declaration revealed divisions on whether to start negotiating a peace agreement or to fight to the death, on one issue all were united: that the Emperor, who in formal terms was the supreme authority in Japan, must not be subjected to prosecution for war crimes. It was this implication of the Declaration which was most important to the members of this Council and reflected Hirohito's divine status within Japanese society.[6] In light of the Allies' arrests of high-ranking Nazis in the weeks following German surrender, members of the Council had good reason to suspect that the Allies had a similar fate in mind for them and their Emperor. In the end, no Japanese response to the Declaration was made until after the Allied use of atomic weapons against Hiroshima and Nagasaki on 6 and 9 August respectively.

The vital significance of the fate of the Emperor in Japanese calculations at this time is reflected in the response eventually made: on 10 August, Japan conditionally accepted the Declaration's terms, 'with the understanding that the said declaration does not comprise any demand which prejudices the prerogatives of His Majesty as Sovereign Ruler', and a request that this qualification be expressly acknowledged by the Allies.[7] The Allied reply stipulated that the Emperor would be subject to the authority of the Supreme Commander of the Allied Powers (SCAP) General Douglas MacArthur; outlined what the Emperor would be required to do to effect the surrender; and simply stated that 'the ultimate form of government of Japan shall, in accordance with the Potsdam Declaration, be established by the freely expressed will of the Japanese people'.[8] On this basis, Japan communicated its final acceptance on 14 August, and signed the instrument of surrender on 2 September.

Once surrender had officially taken place, the task of occupation began. Confirming the implication from earlier Allied correspondence that the Emperor would not be treated as a common war crimes suspect, the US interdepartmental committee responsible for occupation policy directed MacArthur in September to take no action against the Emperor, despite some opposition from other Allies.[9] However, personal impunity for the Emperor did not extend to his intimates or other members of the royal household, with MacArthur ordering the arrest of Kido, the Emperor's chief adviser, and two princes towards the end of 1945. The Japanese government failed to secure a delay of the arrest of Prince Nashimoto; two days after the arrest order concerning Prince Konoye[10] and Kido, the Emperor volunteered himself for trial 'as the one to bear the sole responsibility for every political and military decision made and action taken by my people in the conduct of the war'.[11] However, in light of MacArthur's existing instructions not to arrest the Emperor, nothing came of this rather astonishing offer. While Kido was later taken into custody and prosecuted by the IMTFE, Prince Konoye preferred suicide to trial.[12] The way in which the Emperor's fate was interwoven with the peace terms, and the decision not to prosecute him, would complicate greatly efforts to hold elites criminally responsible for aggression.

It was not just the choice of who to arrest that strongly reflected US political preferences – the question of what to do with them was also determined by American priorities. Thus, MacArthur proclaimed the creation of the IMTFE on 19 January 1946, approving its functions, jurisdiction and constitution the same day. As a SCAP initiative, the IMTFE was controlled more directly by US interests than the International Military Tribunal at Nuremberg. While at Nuremberg, decisions concerning judicial appointments were made at the highest tiers of government by the USA, UK, Soviet Union and France, with the judges themselves electing a president from among their number, at Tokyo, it was MacArthur who exercised both of these powers. MacArthur himself also retained the right to review the sentences imposed by the IMTFE and reduce them if necessary, a power at Nuremberg reserved by the Control Council for Germany.[13]

By all measures, the Tokyo Trial took on mammoth proportions compared to its Nuremberg counterpart. From indictment to judgment, the Nuremberg process had lasted just under a year; the Tokyo Trial went on for just over two and a half years. The sheer number of people present in the courtroom at any one time was greatly expanded at Tokyo on account of eleven powers being entitled to appoint associate prosecuting counsel[14] and the use of both Japanese and American defence counsel in the proceedings. Relaxed rules of evidence and the burden of translation at Tokyo exponentially increased the amount of paper required to service the Trial: for its duration, the Trial took up a quarter of the Occupation Forces' total paper supply, and at one point more paper had to be flown in from the USA exclusively to meet the Tribunal's requirements.[15] Reflecting this greater complexity, one concurring opinion, two dissenting opinions and three separate opinions were recorded in addition to the majority judgment.

Hence, from the closing days of World War II in the Asia-Pacific onward, it was evident that the circumstances in which the Pacific War would end were very different from those in Europe. In particular, the high importance Japanese leaders placed on the sovereign immunity of the Emperor, in conjunction with the formal responsibility assumed by the USA for every aspect of Japanese surrender and occupation, were calculations unique to the Pacific War which impacted directly on the decision of whether or not to prosecute the crime of aggression at Tokyo, and if so, how to prosecute it.

The decision not to prosecute Emperor Hirohito

While the decision not to prosecute the Emperor, or even compel him to testify as a witness, was explicable according to a variety of political rationales,[16] this decision significantly eroded arguments in support of the prosecution of Japanese defendants for the crime of aggression. Emperor Hirohito had been the Japanese head of state at all material times before and during World War II; in terms of formal position he had been Hitler's equal. Moreover, the extreme turbulence experienced in Japanese politics before and during the war meant that Hirohito was virtually the only constant position-holder throughout this period of interest, and thus he was uniquely situated to give evidence about the protagonists of, and the events leading up to, Japanese involvement in World War II.[17] If the purpose of the crime of aggression was to hold individual leaders to account for their contribution to the waging of aggressive war, it was difficult to justify Hirohito's immunity from prosecution, especially in light of his status as ultimate commander of Japan's combined armed forces.[18] Even if it was true that in practice, Hirohito's authority was significantly fettered by custom and that therefore he was more like a figurehead, one would expect this to be reflected in the outcome of the trial process; this claim does not, on its own, justify no prosecution of the Emperor at all. While Hirohito enjoyed immunity from prosecution, on what basis could any of his own ministers or other subordinates be prosecuted for the so-called 'leadership' crime of aggression?

Although this contention could be used to challenge the trial of any of the Tokyo defendants for the crime of aggression, it was an especially powerful argument in relation to Kido. From 1930 onward, Kido was a top official in the Japanese imperial court, and from 1940 he became Hirohito's closest adviser.[19] Other than brief periods as Minister of Education (1937), Welfare (1938) and Home Affairs (1939), Kido's exclusive responsibilities were to Hirohito. If Hirohito was immune from prosecution, it is very difficult to understand how his most senior adviser could simultaneously be convicted of the crime of aggression against four states by the IMTFE – yet this was precisely the outcome of the Tokyo judgment.

Thus, the significance of Hirohito's future in the Japanese decision to surrender, and the SCAP decision not to prosecute him, were both important political factors which eroded any arguments in favour of a trial of the remaining Japanese leaders for the crime of aggression. Such problems were entirely avoided at Nuremberg as a consequence of Hitler's suicide. The difficulties caused by the lack of justification for proceeding with a trial of Japanese leaders for the crime of aggression in light of Hirohito's immunity was noted by both President Webb and Judge Bernard in their separate opinions within the Tokyo judgment.[20]

Evidence and the crime of aggression

Another condition of the Japanese surrender which undermined arguments in favour of prosecuting the Japanese defendants for the crime of aggression was a relative lack of probative evidence on which to build a case against them. In the German context, orders from Berlin to destroy archives as Allied forces entered Germany were largely ignored, and thus the overwhelming bulk of the archives remained intact, providing the Allies with, quite literally, thousands of documents outlining in great detail the plans, practices, participants and policies within the Nazi regime.[21] The comprehensiveness and very high quality of this documentation provided excellent evidentiary basis upon which to proceed with a criminal prosecution of aggression against the Nuremberg defendants; there were plenty of 'smoking guns' with their fingerprints all over them.

At Tokyo, however, the documentary evidence was not of the same standard: many Japanese had in fact destroyed, changed, or hidden incriminating evidence, or falsified records, immediately preceding the American landing.[22] Indeed, with a twelve-day interval between the Allied acceptance of Japan's surrender and the arrival in Tokyo of the first party of Americans, there was ample opportunity to destroy the most damning evidence: Brackman reports that among those documents destroyed at this time were the transcripts of all imperial conferences, all the records of the Supreme Council for the Direction of the War, all the deliberations of the Cabinet and Privy Council, all files on prisoners of war, all orders and plans concerning the attack on the Philippines and Southeast Asia, and all the documents in relation to the Manchurian and Chinese campaigns.[23] The evidence that remained was either of lesser importance or of more questionable reliability.[24] Consequently, the prosecution's case largely relied on the diary of Kido, who had voluntarily surrendered it to the Allies.[25] As a result of this reduction in the qualitative standard of evidence, the very complete picture of events achieved at Nuremberg was not possible at Tokyo, resulting in many gaps concerning issues crucial to the case, such as the relationship between different political factions within the government at certain times and how powers were divided and exercised among important individuals. In these circumstances, it is difficult to see how a trial of Japanese leaders for the crime of aggression could be pursued without either substantial risk of reducing normal thresholds of criminal responsibility to virtually nil – in effect creating a 'guilty until proven innocent' principle – or acquittals on a large scale.[26] Yet another significant obstacle arising out of the unique context of the Pacific War discouraged the prosecution of Japanese elites for the crime of aggression.

The crime of aggression and the circumstances of Japanese involvement in World War II

A third factor problematising the decision to try Japanese leaders for the crime of aggression was the difference between Japanese and German conduct itself in relation to World War II. What facts could be adduced at Tokyo in light of the evidentiary challenges already mentioned suggested that no easy analogy between the German and Japanese roles in World War II could be made. The general history of Germany immediately prior to, during and after World War II is reasonably straightforward and very familiar: the Nazi Party, with Hitler as its dictatorial leader at all material times, successfully seized power at an early stage, organised and controlled German domestic life according to Nazism's ideological aims, and in pursuit of these aims, from 1938 to 1945 it embarked upon the gradual German conquest of Europe via a program of false assurances, invasion and annexation.

Conversely, the history of Japan reveals broad support at all levels for the pursuit of Japanese regional domination, but significant differences of view as to how to achieve this. A bitter struggle ensued in leadership circles between a faction which supported wholeheartedly the use of force and Japan's formal alignment with Germany and Italy to attain this objective, and others who advocated different, less immediately confrontational approaches. This struggle was enabled by a political system which encouraged power rivalries between different organs of government by assigning to each of them an exclusive sphere of authority, and making them and cabinet ministers directly answerable to the Emperor, not to the Prime Minister.[27] While this separation of powers was designed to restrain any one organ of government from gaining too much political clout, it also meant that it was very difficult to pinpoint from among these organs which individual or individuals exercised actual decision-making authority for Japan on a particular issue at a specific point in time. For instance, despite the extensive powers invested in the Emperor under the 1889 Constitution, tradition dictated that he rarely meddled in politics or administration. Instead, the Emperor was expected to endorse the collective advice of cabinet and military heads on matters of policy.[28] Formal imperial statements were in fact drawn up by the Cabinet or military and had to receive initial approval from another body, the Privy Council, before the Emperor signed them. Similarly, in relation to the appointment of senior officials, Hirohito was supposed to act according to the wishes of yet another set of advisers. However, in other ways, he was able to exercise great influence by using occasions on which he met with senior officials or military chiefs to question them, issue general guidelines and express his own opinion about their work. In addition, when his advisers were divided, Hirohito would personally intervene to decide the issue.[29] Clearly then, identifying responsible individuals and groups within the Tokyo regime was always going to be a much more difficult task than in a centralised dictatorship like Nazi Germany.

In addition, a procedural rule insisting upon unanimity of cabinet decisions or in the event of disagreement the formation of a new cabinet, also had an impact during this struggle, and resulted in fifteen different Japanese cabinets in seventeen years. This constant political volatility meant that, unlike the German scenario, no clear pattern or system of conduct could be discerned which encompassed all the alleged counts of Japanese aggression; opportunism provided a better explanation of Japanese acts during this period than ideology. Apart from general economic motivations, Japan's hostile actions in China in 1931 had few obvious connections in terms of actors, methods or immediate objectives with, for example, the attack on Pearl Harbor ten years later. This procedural rule also complicated substantially efforts to ascertain the degree to which each defendant was individually responsible for the decisions of the group. For example, what degree of responsibility, if any, would an individual merely acquiescing in a decision to proceed with war face, as opposed to an individual who actively supported this decision? Were an individual's intentions relevant? Were the prevailing political circumstances relevant, and if so, how could these be taken into account in the judicial determination as to whether or not an individual was criminally responsible for aggression? These difficult questions were evaded at Nuremberg, where Nazi Germany's totalitarian political structure and strong evidence of how, and by whom, political powers were exercised made the task of tribunal adjudication comparatively easy.

Eventually, through the use of intimidation tactics, deception and even assassination, Japan's militaristic faction gained the upper hand over its uncoordinated opponents and in effect exercised a controlling influence over the government of Japan, though many ostensibly important positions remained occupied by those outside of, or unsympathetic to, this faction. Even in relation to this faction, there was no evidence of a 'conspiracy'[30] in the Nuremberg sense: initially, individuals, usually of lesser ranking, who supported the use of force in the advancement of Japan's goal either acted alone or in small groups, simply exploiting as much as possible their existing official positions to achieve the hostile engagement of the Japanese military in China.[31] While top élites may have acquiesced in or at least failed to prevent these actions, few of them could properly be accused of the same type or level of positive acts in pursuit of warmongering for which the Nazi leaders were convicted. In short, the facts could not be easily moulded to the crime of aggression category prosecuted and developed at Nuremberg. Hence, even if evidence of the German standard was available in the Tokyo case, it was likely that a tribunal would come under heavy pressure to either throw out the case against Japanese leaders, or return many 'not guilty' verdicts on the basis of different facts.

The combination of the prior political decision not to prosecute the Emperor, patchy evidence and circumstances significantly different from the German situation were conditions so detrimental to any possible rationale in favour of the prosecution of Japanese leaders for the crime of aggression that they should have been sufficient to reject this possibility outright. While an argument was made at Nuremberg that the blatant wars of conquest embarked upon by Germany were classifiable under this heading on the basis of pre-war efforts to criminalise aggression and outlaw war 'as an instrument of national policy',[32] it was a much greater leap to suggest that Japan's pursuit of regional domination by a range of means, many of which fell short of wars of conquest, also constituted crimes of aggression. Whereas it could reasonably be argued that moral outrage at the horrors of World War I had brought the acceptability of wars of conquest to an end, to the extent that Japan achieved its objective by means other than wars of conquest, such as duress, treaty, installation of a puppet regime and similar, no possible case could be made. On the contrary, a state's pursuit of its economic goals by these means was a relatively regular feature of international relations. Put simply, whether because of the immunity of the Emperor, a lack of probative evidence necessary for a legal case or different facts, the Tokyo scenario was ill suited to a Nuremberg-style trial of its vanquished leaders for the crime of aggression.

The crime of aggression in the Tokyo judgment

In these circumstances, it is unsurprising that the Tokyo judgment followed the prosecution's case much more closely than did the Nuremberg judgment. With an even less secure political, moral and legal foundation than that supporting the prosecution of German leaders for aggression at Nuremberg, the Tokyo Tribunal had few guidelines on which to draw in coming to its conclusions. This left the Tokyo Tribunal with only initial American political preferences in favour of prosecuting Japanese leaders for aggression, and hence it is these that are expressed to a very large extent in the Tokyo judgment. By contrast, the relatively stronger basis underpinning the Nuremberg prosecution ensured a more independent Tribunal and hence a judgment which did more than merely confirm the charges against the defendants. This distinction between the judgments is demonstrated in a number of ways.

For instance, the notion of conspiracy upheld by the Tokyo judgment, as compared to that supported by the Nuremberg judgment, reveals the ongoing impact during the Tokyo Trial of the extremely weak legal basis on which it was founded. At Nuremberg, it will be recalled from Chapter 4 that the IMT rejected the prosecution's attempt to have conspiracy recognised as a stand-alone international crime, and adhered strictly to the terms of the Nuremberg Charter, under which conspiracy was relevant in relation to the crime of aggression only.[33] The same conservatism was not evident in the Tokyo judgment. There, prosecutors went even further than their Nuremberg counterparts, not just separating out the conspiracy charge, but expressing it in language radically different from that used in the Tokyo Charter, which largely followed the Nuremberg provision.[34] Hence, all of the Tokyo defendants were charged with an ongoing conspiracy between 1928 and 1945, the aim of which was:

> that Japan should secure the military, naval, political and economic domina-
> tion of East Asia and of the Pacific and Indian Oceans, and of all countries
> and islands therein and bordering thereon, and for that purpose should alone
> or in combination with other countries having similar objects, or who could
> be induced or coerced to join therein, wage declared or undeclared war or
> wars of aggression and war or wars in violation of international law, treaties,
> agreements and assurances, against any country or countries which might
> oppose that purpose.[35]

Apart from reading down the geographical boundaries of this charge,[36] and despite its expansive terms, which brought into question whether what was being alleged even fell within the ambit of the crime of aggression as stipulated by the Tokyo Charter, the Tokyo Tribunal upheld this charge.[37] It made this decision based on far less probative evidence than that relied upon at Nuremberg.[38] Worse, the wide scope of this charge and its vague language simultaneously broadened the range of persons likely to be found liable, while making it much more difficult for them to defeat this charge. As a result, twenty-three of the twenty-five Tokyo defendants against whom a judgment was entered[39] were found guilty of conspiracy. More-over, two of these were convicted of conspiracy despite being acquitted of waging aggressive war, suggesting a reversal of the Nuremberg conclusion – namely that conspiracy *was* a stand-alone crime in international law, though few, if any, refer-ences could be used in support of this claim. The Tokyo Tribunal's acceptance of the prosecution's broad conspiracy claim also made it easier to implicate the Tokyo defendants in the waging of aggressive war, and thus twenty-two of them were convicted of this charge.

Another indication that the Tokyo Tribunal lacked independence was the fact that only one defendant was acquitted of all aggression charges made against him.[40] Although this is not necessarily proof of a politically controlled tribunal, in light of the flaws undermining the Tokyo Trial from the start, several acquittals on aggression would have been a reasonable prediction had general legal princi-ples prevailed in the judgment. By comparison, at Nuremberg, ten defendants were acquitted of aggression charges.[41]

There are many other procedural features of the Tokyo Trial which suggest that its outcome was largely a foregone conclusion once the American decision to proceed with prosecution had been made. Some of these include the wording of the Tokyo Charter compared with its Nuremberg counterpart;[42] partiality on the part of some of the judges;[43] the change in evidence admissibility rules half-way through the Tokyo Trial, which disproportionately disadvantaged the defence; the Tokyo Tribunal's insistence that defence evidence in mitigation of sentence be submitted before its verdict was even released; and the absence of certain judges for periods of time without provision of an alternative.[44]

However, perhaps the ultimate indication of the supremacy of political forces in favour of the prosecution of the crime of aggression at the heavy expense of legal principles in the Tokyo case was the fact that not one of the eighteen Japanese defendants sentenced to imprisonment served the full term of his sentence. While four died in prison,[45] fourteen were paroled in the 1950s.[46] Of these fourteen, thirteen had originally been given life sentences. Shigemitsu, who was sentenced to seven years' imprisonment, was the first to be released in 1950, and four years later he reassumed his position as Foreign Minister of Japan. In contrast, at Nuremberg, four of the seven defendants served their full sentence.[47] The mass release of Japanese defendants might be explained as a response to recognition of the significant and numerous factors originally militating against the decision to prosecute Japanese leaders for aggression, which subsequently coloured the process and outcome of the Tokyo Trial, or as a response to changed political conditions. Either way, this action seriously undercuts the view expressed in the Nuremberg judgment, that initiation of a war of aggression constitutes 'the supreme international crime, differing only from other war crimes in that it contains within itself the accumulated evil of the whole'.[48] From this, it is apparent that the crime of aggression at the Tokyo Trial simply provided a rationale for effectively ousting particular Japanese elites from power during the US occupation of Japan.

Conclusion

The Tokyo Trial may be interpreted as a cautionary tale about the limitations on what cosmopolitan-inspired legal mechanisms can achieve in the international arena when pursued purely out of narrow, political self-interest despite factual circumstances which defy legal classification. While at Nuremberg, the decision in favour of prosecuting the crime of aggression was facilitated by Hitler's suicide, high-quality documentary evidence and a reasonably clear case history revealing a series of wars of conquest planned and implemented from the highest levels of government authority, the absence of these facilitating factors in the Tokyo circumstances militated strongly against the criminal prosecution of aggression there. Despite these major obstacles, and in accordance with American political priorities, the decision was made to proceed with the Tokyo Trial and the prosecution of aggression. However, the impact of these obstacles continued to be significant, resulting in a judgment and verdict that was much more questionable than the Nuremberg outcome. These weaknesses were exacerbated by a range of procedural problems with the Tokyo Trial which unfairly helped the prosecution's argument and hence demonstrated further the centrality of political objectives at Tokyo. As a result, with little guidance from the law, it was reasonably predictable that the majority of judges at Tokyo would affirm the prosecution's case to a very great extent. Since this time, the Tokyo Trial has usually been described in negative terms, and the value of the Tokyo judgment as a source of law has proven extremely limited – unlike Nuremberg, which is frequently relied upon in both modern-day case law and academic debate. To the small extent that the Tokyo jurisprudence is discussed today at all, it is the dissenting opinions of Bert Roling and Radhabinod Pal which attract the most attention, both of whom were critical of the conclusions drawn by the majority of judges.[49]

Over and above anything else, the decision to proceed with a trial of the Japanese defendants for aggression was dictated by the requirements of the American occupation force, led by the SCAP. This decision was not altered even though it became apparent that such a trial would be beset by overwhelming legal problems of a kind unknown at Nuremberg. In this way, the prosecution of the crime of aggression at the IMTFE and the Tokyo Trial's outcome are much more obvious exercises of naked political power than the Nuremberg experience. The Tokyo Trial demonstrates how easily ostensible cosmopolitan projects – such as holding individuals responsible for 'crime[s] against civilisation'[50] – can be hijacked by the most powerful states to justify what in fact is nothing more than an outcome reflecting their own, individual, narrow self-interest. The result is bad case law which itself undermines the role of those rules and standards which have a genuine claim to represent international law. Thus, it is evident that cosmopolitan changes must reflect, and take sufficient heed of, prevailing political and legal conditions in order to avoid a counter-productive outcome.

6 The UN's 'definition' of state aggression, 1944 to 1974

In Chapter 3, it was demonstrated that the weakness of the League Covenant's concept of aggression as a moral trigger for collective security action led to efforts by members to *define* aggression, with a view to creating an unambiguous, legally proscribed act. In the end, however, no consensus on a definition of aggression emerged, and the League was eventually destroyed by the onset of World War II.

Despite this early lack of success – and Wilson's prior rejection of legal approaches to aggression – from the 1940s onward the idea re-emerged of making more precise through legal definition what state aggression comprises. Attempts towards this goal were made over a thirty-year period; yet three separate political struggles prevented any progress from being made. The first struggle, which took place during the UN Charter negotiations, existed initially among the great powers, all of whom sought to promote a new international security organisation in their own, individual self-interests. From the initial plans discussed among the great powers, it is evident that they were divided on the role of aggression. Once the broad outline of the new organisation had been thrashed out among the great powers, a second struggle emerged, this time between the great powers collectively on the one hand and the small and middle powers on the other. The great powers' division over aggression was resurrected, with the small and middle powers pushing for a definition of aggression to be included in the founding document of the new organisation as a way of subjecting the great powers to the force of law, both compelling and limiting their actions. Although the small and middle powers lost this battle, the issue of defining aggression continued in the post-Charter period. While UN committees consistently approached the problem of aggression as simply a question of legal definition, the disputes played out in these committees reflected a third political struggle: the Cold War conflict between the USA and the Soviet Union, as well as their respective allies.

Once again, it is revealed in this chapter that the narrow self-interest of states acts as a significant constraint on broader cosmopolitan goals such as the further development of international law. This chapter shows this to be true even in relation to those basic values which attract universal condemnation, such as aggression. Thus, the significance of favourable political conditions as a necessary foundation for cosmopolitan progress cannot be underestimated. Before examining attempts to define aggression in the UN period, it is important first to understand how the notion came to be included in the UN Charter, particularly after the controversy it generated in relation to the League.

Aggression in the United Nations Charter

Pre-Dumbarton Oaks Conference

Planning for the maintenance of peace and security post-World War II via a form of international organisation commenced soon after hostilities began in 1939, and again was largely spearheaded by the USA. While the first State Department committee assigned to this task was established at the beginning of 1940,[1] its efforts were soon interrupted by the more immediate challenges posed by Hitler's march across Europe. Subsequent planning attempts met with the same fate until December 1943, when the Department's Informal Political Agenda Group was officially charged with this duty.

It was this group which examined all the major issues concerning postwar security and drew up comprehensive drafts for an international organisation, which were then forwarded to the President for his consideration and comment. Like Wilson, Roosevelt preferred an international organisation of universal reach, rather than one comprising a system of bilateral alliances or regional groupings;[2] however, he was also keen to avoid comparisons between the new organisation and the failed League of Nations, or characterisations of the new organisation as some form of world superstate. Thus, he supported a decentralised organisation in which security decisions would be made collectively by the USA, UK, China and the Soviet Union on a 'unanimity with abstention' basis.[3] Roosevelt communicated these views and his general approval of the group's proposals to the Department in February 1944; a more detailed draft was then produced, which laid the foundations of the Department's submission to the Dumbarton Oaks Conferences. This submission became the unofficial working document of those conferences.[4]

On the other side of the Atlantic, the UK turned its attention in a serious way to postwar planning in autumn 1942. However, real progress was slow until August 1943, owing to major differences of opinion between the Foreign Office and the Prime Minister about the new international organisation. While the Foreign Office supported Roosevelt's plan for a universal organisation in which the Big Four held a controlling interest, Churchill vigorously defended a regionally organised structure, and saw little merit for the UK in the universalist, Big Four plan. For Churchill, Europe, her recovery and the containment of the Soviet Union were the central concerns, and these priorities should have been strongly reflected in British proposals for the postwar international organisation.[5] Finally at the Quebec Conference in August 1943, Churchill reluctantly accepted Roosevelt's proposal for a universal security organisation, thus clearing the way for more comprehensive British plans to be drawn up. By April 1944, a British interdepartmental committee had drafted five memoranda outlining the preferred contours of the new organisation from the British perspective.

The second memorandum, known as Memorandum B on peace and security, skilfully relied on the perceived drafting errors of the League Covenant to argue forcefully for the British position. As in the negotiations leading up to the establishment of the League, the UK opposed any undertaking to guarantee members' 'territorial integrity' or 'political independence', for the reason that such a guarantee would make the new organisation vulnerable to allegations of preserving the status quo and making peaceful change of borders impossible. The difficulty of defining 'political independence' was also raised as a reason not to make it the subject of a guarantee. In a similar vein, the UK opposed any reference to 'justice' in dispute settlement, as a consequence of its 'ambiguous legalistic implications'[6] and out of recognition that, in certain circumstances, maintaining peace may mean that some members must bear lesser injustices.

The UK view was also highly sceptical of any attempt to use the term 'aggression' in relation to the new organisation. Memorandum B pressed the position that making the punishment of aggression the foundation for League action under article 10 of the Covenant had been a grave error. This stipulation meant that too much League time had been wasted trying to define aggression in light of each set of circumstances coming before the League, which had aided aggressors by delaying the League's response to their acts.[7] Yet it was also probable that a strict definition of aggression would also impede the new organisation in the fulfilment of its peace and security functions. Consequently, with regard to the constitutional documents of the new organisation, the UK rejected the inclusion of a list of circumstances amounting to aggression in relation to which the new organisation would act. Rather, it preferred to afford the new Council a high level of discretion on this issue, empowering it to act 'in accordance with the principles and objects of the Organisation'.[8] Hence, it appeared that at least one of the major powers was mindful from the outset of the moral and legal risks generated by placing 'aggression' at the centre of international security arrangements.

By contrast, the Soviet perspective viewed aggression – more specifically, the prospect of revived German aggression, and ways of preventing this possibility – as the *raison d'être* of the new postwar organisation. On this basis, Stalin, like Churchill, initially favoured some form of regional organisation for Europe, though he too eventually came to support Roosevelt's worldwide aspirations. Beyond these very vague indicators, specific Soviet ambitions for the new organisation at this time were opaque.[9] However, it was clear that the Soviet Union was preoccupied with how the new organisation would serve its own security interests; other proposed features of the new organisation – such as an economic and social council and an international court of justice – were of little importance in Soviet eyes.[10]

Dumbarton Oaks Conference, August to October 1944

These initial views were further developed and argued out at Dumbarton Oaks. In the first and most important round, with the US, UK and Soviet Union in attendance, the difference between British and Soviet views on the relevance of the concept of aggression in the new organisation became even sharper. In accordance with the Soviet view that the primary purpose of the Security Council was to keep aggression in check, it insisted that the term be expressly included in the Charter provisions dealing with the scope of the Council's powers.[11] The Soviet delegation reasoned that the term 'aggression' had gained in prevalence in the preceding years, particularly as a consequence of certain prominent pronouncements by the major Allied powers themselves.[12] This justified an explicit reference to aggression in the new organisation's constitution. In addition, the Soviet Union failed to see how peacekeeping could take place unless based on the fundamental aim of punishing aggressors. The Soviet Union envisaged the Security Council as the institutionalised version of the USSR–US–UK wartime alliance, with the Security Council using its superior military power to combat future aggressors as the wartime alliance had done against Nazi Germany.[13]

In response, the UK largely reiterated the reasons outlined in Memorandum B for omitting the term 'aggression'. The League's history of time-wasting and failure caused by placing the concept of aggression at the heart of its security provisions could only be overcome by abandoning the concept altogether and instead substituting more practical terminology, such as 'breach of the peace'. On this point the UK had the support of the US, which viewed the phrase 'act of aggression' as overloaded with moral implications.[14] In a shift away from its prior role promoting the concept of aggression for the purposes of international security and prosecuting warmongering state leaders, the US now preferred the abandonment of 'aggression'. Instead, it favoured less morally charged language like 'breach of the peace', which it felt would in any case still capture conduct falling within the 'aggression' category.[15] Despite the best arguments of the USA and UK, the Soviet Union refused to yield on the importance of incorporating the concept of aggression into the constitution of the new organisation. Thus, the compromise formula empowering the Security Council with respect to a 'threat to the peace, breach of the peace or act of aggression' was agreed upon, and formed part of the Dumbarton Oaks Proposals, which were later used as the basis of discussions at San Francisco.[16]

On the related issue of whether to include a definition of aggression in the new organisation's charter, the British position easily triumphed. The great technological advances in warfare experienced in the first part of the twentieth century, coupled with the uncertainty of not knowing how warfare might develop in the future, highlighted the need for the Security Council to be able to exercise its full powers unencumbered by definitions or other potential fetters.[17] Whether convinced by these arguments, or merely eager to protect their own freedom of action, the Americans and Soviets agreed with the British to exclude a definition of aggression from the final text of the Dumbarton Oaks Proposals.[18] Defining state aggression for legal purposes in the founding document of the post-World War II security organisation had been rejected by the major powers in favour of a general reference to aggression only – though it would not be long before this decision would be subject to renewed debates.

United Nations Conference on International Organisation, San Francisco, April to June 1945

At San Francisco, where fifty governments met to discuss the Dumbarton Oaks Proposals for the new international organisation, the issue of defining aggression in the Charter was again raised. Many delegations, particularly from among the smaller states, were extremely reluctant to leave the Security Council with the broad, sweeping discretionary powers it enjoyed under the Proposals.[19] The smaller powers feared that the great powers might use such a provision to justify action in circumstances more politically expedient for them than strictly international security-threatening.

To this end, draft amendments to the Proposals from Bolivia and the Philippines were circulated on 5 May, both of which included definitions of aggression.[20] At the meeting of Committee III/3 on 18 May, which addressed the new organisation's enforcement arrangements, these states jointly proposed a motion compelling immediate Security Council intervention in the event of at least one of the circumstances specified in the Bolivian amendment actually taking place.[21] This motion attracted support from a range of small and middle powers, including Uruguay, Mexico, Colombia, Egypt, Ethiopia, Guatemala, Honduras, Iran, Mexico and New Zealand. Delegates from these states reiterated similar arguments in favour of definition to those presented by China at Dumbarton Oaks – namely, (1) it was preferable to know in advance what acts comprised aggression and hence would attract sanctions; (2) the Security Council would be aided in its work by the incorporation of a list of specified aggressive acts into the Charter; and (3) the list did not have to be exclusive, and thus the Security Council would still be able to act in situations falling outside the scope of the list.

In an effort to resolve the crucial problem of enforcement, which had also plagued the League, this group of states argued further that the Charter should make explicit that the occurrence of any of the circumstances contained in the Bolivian list should give rise to *automatic* Council action. This would provide assurance that the Council would indeed act in the listed situations. Specifying circumstances in the Charter where action would be automatic was also crucial if the Council's voting procedure was going to allow just one veto from any of the permanent members to paralyse it. At least the first three circumstances in the Bolivian list were uncontroversial, in terms of requiring enforcement action in response; moreover, it was the collective view of the supporting states that 'the Organisation must bind itself to oppose lawless force by lawful force in certain cases where action should be obligatory'.[22]

Opposition to the motion was expressed by a diverse collection of small states and great powers, namely Czechoslovakia, the Netherlands, Norway, Paraguay, South Africa, the UK and the USA. They countered that it was not possible to stipulate all acts that comprised aggression, and even if a non-exhaustive list format was accepted, that could promote the exclusion of unlisted acts from Council consideration.[23] The difficulties of defining aggression ahead of time were also raised; by contrast, identifying an aggressive act after its occurrence would be 'simple'.[24] Automatic Council action was unwise and potentially hazardous because it might compel premature enforcement action. In relation to the substance of the Bolivian list, opponents argued that any act classified as aggression could also be considered a 'legitimate act of self-defence'[25] in certain circumstances; and that some of the terms in the Bolivian list, such as 'intervention', would themselves require further definition. For these reasons, it was safer to empower the Council with full discretion to decide when aggression had occurred.

At the next meeting of Committee III/3, the fate of the Bolivian/Philippines motion, and with it the issue of defining aggression in the Charter, was sealed: on this occasion, France and the Soviet Union, among others, also stated their opposition to the motion. Thus, with four of the great powers having registered their disapproval, it was unsurprising that the motion was defeated by a vote of twenty-two to twelve.[26] Subsequently, the issue of aggression was not brought up again at San Francisco. Thus, the Dumbarton Oaks approach – which expressly included aggression within the remit of the Security Council's powers in response to Soviet views of the punitive role of the new organisation, and yet left this term undefined by agreement of the great powers – was adopted into the final text of the UN Charter.[27] By including references to aggression in the UN Charter without further definition – thereby avoiding the creation of a clear legal obligation to act in particular, identified circumstances – the great powers had, in their own best interest, ensured that they retained ultimate discretion in relation to international security matters.

Defining aggression at the United Nations

In the early UN period, it soon became evident that military action would be authorised very exceptionally by the Security Council as a consequence of growing Cold War tensions. As the split intensified between the Soviet Union and its allies on the one side, and the US and its allies on the other, the likelihood increased of one of the P5 states exercising its veto power in the Security Council in pursuit of its own, individual priorities with respect to this broader conflict, thus reducing even further the probability that any given situation requiring Security Council response would actually receive one. Impotence in the Security Council caused by Cold War divisions started to encourage states with complaints concerning international security to go to the General Assembly instead. The complaints raised in the General Assembly of 'threats to the political independence and territorial integrity' of Greece,[28] of China[29] and of 'hostile activities' in Yugoslavia[30] are cases in point.

It was against the backdrop of Cold War paralysis in the Security Council that in 1950 the General Assembly referred to the International Law Commission for its consideration the 'Duties of States in the event of Outbreak of Hostilities'.[31] Inevitably, albeit indirectly, examination of this topic raised once again the prospect of defining aggression. By 1952, the Secretary-General had produced a comprehensive report outlining the arguments for and against defining aggression by international agreement. Although these arguments were largely irreconcilable with one another, each relying on a vision of international relations which strongly conflicted with the perspective underpinning the other side,[32] the General Assembly decided that same year to convene a special committee to consider the issue of defining aggression, in association with a possible code of international criminal offences against the peace and security of mankind.[33]

If the pro-definition camp was correct, the practical effects of a definition of aggression – for instance, providing states with guidance on prohibited behaviour and the limits of self-defence; educating and empowering public opinion; and assisting the international organs responsible for making determinations – might help to overcome the significant political obstacles preventing the Security Council from fulfilling consistently and in all respects its peace and security duties. For this important reason, a definition of aggression was considered by the General Assembly to be worth pursuing, even if initial indicators of the success of this task were less than promising. It was thought that if the lawyers could define aggression successfully, the political stagnation on international security matters provoked by the Cold War might be circumvented.

In total, the General Assembly convened four committees to define aggression in the lead-up to the General Assembly's Definition of Aggression of 1974. Although the four committees throughout their deliberations continued to approach the issue of defining aggression as a legal exercise, the influence of political considerations in the committees' meetings was strong and constant, with views often split down Cold War lines. Thus, the more the committees doggedly pursued attempts to paper over political divisions by negotiating a supposedly legally binding definition of aggression, ironically the more they highlighted the political differences that existed. Finally, after a significant verbal confrontation between the USA and the Soviet Union at the 1968 meeting of the fourth committee, the enduring political nature of the problem of defining aggression was noted, clearing the way for the very fragile consensus underpinning the General Assembly Definition of Aggression to be brokered. It is to the deliberations of these committees that we now turn.

1953 Report of the special committee on the question of defining aggression[34]

From this report, it is clear that very little agreement existed about any aspect of the task of defining aggression, and that the positions taken by delegates on these issues were strongly influenced by Cold War considerations. While France, the UK and the Netherlands favoured a narrowly construed definition of aggression informed by the Charter obligation to refrain from the threat or use of force and the right of self-defence, other states, including the Soviet Union, Poland, Mexico, Bolivia and Iran argued in favour of a definition which was not restricted to issues of armed force but also took into account the Charter principles of sovereign equality,[35] non-intervention,[36] equal rights and self-determination.[37] The Soviet Union, Bolivia and Iran were joined by Syria and the Dominican Republic in the view that certain economic conduct fell within the scope of the Charter meaning of aggression, while the UK and Brazil contended that it did not. In support of the latter state, the USA noted that 'serious consequences might result from extending the idea of aggression', which included a weakening of the concept as a whole.[38] The Soviet Union and others also advocated including acts of an ideological nature in the definition, such as the encouragement of 'war propaganda'.[39] This again was opposed by two leading members of the Western bloc, the USA and the UK.

Even the form a definition of aggression should take provoked controversy. Three possible kinds of definition – general, enumerative, or a combination of both – were identified. While those in favour of a general definition argued that it would provide sufficient flexibility to address unforeseen circumstances and would contribute to the evolution of international law, critics like Poland argued that a general definition would be futile in the absence of a statement of elements constituting aggression, because making a determination in accordance with a general definition would require protracted discussions, thus impeding a timely UN response if indeed aggression had been committed. Those such as the Soviet Union and Poland who supported an enumerative definition – namely a list of condemned acts – believed this would make the determination of aggression easier by placing the burden of proof on the alleged aggressor, rather than on the victim. However, critics like the UK and China[40] opposed this approach on the basis that it would make more problematic the restoration of peace; it would make determinations of aggression automatic; and it would help would-be aggressors to avoid a determination against them simply by engaging in conduct outside the scope of the definition. A definition which combined a general statement and a list of acts was viewed by supporters as embodying the merits of both approaches, while opponents contended it would simply unite the defects of the two approaches.

The effect of a definition of aggression was perhaps the most contentious issue in this and subsequent committee meetings; disagreement was so entrenched that delegates were forced merely to repeat the same views stated by the Secretary-General in his report of the year before. Thus, proponents of definition, such as the Soviet Union, Iran, Syria, Poland, Bolivia and Mexico, claimed it would contribute to the evolution of international law; provide guidance to international organs, facilitating less subjective decision-making; educate public opinion and discourage potential aggressors. Opponents of definition[41] responded that it would not deter potential aggressors but would only encourage them to adopt different techniques; it would impede international organs in their assigned task of determining the aggressor; and history had shown that a definition was both unnecessary and virtually impossible to reach through consensus. Norway pointed out that the real difficulty of judging whether or not aggression had taken place was a result of the difficulty of discovering the facts in a given situation of high conflict. The existence or otherwise of a definition of aggression was a secondary matter; a definition would only be of use provided preliminary agreement on the facts existed.[42] Thus, in practice, it was not whether a specific act was aggressive or not that divided opinion among states – rather, it was whether that act had in fact taken place.

Some committee members emphasised that a definition would exert immense moral authority over those bodies exercising international peace and security functions, while the Dominican Republic argued that a definition, if adopted as part of a General Assembly resolution, might become recognised as a general principle of international law, in which case its effect would be 'questionable'[43] – that is, more significant than a purely moral obligation. Other states, such as Poland, tried to shut down any future discussion on the effect of definition by arguing that GA Res 599[44] and GA Res 688[45] had settled the matter – in favour of definition – for good. While all parties were united in opposing aggression, beyond this, the depth of divisions over the details – and how these often fell down Cold War lines – was readily apparent.

1956 Report of the special committee on the question of defining aggression[46]

In 1954, the original special committee of fifteen members was expanded to nineteen members, and in GA Res 897(IX)[47] and GA Res 898(IX),[48] work towards the Draft Code of Offences Against the Peace and Security of Mankind and the establishment of an international criminal court was suspended until the special committee on defining aggression had submitted its report.[49] The 1956 Report reveals little progress on the substance, purpose and effect of a definition of aggression since 1953.

Once again, the content of a definition was hotly debated, with positions on various proposals being largely determined according to Soviet or Western bloc membership. Seven draft proposals in total were submitted to the 1956 Committee by the Soviet Union and her friends and allies, including Paraguay, Iran, Panama, China, Iraq, Mexico, the Dominican Republic and Peru. The USA expressly criticised six of these drafts.[50] The UK joined the USA in criticising four of these, and formally associated itself with American criticisms in relation to the Soviet draft. In particular, the centrality of the priority principle – namely the state who first commits any act listed as prohibited should be declared 'the attacker' – in the Soviet draft attracted serious opposition from the USA, the UK and the Netherlands. By contrast, Soviet Bloc members Poland and Czechoslovakia, as well as firm Soviet friend Syria, spoke in favour of the Soviet draft.[51] While states such as Yugoslavia[52] expressed their opposition to the inclusion of notions of economic, ideological or indirect[53] aggression in a definition, others including the Soviet Union, Paraguay, Iran and China still pushed for the same.

As in 1953, the basic issue of what a definition of aggression would achieve – described quaintly in UN documents as 'the possibility and desirability of a definition'[54] – remained controversial. While states including the Soviet Union, Czechoslovakia, Iraq, Poland, the Netherlands, Mexico, Syria, Paraguay and Peru felt that a definition was possible and desirable for international peace and security purposes, others lamented the fact that any definition would not be binding, and therefore would, at best, provide guidance. For this latter reason, certain delegates continued to argue that a definition would, in reality, be useless. This discussion also raised the issue of which international bodies were meant to be guided by a definition. While some states such as the Soviet Union contended that any definition was for use by the Security Council only in the performance of its peace and security functions, others claimed on the basis of GA Res 377A (V)[55] that in certain circumstances the General Assembly might also be empowered to determine the aggressor.[56]

Further, extended debate on the definition's effect merely reinforced the same old intractable divisions described in the Secretary-General's 1952 Report.[57] Thus, China doubted the utility of a definition in an international community 'where everyone freely carried arms, everyone freely produced arms, where no police force or courts with compulsory powers existed';[58] the USA cited the 'mischief and confusion'[59] that a definition could bring to the fulfilment of the UN's peace and security functions; and the UK restated that a definition might in fact encourage a potential aggressor by de-emphasising the significance of acts falling outside the definition's scope. In response to this latter concern, 'almost all'[60] committee members agreed that the Security Council should retain and exercise its freedom to identify as aggression acts not specifically enumerated in the definition, in appropriate circumstances. However, the Netherlands and Norway questioned the extent to which a definition could perform its apparent guidance role if a provision to this effect was incorporated into the definition.[61] Despite this view, states such as Syria, Yugoslavia and Peru continued to argue respectively that it was desirable to bind the Security Council, at least morally, to identify aggression when the definition's listed acts occurred; that a definition would make a significant contribution to the maintenance of peace and security; and although it was probable that any definition would display some flaws, 'a legislator should not insist on formulating only perfect rules'.[62]

In light of the continuing and irresolvable differences of opinion symptomatic of the broader Cold War conflict which were expressed in the 1956 Report, the General Assembly decided in 1957 to postpone consideration of the question of defining aggression for two years, at which time a third special committee would be convened.[63] In 1959, this third committee of twenty-one members met; with Cold War tensions still operating, political differences continued to make defining aggression impossible, and the third committee adjourned until 1962. Again for this reason, the third committee adjourned its deliberations two more times, thus suspending further work until 1967. In that year, a Soviet request to the General Assembly about the 'Need to Expedite the drafting of a definition of aggression in the light of the present international situation'[64] resulted in the establishment of yet another special committee, this time of thirty-five members, which commenced work in 1968. Thus, although formal meetings continued in the decade following 1957, practical progress towards a legally binding definition of aggression was put on hold in response to divisive political conditions.

Work of the special committee on the question of defining aggression from 1968 onward[65]

By 1968, the international political climate had shifted away from the intense acrimony which typified the early years of the Cold War towards a slightly more conciliatory environment. The Sino-Soviet split from the late 1960s onward diverted the attention of China and the Soviet Union from attacking US interests, and simultaneously presented the USA with new opportunities to further its political leverage over one, or possibly both, powers.[66] In addition, by this time both the Soviet Union and the USA began to feel the heavy economic strain of their global competition, in particular with respect to the nuclear arms race and the Vietnam War respectively, and hence they also had a clear financial interest in achieving a form of *rapprochement*. In these relatively less confrontational conditions, the chance to make some progress towards a definition of aggression was grasped by the General Assembly.

However, the warming of relations between the superpowers would take a few years yet, as the 1968 committee meeting attested. This meeting proved to be explosive by UN standards. While discussing the perennial issue of what would be achieved in international peace and security terms by a definition of aggression, and after the same old pro-definition argument about guidance 'for Member States and the United Nations'[67] had been reiterated, the Soviet Union used the occasion to declare unilaterally that the USA had committed aggression in Vietnam, a view backed up by Algeria, Bulgaria, Romania and Syria. Not content to stop there, the Soviet Union added that the USA had also committed other acts of aggression in Latin America, Cuba, Panama and the Dominican Republic. In response, the USA indicated that in relation to the Vietnam conflict it was only North Vietnam and its supporters that were the aggressors. Further, the USA reminded the Soviet Union that it occupied 'the almost unique position among world Powers of having been formally judged an aggressor by a world body', and pointed out that 'the Hungarian people must draw cold comfort from the pious declaration of the Government of the Soviet Union that no State could invade another State'.[68]

This exchange illustrated very clearly how irrelevant a legal definition of aggression was for the maintenance of international security in political circumstances where the great powers were locked in battle among themselves. This point was not lost on certain members of the committee: the 1968 Report indicates that doubts were expressed by certain states concerning the value of a definition, with some of them still questioning 'the advisability of defining aggression at all'[69] just five years before the General Assembly Definition of Aggression. Finally, it was this latter group which succinctly identified the true source of the political problem lurking beneath efforts to define aggression:

> The main thing needed to deter or suppress aggression was not to have a definition, but to ensure that the system of collective security would be applied and until now it was not the absence of a definition of aggression

which had hampered the organs of the United Nations in their efforts to maintain peace and security. Success or failure had depended on the willingness, or lack of willingness, of States Members to respect their Charter obligations. Consequently there was the danger that a definition would create an illusion of accomplishment when none in fact had been made.[70]

The implication of this apparently long-forgotten insight – that no development of international law, such as a definition of aggression, could successfully conquer international political conditions in which no compulsory law enforcement mechanisms existed, let alone where the great powers were each competing for world supremacy – dealt a serious blow to the pro-definition camp. Being compelled to concede that even with a definition of aggression, Charter obligations in relation to international security were unlikely to be enforced in light of the superpower global competition meant that pro-definition states had no option but to return to their original, rather weak starting point: that a definition could still act as a useful, non-binding guide to decision-making bodies.

Following these events, it is unsurprising that the three draft proposals which dominated the attention of the 1969 committee reaffirmed the non-binding nature of a definition of aggression vis-à-vis the Security Council's powers.[71] With this agreed, the other issues raised by the task of defining aggression seemed to fade into insignificance. If, in the prevailing Cold War climate, a definition could at best only guide the Security Council in its peace and security functions, neither restricting the Security Council's discretion to those acts listed in a definition, nor compelling the Security Council to determine aggression when any of the listed acts occurred, then neither the legal task of defining aggression, nor any particular definition, were any longer of crucial importance for international security. This growing realisation during the committee's 1970 to 1972 sessions facilitated compromise among the states, later making possible the adoption of the General Assembly Definition of Aggression in 1974.

If, by 1968 onward, it was recognised that inhospitable Cold War conditions limited what a definition of aggression could achieve, why did the committee continue with its deliberations until 1974, when the General Assembly Definition of Aggression was adopted? The answer to this question lies in the General Assembly's 1954 decision to postpone work on the related questions of the Draft Code of Offences against the Peace and Security of Mankind, and on the international criminal court, until a definition of aggression was accomplished. The desire to reopen these other issues thus provided strong motivation for a definition of aggression, separate from arguments about the inherent value of such a definition itself. Hence, at the 1973 meeting of one of the UN's subsidiary organs, where the committee's incomplete draft definition was discussed, a view stressing the importance of reaching consensus on a definition of aggression was stated thus:

a modest compromise now was more important than continuous deliberations on a more comprehensive definition; a limited consensus could clear the way for continuing efforts to codify and progressively develop international law in some important fields....[72]

The significance of this motivation over and above the substance of a definition of aggression is apparent in the text of the General Assembly Definition of Aggression, which simply preserved in its text many of the outstanding differences of view generated by conflicting political ideologies which were expressed during the deliberations of the UN committees since the early 1950s. Thus, in the General Assembly Definition of Aggression, the status of 'economic' and 'ideological' aggression was left open, and references supporting both the narrow and wide constructions of the Charter meaning of aggression were included.[73] These kinds of loopholes reveal that the General Assembly 'Definition' of Aggression in fact defined very little; instead, this resolution demonstrated the continuation of Cold War political divisions during and after its adoption. Consequently, the thirty-year effort to define state aggression has shown how powerless developments of international law for maintaining international security are in the face of great power struggles which threaten the prevailing balance of power.

Conclusion

This chapter further reinforced the folly of seeking to push the evolution of international law beyond prevailing political constraints. Over the period examined, three different sets of political tensions militated against defining state aggression as a matter of law. The first set of tensions arose in the mid-1940s among the great powers themselves, two of whom opposed altogether the inclusion of the concept of aggression in the UN Charter on the basis of the challenges it posed in the League context. Despite this opposition, a compromise was brokered with the Soviet Union and aggression was referred to in the draft Charter, though in the interest of preserving great power discretion it was not defined. At San Francisco a second set of tensions emerged, this time between the great powers and the small and middle powers. The latter powers, wary of the wide margin of discretion left to the great powers under the draft Charter, attempted to resurrect the debate on defining state aggression in the Charter in order to constrain this discretion. Confronted with the political circumstances of unanimous great power opposition, however, this move was blocked, and aggression was left undefined in the final document.

Nevertheless – and undeterred by the political battles mentioned above which revealed the political, not legal, nature of the problem of aggression – the issue of bringing the force of law to a definition of state aggression was once again revived in the early UN period. Over more than twenty years, and blind to the real source of difficulty masked by efforts to 'define' aggression, committee after committee met to discuss the substance, form and effect of a definition of state aggression, with no consensus achieved. On the contrary, the universal negative value associated with aggression did not translate into its legal definition at all; rather the discussions about defining aggression as a legal matter *themselves* reflected a third set of political tensions: the Cold War conflict. This is apparent from the dramatic outbursts by the USA and the Soviet Union in the 1968 committee meeting, and even from the final text of the General Assembly Definition of Aggression itself.

It was not until 1968 that the lessons of 1928 were properly learned – namely, that 'in existing circumstances ... no practical result' would emerge from efforts to establish advance, strict criteria for determining an aggressor.[74] In both eras, it was the self-interest of the great powers in maintaining their freedom of action that was the true political reason behind the failure of legal efforts to define state aggression. Put another way, the lack of sufficient great power support for effective peaceful change mechanisms – such as a world legislature, executive and judicial authority backed up by binding enforcement powers – meant that approaching the task of defining state aggression as a legal issue was an extremely premature act doomed to failure. In fact, as demonstrated in this chapter, it was more the desire to revisit other topics which, in a short-sighted decision by the General Assembly, had been postponed pending arrival at a 'definition' of aggression which led to the General Assembly Definition of Aggression, and not the achievement of a new-found international political consensus which could be used in support of a legal definition. Thus, the General Assembly Definition of Aggression should be viewed as a necessary institutional hurdle for the topics of an international criminal code and court to be reopened, rather than the ultimate statement of what conduct precisely constitutes aggression under international law.

7 The International Law Commission's attempts to criminalise state aggression, 1946 to 1998

In the last chapter it was demonstrated that the General Assembly established various special committees over a long period of time to define state aggression, based on the faulty characterisation of aggression as a problem in need of legal solution. From the advent of the UN organisation, however, defining state aggression was only one of the legal solutions sought by the General Assembly. Thus, in the late 1940s to early 1950s, around the same time that the first special committees were debating a definition of aggression, the General Assembly tasked the International Law Commission with developing proposals for an international criminal code and an international criminal court. On the basis of the Nuremberg precedent, such a code was inevitably going to include the crime of aggression. However, unlike at Nuremberg, the main focus of ILC efforts was not on individual criminal responsibility but on establishing the crime of *state* aggression. As already shown, the assumption that the problem of state aggression could be addressed simply by reaching a consensually agreed definition which would then bring the force of law to bear on any proscribed acts within the definition was misguided at best. To go further than this and assert that aggression was not just a breach of the law of nations but in fact a stand-alone *crime committed by states* was an even greater flight of fancy as regards what international law could achieve in relation to intransigent political constraints. Despite the ILC recognising as early as 1953 the uselessness of attempting to define aggression, its efforts to criminalise state aggression were nonetheless postponed pending definition of state aggression by the General Assembly's special committee on that topic.

By linking formally ILC efforts to criminalise state aggression and the General Assembly Definition of Aggression, when the ILC finally resumed its work in 1981, it remained preoccupied with reconciling the idea of state and individual criminal responsibility for aggression, desperately trying to find some use for the General Assembly Definition of Aggression in an international criminal law context. This preoccupation continued until the mid-1990s, when individual criminal responsibility once again took centre stage, as it had done originally at Nuremberg. The ILC's work towards criminalising state aggression had once again shown that approaching the problem of state aggression as just a question of law – whether as a breach of international law requiring more precise definition, or as a more serious, international criminal act – was erroneous, and that no attempt to frame the issues legally would overcome the political disagreements the problem provoked. Rather, the political tensions over aggression would simply be played out by states in legal form.

Aggression as a crime: 1946 to 1954

The *crime* of aggression was considered initially by the General Assembly in relation to two separate, but related, topics: (1) the codification of international law; and (2) an international criminal jurisdiction. The thrust of debates on these topics during this period concerned aggression as a state crime, with individual criminal responsibility as a secondary consideration. It is to these debates that we now turn.

The codification of international law

In an effort to contribute to the further development of international law, in 1947 the General Assembly directed the ILC to extrapolate the relevant tenets of international law from the Nuremberg Charter and judgment, and to draft a code of offences against the peace and security of mankind.[1] The ILC held its first session in 1949; the following year, the Special Rapporteur for this topic submitted his report on a draft code. Even at this stage it was evident to the ILC that insistence on defining aggression was futile. Quoting Soviet objections to the American proposal to insert a definition of aggression into the Nuremberg Charter in 1945,[2] the Special Rapporteur reasoned as follows:

> When people speak about aggression, they know what that means, but, when they come to define it, they come up against difficulties which it has not been possible to overcome up to the present time.... For the[se] reasons ... we suggest that the International Law Commission abstain from any attempt at defining the notion of 'aggression'. *Such an attempt would prove be a pure waste of time.*[3]

While the ILC thus refrained from attempts to define aggression exhaustively in its 1951 Draft Code, its provisions setting out liability for aggression went far beyond the Nuremberg and Tokyo Charters, expressing responsibility in terms of state, rather than individual, conduct:

The following acts are offences against the peace and security of mankind:

1   Any act of aggression, including the employment by the authorities of a State of armed force against another State for any purpose other than national or collective self-defence or in pursuance of a decision or recommendation by a competent organ of the United Nations.
2   Any threat by the authorities of a State to resort to any act of aggression against another State....[4]

The intention of the ILC was to criminalise every act of aggression committed by a state,[5] thus endorsing a conclusion that the judges at Nuremberg were careful to avoid – namely, that states *themselves* were capable of, and could be held responsible for, committing international crimes. However, the 1951 Draft Code also recognised the criminal responsibility of individuals 'acting on behalf of the State', and suggested in certain circumstances that such responsibility might also extend to private individuals.

This explicit extension to states of criminal responsibility for aggression was not the only massive leap since Nuremberg. Whereas in the Nuremberg Charter the major war criminals were charged with, *inter alia*, 'initiation or waging a war of aggression', the 1951 Draft Code criminalised all 'acts of aggression'. This potentially extended the scope of the crime of aggression to include conduct not limited to the use of armed force, and deliberately invoked the language used in the UN Charter's provision relating to the Security Council's role.[6] Again, at Nuremberg, judges were circumspect on the issue of non-military aggression, stopping short of finding aggression against Austria and Czechoslovakia where no armed resistance to German occupation arose.[7] Hence, the 1951 Draft Code incorporated into its terms controversial inferences intentionally left vague by the Nuremberg judges.

The 1954 Draft Code produced by the ILC was identical to the 1951 Draft Code, save for the addition of a crime against UN personnel. By choosing to focus on state crimes, the ILC had left its 1954 Draft Code vulnerable to being associated with the wrong-headed decision by the General Assembly to establish a special committee to 'define' state aggression. This association was formalised by GA Res 897,[8] which delayed further consideration of the 1954 Draft Code until the 'definition' of aggression was complete. By ignoring the lessons of Nuremberg – namely limiting international criminal responsibility for aggression to individuals and adopting a very conservative approach with regard to the state implications of such responsibility – the ILC needlessly halted work on an international criminal code until the General Assembly Definition of Aggression of 1974 had been passed.

International criminal jurisdiction

This emphasis on state criminality rather than individual criminal responsibility for aggression was also evident in relation to the topic of an international criminal court, and was perhaps even more controversial than in the context of an international criminal code. Despite the Nuremberg and Tokyo trials, nowhere in the UN Charter was the future prosecution of international crimes mentioned; the sole judicial body the Charter expressly recognised was the International Court of Justice, a court which could rule only on interstate disputes and only with state consent.[9] In fact, under the Charter, the exclusive entity with supranational powers was the Security Council, and these powers were only exercisable in very limited, and serious, circumstances – that is, for the maintenance or restoration of international order.[10]

In 1948, the General Assembly called upon the ILC to:

> study the desirability and possibility of establishing an international judicial organ for the trial of persons charged with genocide or other crimes over which jurisdiction will be conferred upon that organ by international conventions.[11]

While this request refers to individual criminal responsibility only, the Special Rapporteur advised in his 1950 Report that international criminal jurisdiction should be exercised over *states and* individuals – a clear indication of the ILC's preference for a supranational criminal court. This preference is also reflected in the Report's recommendation that the power to initiate international criminal proceedings reside solely with the Security Council.[12] Despite this attempt at resurrecting the possibility of state criminality it was soon dropped, with the 1953 Draft Statute for an International Criminal Court applying expressly to natural persons.[13] Politically, the notion of expanding the range of supranational powers exercisable by international bodies less than a decade since the establishment of the UN organisation – let alone as the Cold War conflict was intensifying – was a complete non-starter, and had to be abandoned.

Even with the highly controversial question of state criminal responsibility side-stepped, other overwhelming difficulties confronted the ILC in its consideration of an international criminal court. Just as legal debates over the 'definition' of aggression in the General Assembly special committees were simply the means through which long-standing political disagreements among states were communicated and fought, the same was happening in the ILC in relation to the establishment of an international criminal court. Thus, at the meeting of the 1953 Committee for an International Criminal Jurisdiction, vastly contrasting opinions were expressed on basic political questions that required resolution long before the details of an international criminal court could be finalised. These basic questions included the appropriateness of an international criminal jurisdiction in light of the state of international law and international relations in 1953; the relationship between the administration of international criminal justice and the maintenance of peace; the purpose of an international criminal court; the relationship between an international criminal court and the UN; and the standards which a proposed international criminal court would need to live up to. While the UN Report about the meeting of the 1953 committee carefully avoided associating individual ILC members with particular positions in relation to these questions, the high level of disagreement is apparent.[14]

This lack of consensus was reflected in the 1953 Draft Statute, where several provisions in fact incorporated a choice between two possible alternatives. Thus, each of articles 7, 8, 9 and 11 concerning the procedure for electing judges listed two different alternatives, and article 29 presented options on which entities should be entitled to exercise powers relating to the initiation of proceedings. Papering over conflicts concerning what types of conduct should be prosecuted by an international criminal court, the 1953 Draft Statute conferred jurisdiction simply over 'crimes generally recognized under international law',[15] apparently leaving it to a future international criminal court itself to decide what this meant. This high level of political disagreement underpinning these ostensibly legal questions meant that the Committee was unable to decide even whether it was possible, practicable and desirable to create an organised international criminal jurisdiction, let alone determine the finer points of such a jurisdiction. Despite this significant obstacle, the members of the Committee concluded that:

> on the basis of the preparatory studies made by the General Assembly and both the Special Committees on International Criminal Jurisdiction the moment had come for the General Assembly to decide what, if any, further steps should be taken toward the establishment of an international criminal court.[16]

Clearly, any further consideration of the 1953 Draft Statute could not occur in isolation from the 1954 Draft Code. Thus, having already postponed work on the 1954 Draft Code until the General Assembly 'defined' aggression, GA Res 898 now also postponed further efforts on the 1953 Draft Statute until such 'definition' occurred *and* the General Assembly once again took up consideration of the 1954 Draft Code. The postponement of both the 1953 Draft Statute and the 1954 Draft Code had the effect of elevating, for procedural reasons, the importance of achieving a General Assembly 'definition' of aggression, in circumstances where the value of such a 'definition', for any other purpose, was far from evident, as Chapter 6 demonstrated. The ILC's insistence upon advancing the idea of *state* criminality with little, if any, regard for the sharp Cold War political divisions of the time, or the disastrous political consequences of holding Germany morally responsible for World War I at Versailles, led in effect to the twin topics of an international criminal code and an international criminal court being shut down by the General Assembly indefinitely, only a few years after they had been placed on the agenda. As we shall see in the next section, because of the General Assembly's decision to link together its definition of aggression, the 1953 Draft Statute and the 1954 Draft Code, the politically charged issue of state responsibility for the crime of aggression continued to infect efforts towards creating an international criminal jurisdiction even in less hostile international political conditions.

Aggression as a crime: 1981 to 1996

It is evident from the previous chapter, that the General Assembly Definition of Aggression was more the result of a renewed desire to reconsider the linked issues of an international criminal code and court than a dramatic shift towards political consensus on the nature of aggression after years of wrangling. Given the outstanding political conflicts of 1953 to 1954 over international criminality and aggression, combined with the lack of further consideration of these topics in the interim period, it is not surprising that the criminality of aggression received only a token acknowledgement in the General Assembly Definition of Aggression. Its article 5 simply provided that 'a war of aggression is a crime against international peace' and 'aggression gives rise to international responsibility'. This token recognition reflected the discussions in the General Assembly's various special committees, where it was clear that committee members mainly viewed their task in international peace and security terms, rather than through the lens of international criminal law.

Thus, although the passage of the General Assembly Definition of Aggression was a welcome development in that it cleared the way procedurally for reopening efforts towards an international criminal code and court, it was hardly a celebration. For even post-'definition', it was not at all clear what relevance, if any, the General Assembly Definition of Aggression had in an international criminal law context. The ongoing emphasis on somehow incorporating the long-awaited, over-hyped General Assembly Definition of Aggression into an international criminal code ensured that state responsibility for the crime of aggression continued as a live topic long after its expiry date.

The Draft Code

After a twenty-seven-year hiatus, it was not until 1981, as the Cold War entered its final years and seven years after its Definition of Aggression, that the General Assembly invited the ILC to resume its activities with respect to producing a new Draft Code.[17] A Special Rapporteur was appointed, who generated nine reports on the topic between 1983 and 1991.[18] Making up for lost time, the Special Rapporteur in his second report recommended that the offences listed in the 1954 Draft Code, including aggression, should remain. He also noted that certain delegations favoured the addition of economic aggression as a specific offence, though he acknowledged the difficulties with this proposal, and suggested it was a turn of phrase 'more suited to political than legal parlance'.[19]

In 1986, the Special Rapporteur's Report included provisional articles for an updated Draft Code. Despite the only very tenuous link between the General Assembly Definition of Aggression and the crime of aggression, preoccupation with this relationship now infected the ILC's efforts to produce a Draft Code. Consequently, article 11 of the 1986 Draft Code detailed word for word many of the paragraphs comprising the General Assembly Definition of Aggression. In fact, the only substantive sections of the General Assembly Definition of Aggression that were excluded from the 1986 Draft Code concerned evidence and interpretation, omitted on the basis that these were 'matters within the competence of the judge'.[20] The crime of aggression was now defined in the 1986 Draft Code as:

> the use of armed force by a State against the sovereignty, territorial integrity or political independence of another State, or in any other manner inconsistent with the Charter of the United Nations, as set out in this definition,[21]

and the series of qualifying acts from the General Assembly Definition of Aggression was listed. Although the Definition was addressed clearly at states' responsibility for aggression, it was imported into the Draft Code, which under its own terms limited responsibility to 'any *person* who commits an offence against the peace and security of mankind'.[22]

Regardless of this tension, the influence of the General Assembly Definition of Aggression persisted, also featuring in the 1988 Draft Code. Worse, the Special Rapporteur at this time appeared to broaden to infinity the range of potential acts which could be classified as aggression by including the words 'in particular' at the start of the list of acts taken from the Definition, though this idea also provoked disagreement. With the Cold War coming to an end at this time, it is unsurprising that ILC members from great power states such as the USA, France, China and the Soviet Union, among others, all opposed the addition of 'in particular', while members from smaller powers such as Bahrain, Brazil and Mexico supported it.[23]

In an attempt to unite the Definition with individual criminal responsibility, an article was proposed that 'any individual to whom acts constituting aggression are attributed under this Code shall be liable to be tried and punished for a crime against peace'. On its face, this statement seemed to be self-evident in light of the Nuremberg precedent. Yet to some, it had no place in the Draft Code on the basis that it was redundant, vague or dangerous. Finally, in an effort to avoid the political storm generated by the prospect of an international criminal court, the 1988 Report included a proposal that 'any determination by the Security Council as to the existence of an act of aggression is binding on national courts', though a divergence of views even on this more conservative idea existed. Once again, discord surrounding essentially political issues such as whether or not to establish an international criminal court and the relationship between political and legal organs in determining the existence of a crime of aggression were noted on the ILC's record, leaving them intact for future meetings.

While the General Assembly Definition of Aggression remained in the Draft Code, very little progress was made on these matters; trying to join in abstract terms state and individual responsibility for aggression was proving politically impossible. In 1991, the member from France expressed his total opposition to the inclusion of the Definition in the Draft Code, and suggested the only way forward was for the Draft Code:

> to indicate that aggression constituted in itself a crime against the peace and security of mankind, with the consequences defined under the Code, and to leave it to the courts which had jurisdiction, in other words, to domestic courts or to a future international criminal court, to decide, in the light of the facts of the case and in accordance with general principles of international law, whether aggression had occurred and to draw the appropriate conclusions.[24]

However, this view failed to gain favour, and the General Assembly Definition of Aggression remained in the Draft Code.

It was not until 1995 that the stranglehold of the Definition over the Draft Code eased. On the advice of the Special Rapporteur, the Definition's list of acts qualifying as aggression was omitted altogether from the Draft Code, a consequence of the great amount of criticism this list – and attempts to recast it – had attracted. The introductory statement from the General Assembly Definition of Aggression was also expressly rejected in favour of wording that more accurately reflected article 2(4) of the UN Charter. Nevertheless, opinion remained divided: reasons given for opposing this newly redrafted provision included its reference to the phrase 'in any other manner inconsistent with the Charter of the United Nations', which some felt would itself result in many controversies; the lack of distinction between major and minor uses of force; and the provision being 'too close'[25] to the text of article 2(4) of the UN Charter. Others appeared willing to tolerate the redrafted provision only on the basis that any other formulation attracting consensus might take years; that the provision was viewed as merely a 'first stage';[26] and because 'it was pointless to devote too much attention to the problem of aggression, which could never be solved'.[27] Tellingly, no member spoke in full support of the redrafted provision.

Finally, the last remaining trace of influence from the General Assembly Definition of Aggression – namely the long-held view that there was a need for a paragraph 'defining' aggression – was knocked out of the Draft Code in 1996, when the provisions on aggression were compressed into one article simply outlining in general terms the basis of individual responsibility for aggression:

> an individual who, as leader or organizer, actively participates in or orders the planning, preparation, initiation or waging of aggression committed by a State shall be responsible for a crime of aggression.[28]

Thus, via a very circuitous route, drafters had finally achieved their original purpose: that is, setting down the conditions in which individual responsibility for the crime of aggression would arise. After a fifty-year period, their efforts had led them back to a variation of the Nuremberg approach. The fact that a general statement of liability – not a 'definition' of aggression per se – had been the linchpin of the Nuremberg trial, and that the jurisprudence emanating from Nuremberg was generally considered good law, was finally remembered.

The evolution of the Draft Code demonstrates that early efforts to advance too far and too fast the scope of the crime of aggression as the Security Council stagnated due to growing Cold War tensions completely overtook the ILC's early work on the Draft Code. By contrast, the 1996 Draft Code represented the completion of a full circle: the emphasis on criminal responsibility for state acts in the 1950s as the Cold War intensified had, towards the end of the Cold War, eventually given way to individual criminal responsibility for international crimes, as per the original Nuremberg precedent of 1946. Having abandoned efforts to impose state responsibility for international crimes, the General Assembly brought the 1996 Draft Code to the attention of the Preparatory Committee on the Establishment of an International Criminal Court. Since this time, no further steps to bring the 1996 Draft Code into force have been taken.[29]

The Draft Statute

Placing individual criminal responsibility once again at the heart of efforts to establish an international criminal code also revived the idea of an international criminal court. In 1989, in response to a General Assembly request, the Special Rapporteur for the Draft Code included consideration of the establishment of an international criminal court in his report from 1990 onward.[30] The end of the Cold War produced political fluctuations resulting in varied responses to the question of which crimes to include within the jurisdiction of an international criminal court. While in 1990, the Special Rapporteur envisaged that this question would be determined primarily by reference to a finalised Code of Crimes against the Peace and Security of Mankind, by 1992, he was proposing exclusive and compulsory jurisdiction over five listed crimes – none of which included aggression – plus jurisdiction over other crimes on the basis of consent from particular states with an interest in the matter.[31] However, just a year later, the Special Rapporteur once again suggested the jurisdiction of an international criminal court remain contingent on the 'adoption of a criminal code'; in the absence of such a code, the ambit of an international criminal court would be determined by special agreements between state parties or by a unilateral state declaration.[32]

In 1994, the ILC adopted a Draft Statute, and recommended to the General Assembly that it organise an international conference at which this draft might be considered. The 1994 Draft Statute conferred jurisdiction to an international criminal court over aggression, genocide, crimes against humanity, war crimes, and serious crimes established by treaty.[33] The inclusion of the crime of aggression was explained by the ILC in its commentary to this provision in the following terms:

> a court must, at the present time, be in a better position to define the customary law crime of aggression than was the Nuremberg Tribunal in 1946. It would thus seem retrogressive to exclude individual criminal responsibility for aggression (in particular, acts directly associated with the waging of a war of aggression) 50 years after Nuremberg.[34]

However, the ILC also noted 'the difficulties of definition and application',[35] and, in light of the Security Council's peace and security duties, suggested that some stipulation be included permitting prosecution by an international criminal court of the crime of aggression only after the Security Council had determined that the relevant state committed an act of aggression.[36] The task of 'defining' aggression – which had tormented both the General Assembly and the ILC's negotiations over an international criminal code – was thus resurrected in the context of an international criminal court.

In accordance with the ILC's recommendation, the General Assembly agreed to establish an ad hoc committee to meet in 1995 to consider the 1994 Draft Statute.[37] While the ad hoc committee could agree in principle to the inclusion of genocide, war crimes and crimes against humanity within the jurisdiction of an international criminal court, no consensus on including the crime of aggression was achieved. By 1995, the 'international crimes generally recognised' in the 1953 Draft Statute evidently did not cover the crime of aggression. Just as the legal dead-end of 'defining' aggression had swamped efforts in relation to the Draft Code, the advantages or difficulties of a definition of aggression were now being cited by states to support their respective political positions on whether or not an international criminal court should exercise jurisdiction over the crime of aggression. Thus, those advocating prosecution of the crime of aggression by an international criminal court justified their view by reference to the Nuremberg Charter, the General Assembly Definition of Aggression, the 1996 Draft Code and other draft documents, implying that these might provide assistance in 'defining' aggression for the purposes of individual criminal responsibility.

By contrast, those wanting the crime of aggression excluded from the jurisdiction of an international criminal court argued that a definition of aggression would take too long and cause lengthy delays to the establishment of an international criminal court. They also claimed that a definition would have to address excuses and defences such as humanitarian intervention and self-defence. Both the Nuremberg Charter and the General Assembly Definition of Aggression were rejected outright as unhelpful in this context. The old issue about the relationship between the UN – in particular, the Security Council – and an international criminal court was also cited as a rationale for excluding aggression from its jurisdiction. Hence, these latest arguments over a definition of aggression in the context of an international criminal court were just the most recent versions of peripheral, interminable legal debates concealing the true source of difficulty: a lack of political consensus, especially among the great powers, in support of a permanent, international judicial organ with jurisdiction over the crime of aggression.

This firmly entrenched lack of political consensus was only confirmed by the Preparatory Committee for the Establishment of an International Criminal Court between 1996 and 1998. While the same types of legal arguments as advanced in the ad hoc committee were put forward by supporters and opponents alike, a third position also emerged at this time: certain states now claimed to support in theory the inclusion of aggression within the jurisdiction of an international criminal court, but only on the conditions that 'general agreement could be reached on its definition and on the appropriate balance of the respective roles and functions of the Court and the Security Council, without delaying the establishment of the Court'.[38]

With the formation of this third group, attention once again focused upon 'defining' aggression. Coalitions began forming around the various precedents in existence, including the Nuremberg Charter, the General Assembly Definition of Aggression and the 1996 Draft Code. Proposals for defining aggression for Statute purposes were put forward based on these precedents, and the tired legal arguments over whether a 'general' or enumerative definition was better, and whether or not a proposed enumeration should be exhaustive, were revived.[39] For each group in favour of one proposal, there were multiple factions ready to point out that proposal's failings. Thus, the Nuremberg Charter's provision on aggression was considered by opponents as either too imprecise, too limited or too obsolete, while the General Assembly Definition of Aggression was attacked for not addressing *de minimis* considerations or potential defences.[40]

Other delegations refused to be drawn into this never-ending debate, denying the need for a definition of aggression, and arguing in favour of a provision in the Statute reserving the Security Council's powers to determine whether a situation constituted aggression or not. As always, the fundamental issues debated in the Preparatory Committee concerned whether or not to include aggression in the statute establishing an international criminal court, its 'definition' if included and what its inclusion would mean for the relationship between the Security Council and an international criminal court. In these circumstances, it was an understatement to describe these issues as 'an essentially political judgment question which is so far not entirely resolved'.[41] Without such resolution, no amount of legal paper-shuffling would achieve very much.

This was confirmed by the text of the Draft Statute produced by the Preparatory Committee in 1998, immediately prior to the Rome Conference. Although the Preparatory Committee's proposal listed three different alternatives on the crime of aggression, it stated from the outset that while 'a large number of delegations' favoured aggression's inclusion in the Statute, the listing of these three options was 'without prejudice to a final decision' on the crime's inclusion.[42] Without even basic political agreement on whether or not to include aggression, setting out three possible alternatives for its inclusion was premature. Nevertheless, option one outlined in broad terms the prohibited conduct; option two combined a short statement of the conditions attracting liability with the list of qualifying acts from the General Assembly Definition of Aggression; and option three stipulated a more qualified version of option one, with the significant proviso that jurisdiction over aggression was subject to Security Council determination 'regarding the act of a State'.[43]

In line with UN drafting procedure, square brackets surrounded amendments or additions that were still the subject of debate; tellingly, virtually all of the text contained in these three options fell within square brackets, just a few months before the Rome Conference would be convened.[44] By contrast, other crimes within the Preparatory Committee's draft, such as genocide, war crimes and crimes against humanity, not only attracted broad-based political support in terms of their inclusion in the statute, but, as a consequence of the jurisprudence emanating from the International Criminal Tribunal for the Former Yugoslavia and the International Criminal Tribunal for Rwanda, they also benefited from substantial clarification with regard to their substance. A lack of political consensus about subjecting acts comprising the crime of aggression to international adjudication procedures remained the foremost obstacle confronting the inclusion of the crime of aggression within the jurisdiction of an international criminal court.

United Nations Conference of Plenipotentiaries on the establishment of an International Criminal Court, Rome, 15 June to 17 July 1998

The experience of the ad hoc Committee and the Preparatory Committee with respect to the crime of aggression was simply a taste of things to come at the Rome Conference. Even with the end of the Cold War, the profound questions of international organisation raised by the prospect of a permanent international criminal court with jurisdiction over the crime of aggression ensured that divisions among states remained deep and insuperable. Broadly speaking, political affiliations at Rome were split three ways into: (1) the P5 states; (2) the 'Like-minded Group', an association of small and middle powers who strongly supported the establishment of an international criminal court, though their views differed on detail; and (3) the Non-aligned Movement. In relation to the crime of aggression specifically, at least thirty-two[45] small and middle powers expressed their unconditional support for the inclusion of aggression in the ICC Statute during the opening plenary meetings; and another thirty[46] states, including Russia, offered their conditional support – the two most common provisos predictably being the drafting of a 'precise' definition of aggression, and sorting out the relationship between the Security Council and an international criminal court. This split was further complicated by the deafening silence of forty-five[47] states, including France and the UK,[48] that made no mention of the crime of aggression at all in their opening statements, and another five[49] powers, including the USA, which expressed their complete opposition to the crime of aggression within the scope of an international criminal court. With this level of political disagreement, the prospect of the Rome Conference, at the end of its three-week duration, producing a generally accepted way forward for empowering an international criminal court with respect to the crime of aggression was remote indeed.

At Rome, more thorough discussions on the Preparatory Committee's proposals ensued, but without any real progress. During the course of these discussions on 18–19 June, it became evident that many delegations preferred option 3 out of the three Preparatory Committee's proposals, which made an international criminal court's jurisdiction over aggression contingent upon a Security Council determination; combined with those who were willing to consider this option as an alternative to their own first preference, this group was significant in number. However, even among those delegations claiming to support this option, very few were prepared to accept it as is, without any modifications; their support for option 3 was as a 'working basis'[50] only, and they continued to attempt to redraft option 3 in accordance with their own political preferences. Even the key feature of option 3 – namely its dependence on a prior Security Council determination – was not immune from challenge, with states including Non-Aligned Movement members Angola, North Korea and Cuba, as well as Ukraine,[51] opposing a decisive role for the Security Council in this context, with global leaders such as Japan, Russia, France and the UK insisting on the same. Hence, the appearance of even limited consensus around option 3 was in fact chimerical.

Another faction – mainly comprising Middle Eastern states – which expressed support for the inclusion of aggression in principle believed that none of the three options presented by the Preparatory Committee were adequate, and that something closer to the General Assembly Definition of Aggression was required. Others again expressed their opposition to including aggression on any basis, and were joined by a few states who were now openly doubtful about whether the issues raised by the prospect of including the crime of aggression within an international criminal court's jurisdiction could be resolved at Rome.[52] Thus, detailed consideration of the crime of aggression simply splintered even further the original political divisions expressed at the start of the Conference.

Between 20 June and 5 July, the Rome Conference moved on to consider other issues concerning an international criminal court generally, such as questions of standing and other jurisdictional concerns. During this period, three proposals concerning the crime of aggression were distributed, including one from the Middle East grouping mentioned above. However, none of these were included in the Conference Bureau Discussion Paper of 6 July, which included two options only: (1) to accept the Preparatory Committee's option 3 as drafted, or (2) to include no provision on aggression at all.[53] With time running short, some progress towards consensus – or at least a reduction in the various positions taken – was needed, when discussions on aggression resumed on 8 July; however, presentation of these alternatives at this juncture of the Conference merely divided opinions further. While a few delegations were prepared to accept option 1 as currently drafted, others continued to claim their support of this option as simply a 'reference point' for further discussions.[54]

In their responses to the two straightforward choices summarised in the Conference Bureau Discussion Paper, significantly the vast majority of delegations made no reference to either option, merely reiterating the vague and often repeated statement that the inclusion of the crime of aggression in the Statute must be conditional upon (1) an 'acceptable' definition of aggression; and/or (2) agreement as to the relationship between the Security Council and the international criminal court. Interestingly, India – which from the beginning had expressed its thinly veiled opposition to the inclusion of aggression – ostensibly became part of this group of 'in theory' supporters, now claiming that aggression should 'in principle' be included in the Statute 'if properly defined'.[55] Another group of states was even less specific: they simply indicated their ongoing support for the inclusion of the crime of aggression without making any attempt to address the concerns of other delegations. Within this latter group, however, two states were brave enough to point out the real source of the problem underpinning the crime of aggression: Azerbaijan and Ethiopia both highlighted the role of political calculations in resolving the aggression debate.[56]

By this point, the earlier murmurs expressing doubt as to whether consensus could be reached concerning the crime of aggression had turned into a chorus. States from the Like-minded Group started to find reasons to exclude the crime of aggression, including a lack of time to address the issues of definition and the Security Council's role;[57] the possible risk these unresolved issues posed to the outcome of the Conference;[58] and that exclusion was the only 'realistic alternative' if all of the elements of option 1 could not be agreed upon.[59] By contrast, Syria asked aloud why the 1 July proposal which it and other Middle Eastern states had submitted had not been included in the Bureau's discussion paper, and suggested fresh amendments with regard to the preconditions for the international criminal court's exercise of jurisdiction. Exclusionists now also sought to express their opposition in terms of the lack of progress on the crime's definition and the Security Council's role in relation to it.

Reflecting this ongoing diversity of opinion, the Bureau released a second proposal on 10 July, setting a deadline of 13 July for the development of 'generally accepted' provisions about aggression.[60] If none were forthcoming, the Bureau proposed to exclude aggression from the Statute, instead addressing this crime 'in some other manner, for example, by a Protocol or review conference'.[61] From this point, the focus of meetings of the Committee of the Whole shifted away from the secondary issues of definition and the ICC–Security Council relationship back to the basic concern: whether or not to include the crime of aggression in the statute establishing an international criminal court.

Early on 13 July, several delegations once again spoke in favour of including the crime of aggression, with influential Syria threatening to 'reconsider its position with regard to the Statute as a whole' if aggression was excluded from the Statute.[62] At the same meeting, Iran, speaking on behalf of the Non-aligned Movement, also expressed its disappointment that the latest Bureau proposal contained no substantive provision relating to aggression. Later in the day, Egypt explicitly tied its position with respect to the ICC–Security Council relationship generally to a package of its preferred proposals, indicating that it was willing to reconsider its view of the former on condition that, *inter alia*, the crime of aggression was included in the Statute. Most of Egypt's wishes were accommodated in the final document.[63] Certain delegations advocated that it would be preferable to defer consideration of the crime of aggression until sometime after the Conference.[64] Echoing Ethiopia and Azerbaijan, a few Non-aligned Movement member delegations underscored that greater political support would overcome the problems relating to the inclusion of the crime of aggression.[65] The Bureau's deadline of 13 July – the last day on which the crime of aggression was discussed by the Committee of the Whole – came and went, with no resolution of the matter.

The following day, the Non-aligned Movement submitted a new proposal which sought to reconcile these perspectives. It proposed to add aggression as a crime within the international criminal court's jurisdiction, but to postpone this entity's exercise of jurisdiction over this crime pending: (1) elaboration by the proposed, post-Conference Preparatory Commission of the definition and elements of the crime of aggression; and (2) the Preparatory Commission's recommendation that these be adopted by the Assembly of State Parties. Although the wording differs, it is clear from the substance of this proposal that it is the predecessor to article 5(2) of the Rome Statute, which was signed by 120 states just three days later, on 17 July 1998.[66]

Conclusion

In addition to the General Assembly's own efforts to 'define' aggression, this chapter has demonstrated that from the earliest UN years, the ILC turned its attention to the development of an international criminal code and court within which, it was assumed, the crime of aggression would play a central role. Despite the General Assembly referring specifically to the Nuremberg Charter and judgment in its instructions to the ILC, it swiftly forgot the main lessons from Nuremberg. Thus, Nuremberg conservatism which focused on individual responsibility for the crime of aggression, carefully limiting the scope of this crime to particular uses of armed force and deliberately avoiding the issue of state criminality, quickly gave way to the ILC vision of state responsibility for the crime of aggression which included all *acts* of aggression, not just *wars* of aggression. Not content with stretching the Nuremberg precedent to this radically new extent, the ILC combined this approach with the suggestion of an international criminal court which exercised jurisdiction over states and individuals. Predictably, the ILC got nowhere fast with these proposals, which went beyond the pale in political terms. Worse, because the ILC itself chose to focus on the issue of state criminality, its work on the twin issues of an international criminal code and court became tangled up with the General Assembly's efforts to 'define' state aggression, and the decision was made to put the former on hold until a 'definition' of state aggression was achieved. The impact of this decision – given that it was not until the mid-1970s that the General Assembly Definition of Aggression was passed – was to shut down any further work towards an international criminal code and court for in excess of twenty years. A better example of the damage that can be caused when legal drafters, throwing caution (and reality) to the wind, seek to move well and truly beyond that which is politically acceptable by a consensus of states is hard to find. It also highlights just how poor a substitute legal innovation is for political agreement.

It was also shown that the damage caused by this initial wrong turn lasted beyond the mid-1970s, as renewed efforts in the 1980s and 1990s towards an international criminal code and court struggled to incorporate the General Assembly Definition of Aggression within their terms. Only once individual criminal responsibility returned as the main focus of these efforts in the mid-1990s did the idea of establishing an international criminal code and court start gaining momentum. By dropping the preoccupation with state criminality in favour of individual criminal responsibility, the end of the Cold War meant that a new, worldwide consensus in favour of an international criminal code and court emerged. The result of the ad hoc Committee of 1995 and the Preparatory Committee of 1996 to 1998 demonstrated the strength of the political consensus surrounding the international prosecution of individuals charged with genocide, war crimes and crime against humanity. By contrast, the same, tired debates on the crime of aggression continued in these committees, with three distinct camps emerging: those in favour, those against, and those who expressed their support for the crime of aggression 'in theory', pending 'definition' and agreement as to the relationship between the ICC and the Security Council for the purposes of this crime. These deep divisions were maintained at Rome, and with little prospect of moving towards consensus, the inclusion of the crime of aggression within the Rome Statute was by no means assured. In the end, it was the threat of losing support for the ICC as a whole from the pro-crime of aggression states – many of whom were from the Middle East – which led to the crime of aggression being mentioned in the Rome Statute, though the ICC's exercise of jurisdiction in relation to this crime remains blocked once again pending 'definition' and the 'conditions' of such exercise of jurisdiction. Thus – like the General Assembly Definition of Aggression before it – the way in which the crime of aggression has been incorporated within the Rome Statute simply preserves within its terms the ongoing political disagreement at the heart of the problem.

This chapter has also demonstrated that while other international crimes – such as genocide, war crimes and crimes against humanity – have benefited from renewed and sustained political consensus resulting from the end of the super-power conflict, the difficulties associated with the crime of aggression have outlasted the Cold War. This suggests that the challenges which the crime of aggression poses actually run much deeper than any prevailing political climate. As the debates about the crime of aggression in this chapter – and about aggression more generally in previous chapters – have shown, recognition of 'aggression' in international relations raises a number of assumptions about the best form of international political organisation, rule-making and proper authority which are far from being generally accepted. From this perspective it is perhaps not surprising that great powers with an enormous political stake in the status quo – such as the USA and China – openly opposed the Rome Statute, while those with the most to gain from change – arguably the Non-aligned Movement – pushed hard for the inclusion of the crime of aggression. It is to this broader theme that we shall return in the concluding chapter of this book.

8 State aggression at the UN, 1945 to 2009

While the way in which the concept of aggression was incorporated controversially into the Rome Statute means it continues today as a live issue in an international criminal law context, the record of UN organs in the post-Charter period demonstrates how far short it has fallen of playing a central role in maintaining international peace and security. Despite the Soviet Union insisting during Charter negotiations that express powers be conferred on the Security Council in relation to aggression, it has *never* acted as a trigger for peace enforcement in the UN system. At most, the notion of aggression has been used by the Security Council and General Assembly as a form of moral censure against certain states, in particular those resorting to international armed force. However, not all states falling into this category were branded aggressors; in the Cold War period only those not protected by one of the superpowers, or those whose acts were especially outrageous, attracted this label. Yet even condemnation by the Security Council as an aggressor was not sufficient to overcome Cold War divisions and thereby provoke peace enforcement action. Even more interestingly, the General Assembly – formally free of the veto stranglehold the P5 powers exercise in the Security Council, as well as being a more representative body – also refrained from describing major international crises as aggression, though other international uses of armed force did attract this criticism from the General Assembly.

Since the end of the Cold War, with collective peace enforcement action under UN auspices more likely than ever before, references to aggression in the resolutions of both the Security Council and General Assembly have fallen out of favour. Just how unpopular the concept of aggression now is in an international peace and security context is confirmed by recent jurisprudence from the International Court of Justice. When specifically asked to rule on the question of aggression in a particular case, the world's court – and arguably the least political body of the three discussed in this chapter – side-stepped the matter, a dodge criticised publicly and vehemently by two of the judges presiding over the case. From this, the ongoing potency of political factors – especially the influence of the great powers – even in UN organs ostensibly less tied to *realpolitik* is apparent.

Security Council

Despite its power to make determinations as to the existence of a threat to the peace, breach of the peace, or act of aggression under article 39 of the UN Charter, the Security Council exercised this power very infrequently between 1945 and 1990. Cold War competition obstructed consensus in the Security Council on how best to address challenges to international peace and security. In fact, Cold War considerations dominated political activities to such an extent during this time that the Security Council only managed to authorise full-scale peace enforcement action – the most serious Security Council response available – on two occasions: in Korea in 1950, and in Kuwait in 1990. Significantly, the Soviet Union was absent from the Security Council during the vote on SC Res 82, which, despite its title,[1] determined that the armed attack by which North Korea commenced war against the Republic of Korea was a breach of the peace. Similarly, it was only at the tail end of the Cold War, when US–Soviet tensions had relaxed somewhat, that SC Res 660[2] was made possible. But even then, Soviet insistence that the concept of aggression be excluded from this resolution resulted in another determination 'that there exists a breach of international peace and security'.[3] Clearly, by 1990, the Soviet Union had changed its 1944 view, expressed at the Charter negotiations, on the significance of the concept of aggression for collective security purposes. With regional wars classified by the Security Council as breaches of the peace and top-end peace enforcement action authorised on this basis, it is perhaps no surprise that the Security Council has never in its history used its powers under Charter article 39 to determine the existence of aggression.

Given these facts, if the Security Council made no reference to aggression or aggressive activities in any of its resolutions, this might suggest that in the post-Charter period, the concept of aggression has never played any role in international relations, having been supplanted by the categories of 'threat to the peace' and 'breach of the peace' for the purposes of maintaining international order. However, on several occasions, the Security Council has complicated matters by *describing* and *denouncing* an incident as aggressive, though stopping short of a *formal determination* to this effect. The cases of South Africa, Southern Rhodesia and Israel are especially relevant on this point.

From the early 1960s through to the mid-1980s, South Africa was the subject of many Security Council resolutions for its conduct in relation to Angola, Zambia, Lesotho, Botswana and Namibia. On multiple occasions, the Security Council 'strongly condemn[ed]' South Africa for:

1   its 'aggression,[4] its 'latest premeditated and unprovoked aggression',[5] and finally its 'continued, intensified and unprovoked acts of aggression'[6] against Angola;[7]
2   its 'continued collusion … in repeated acts of aggression' against Zambia;[8]
3   its 'premeditated aggressive act' against Lesotho;[9]
4   its 'recent unprovoked and unwarranted military attack on the capital of Botswana as an act of aggression';[10] and

5   its 'utilization of the Territory of Namibia as a springboard for acts of aggression and destabilization of Angola'.[11]

Despite these acknowledgements of the aggressive nature of South African actions – and with the exception of the largely unsuccessful arms embargo established by SC Res 418 of 1977[12] – the Security Council did little more in these resolutions than demand that South Africa desist from its aggressive conduct, and ask other states to help the victims of the aggression. By deliberately refraining from making a formal determination about South African conduct, yet at the same time expressly criticising South Africa's aggressions in its resolutions, the Security Council brought to the world's attention its impotence as the main entity for ensuring international peace and security in the context of an enduring, all-encompassing great power conflict.

Similarly, without formally determining that aggression had been committed, the Security Council was still condemning the ongoing 'provocative and aggressive acts' of Southern Rhodesia against Mozambique[13] and the former's 'continued, intensified and unprovoked acts of aggression' against Zambia[14] ten years after comprehensive sanctions against Southern Rhodesia had first been introduced. Once again, in 1985, the Security Council condemned Israel's 'act of armed aggression', and even went so far as to acknowledge Tunisia's right to reparations from Israel for its raid of PLO headquarters, yet still failed to make a formal determination that aggression had taken place.[15] Further examples also exist of the Security Council invoking the notion of aggression for basic 'naming and shaming' purposes while at the same time giving up the opportunity to make a formal finding of its existence.[16]

Taken together, these examples reinforce the blunt observation made at the 1968 Special Committee on the Question of Defining Aggression: that it is the lack of political will, not perceived difficulties with the concept of aggression itself, which is the real issue preventing the Charter security regime from functioning as designed.[17] Until this underlying problem is addressed, the concept of aggression is destined to be used at most as a term of moral condemnation by the Security Council, other bodies and individual states alike. Without the political will required to back up such condemnation with peace enforcement action, the impact of denunciation on moral grounds remains weak.

However, there is reason to believe that even in the limited arena of international moral standards, the concept of aggression is waning. While the end of the Cold War has facilitated the emergence of a revived UN, including a Security Council which more frequently exercises its powers under article 39, at the same time the Security Council has shifted even further away from the concept of aggression. Virtually all situations subject to a Security Council determination since 1991 have been classified in the 'threat to the peace' category. Thus, events arising out of the implosion of the former Yugoslavia,[18] civil wars in Sierra Leone,[19] Angola,[20] Liberia[21] and Haiti,[22] mutinies in Central African Republic[23] and Ivory Coast,[24] the failure of the Taliban in Afghanistan to 'respond to the demands of' SC Res 1214 of 1998,[25] and the 'magnitude of the human tragedy'[26] resulting from conflict within Somalia's borders have all been held by the Security Council to constitute, or to continue to constitute, 'a threat to international peace and security'. In none of these resolutions has the Security Council described or denounced the acts committed in terms of aggression. To the extent that historical record is any guide, the Security Council's practice during the Cold War of classifying even invasions as 'breaches of the peace', combined with the post-Cold War expansion of the 'threat to the peace' category, would strongly suggest that the concept of aggression has now disappeared from the Security Council's vocabulary with regard to its international peace and security role.

General Assembly

These difficulties in the Security Council have been mirrored in the General Assembly, whether in its emergency special sessions, its general special sessions or its ordinary meetings. During the Cold War, by virtue of the Uniting For Peace Resolution,[27] nine emergency special sessions of the General Assembly were called by the Security Council to address urgent problems of international peace and security in relation to which the proper course of action could not be agreed by the latter body.[28] What is striking about these emergency special sessions is the high frequency of occasions on which the General Assembly, like the Security Council, held back from identifying international conflicts as aggression, despite the General Assembly's more representative composition and formal equality of voting, regardless of the gravity of the situations being addressed. Thus, the General Assembly made no mention of aggression in relation to the 1956 Suez Crisis,[29] the Soviet invasion of Hungary the same year,[30] the 1967 Six Day War,[31] or the 1980 Soviet invasion of Afghanistan.[32] Only three of the ten situations dealt with by the General Assembly in its emergency special sessions refer to aggression at all, and these all took place in the 1980s as the Cold War was coming to an end.[33]

Another way in which the General Assembly followed the lead of the Security Council during the Cold War – despite the former's different role, composition and voting procedures – was by echoing denunciations of aggression first made by the Security Council. Nine years after the Security Council first described South Africa's continued occupation of Namibia as 'an aggressive encroachment on the authority of the United Nations',[34] the General Assembly in 1978 named the South African annexation of Walvis Bay as 'an act of aggression against the Namibian people', and indicated that 'South Africa's illegal occupation of Namibia constitutes a continued act of aggression'.[35] Moreover, the General Assembly condemned South Africa's aggression against Angola, among other states, in 1988, yet South African aggression towards Angola had already been denounced by the Security Council in 1976.[36] While the great powers remained divided on the issue of whether or not to respond to South Africa with military enforcement action, the General Assembly's resolutions added further moral support at best to the existing Security Council resolutions on this matter.[37]

The value of the General Assembly's resolutions as a form of moral support to the decisions of the Security Council is one thing; their worth as tools of moral suasion for compelling Security Council action where great power consensus is absent is quite another. On occasions where the General Assembly has been the first to condemn aggressive activities, the Security Council has not followed suit with corresponding action. For example, while the General Assembly criticised 'acts of aggression' taking place in Central America in 1983, the Security Council made no determination about these events at all.[38]

Even in circumstances where the General Assembly has made a decision relating to international security on the basis that the matter was referred to it by the Security Council as a consequence of great power disagreement, the latter has not followed that decision with peace enforcement action. Thus, while the General Assembly declared at its eighth emergency special session in 1981 'that the illegal occupation of Namibia by South Africa together with the repeated acts of aggression committed by South Africa against neighbouring states constitute a breach of international peace and security', Cold War conflict between the great powers left the General Assembly re-declaring South Africa's conduct as aggression under the terms of the General Assembly Definition of Aggression a further six times, up until 1988.[39] In addition, the General Assembly's conclusion at its ninth emergency special session in 1982 that:

> Israel's decision of 14 December 1981 to impose its laws, jurisdiction and administration on the occupied Syrian Golan Heights constitutes an act of aggression under the provisions of article 39 of the Charter of the United Nations and GA Res 3314

was similarly ignored by the Security Council, though the General Assembly condemned and re-declared this act of aggression every year for seven consecutive years.[40] Despite the General Assembly's best efforts, at no stage did the Security Council make a formal determination that aggression existed in either of these cases. From this, it would seem that the General Assembly's greater willingness to make decisions about the existence of aggression has exercised minimal moral force over the Security Council's hesitancy to do the same.

While in the post-Cold War period the Security Council has abandoned altogether any references to the concept of aggression in the performance of its peace and security functions, opting instead to respond to new challenges by interpreting widely what is meant by a 'threat to international peace and security', the General Assembly continued to hold on to to the notion of aggression, at least until 1994, while at the same time adopting the Security Council's new approach. Thus, the General Assembly referred to 'the aggression against the territory of the Republic of Bosnia and Herzegovina, which constitutes a threat to international peace and security' in 1992[41] and 'the continued aggression against Bosnia and Herzegovina' in 1994.[42] It was also in 1994 that the General Assembly noticeably dropped any references to Israeli aggression or the General Assembly Definition of Aggression from its resolutions in relation to the Golan Heights.[43] Since 1994, the situation in the Golan Heights appears to have been downgraded even further by the General Assembly, which recently 'determine[d] once more that the continued occupation of the Syrian Golan and its de facto annexation constitute a stumbling block in the way of achieving a just, comprehensive and lasting peace in the region'.[44] The ways in which the General Assembly has addressed other situations since 1994 also suggest that the concept of aggression has vanished from its international peace and security terminology, as it has done in the Security Council.[45]

The International Court of Justice

The workings of the International Court of Justice also reflect the strong influence of political factors within the UN system's primary legal organ, especially with regard to questions concerning enforcement of ICJ decisions and concerning international uses of armed force. On the one hand, the requirement that the express consent of both sides to a dispute is given before the ICJ can carry out its adjudication function addresses the problem of enforcement in an international arena typified by the absence of centralised law enforcement mechanisms, by increasing the likelihood that implementation of those decisions will take place. However, on the other hand, this condition also restricts greatly the range of disputes heard by the ICJ in practice, meaning that where relations between states have deteriorated to the degree that allegations of aggression are involved, it is unlikely that all parties will consent to the ICJ's adjudication of the dispute. Even where consent of the parties is initially granted, the outcome of ICJ proceedings is frequently subject to external political developments, reflected in the discontinuance notices filed with the agreement of the parties on the basis that the issues have subsequently been resolved out of court.[46]

As a consequence of ICJ rules and practice, then, it is unsurprising that it has only been confronted with arguments explicitly concerning aggression on two occasions. The ICJ has dealt with these contentions very cautiously. In the *Nicaragua (Admissability)* case,[47] the US argued that Nicaragua's application to the ICJ was inadmissible on the grounds that the crux of Nicaragua's claim was that:

> the United States is engaged in an unlawful use of armed force, or breach of the peace, or acts of aggression against Nicaragua, a matter which is committed by the Charter and by practice to the competence of other organs, in particular the United Nations Security Council.[48]

However, the ICJ rejected this argument on the basis that it was evident that the situation 'demand[ed] the peaceful settlement of disputes'[49] did not concern a continuing armed conflict between Nicaragua and the USA, and was hence properly brought before the ICJ.

As Nicaragua had not expressly alleged aggression in its application, in *Nicaragua (Merits)*[50] the ICJ was able to avoid to a great extent making any important rulings in this area. Instead, it focused on what was meant by an 'armed attack'. In deciding the scope of 'armed attack', the ICJ indicated that article 3(g) of the General Assembly Definition of Aggression reflected the position of customary international law.[51] By narrowly restricting its ruling to this specific provision, it has been suggested that the ICJ has thrown doubt on the status of the rest of the Definition.

By contrast, in *Armed Activities on the Territory of the Congo*,[52] the Congo asked the ICJ to declare *inter alia* that Uganda was 'guilty of an act of aggression within the meaning of article 1 of GA Res 3314 … contrary to article 2 paragraph 4 of the United Nations Charter'.[53] This was top of the Congo's list of requests to the ICJ, and, in light of the seriousness of the events being adjudicated,[54] was a vital part of the Congo's application. The ICJ substantially upheld the Congo's claim, but did so in its own terms:

> the unlawful military intervention by Uganda was of such a magnitude and duration that the Court considers it to be a grave violation of the prohibition on the use of force expressed in article 2, paragraph 4, of the Charter.[55]

This was as close as the ICJ got to *considering* the extent to which Uganda's actions amounted to aggression, let alone to making a finding that Uganda had committed such aggression. Given the Congo's multiple requests throughout the proceedings for a declaration in relation to aggression, the ICJ's evasion of this important question can only be explained by reference to the political sensitivities of the P5 members of the Security Council, and its own record with respect to determinations of aggression. A finding of aggression by the ICJ may have put political pressure on the Security Council to act in circumstances where P5 agreement to act, or acquiescence, could not be guaranteed. It may also have thrown light on the Security Council's own sixty-year failure to determine the existence of even one case of aggression. At the very least, such a finding would bring greater public attention to the conflict, which continues in part to this day and has been described as 'Africa's world war'.[56] The Security Council's failure to address such a flagrant and large-scale conflict would be a very public failure indeed.

While the political ramifications of the ICJ making a determination of aggression may have been significant, ultimately its job, precisely as the UN's primary legal organ, is to consider the legal merits of the case before it, without paying undue attention to such political factors. By avoiding altogether the issue of aggression in the circumstances presented by this case, the ICJ derogated from its own duties, and revealed the high degree to which this formally independent legal body can be influenced by grave political considerations. This point was not lost on two of the judges presiding over this case. Hence, in his separate opinion, Judge Elaraby outlined a range of factors pertaining to this case which:

> require[d] the Court to adhere to its judicial responsibility to adjudicate on a normative basis … the Court should … have embarked on a determination as to whether the egregious use of force by Uganda falls within the customary rule of international law as embodied in GA Res 3314.[57]

By normal judicial standards, Judge Elaraby's conclusion was outspoken: 'I am unable, however, to appreciate any compelling reason for the Court to refrain from finding that Uganda's actions did indeed amount to aggression.'[58]

By comparison, Judge Simma's separate opinion made Judge Elaraby look restrained:

> So, why not call a spade a spade? If there ever was a military activity before the Court that deserves to be qualified as an act of aggression, it is the Ugandan invasion of the Congo. Compared to its scale and impact, the military adventures the Court had to deal with in earlier cases, as in *Corfu Channel*, *Nicaragua*, or *Oil Platforms*, border on the insignificant....
>
> The Council will have had its own – political – reasons for refraining from such a determination [i.e. that the Ugandan invasion constituted an act of aggression]. But the Court, as the principal *judicial* organ of the United Nations, does not have to follow that course. Its very raison d'être is to arrive at decisions based on law and nothing but the law, keeping the political context of the cases before it in mind, of course, but not desisting from stating what is manifest out of regard for such non-legal considerations. This is the division of labour between the Court and the political organs of the United Nations envisaged by the Charter! ...
>
> By the unnecessarily cautious way in which it handles this matter, as well as by dodging the issue of 'aggression', the Court creates the impression that it somehow feels uncomfortable being confronted with certain questions of utmost importance in contemporary international relations.[59]

Thus, even within the ICJ, it seems that the political sensitivities raised by the concept of aggression have infiltrated and prevented the ICJ from fulfilling the most basic of its judicial roles.[60]

Conclusion

Although under the UN Charter the Security Council was empowered to determine the existence of aggression on behalf of the UN organisation as a whole, this chapter has shown what little impact the notion of aggression has had in an international peace and security context since 1945. It was demonstrated that while the Security Council has never made such a determination, preferring instead to classify incidents as breaches of the peace, or, more recently, threats to international peace and security, it had on numerous occasions denounced aggressive conduct during the Cold War. Similarly, the General Assembly over this period also condemned a range of incidents as aggression. However, none of these condemnations seemed to have provoked the Security Council into peace enforcement action, and where major instances of international hostilities broke out, the General Assembly – despite its more equal representation and voting – followed the Security Council by ignoring them. Building on Chapter 7, this suggests that Cold War divisions were not the sole reason behind the failure of the concept of aggression to act as a trigger for collective security, but in fact masked deeper political challenges.

This is confirmed by developments in the post-Cold War era. Since the mid-1990s, the notion of aggression has completely disappeared from the resolutions of the Security Council and the General Assembly, though the former has been more active in peace enforcement terms than ever before. This unease surrounding the concept of aggression has recently spread to the ICJ, the UN's main legal organ, where in 2005 the majority of judges refused to consider, let alone adjudicate, the Congo's request that Uganda's misconduct be declared an act of aggression under the General Assembly Definition of Aggression. This derogation of duty by the ICJ only serves to highlight how susceptible to great power political influence even well-established international legal organs continue to be, even in today's globalised world where many argue that developments such as the expansion and increasing sophistication of international legal regimes are leading towards new global political possibilities.

9   Conclusion

In the first chapter of this book, a comparison of key cosmopolitan and communitarian thinkers provoked two significant questions about the current state of international relations. The first question was whether recent trends are best interpreted as progress towards global democracy, as some cosmopolitans claim, or are better described as a Walzerian 'universal moment' reflecting the communitarian nature of international politics. The second question concerned the role of worldwide, authoritative mechanisms for peaceful change in international affairs. Was the claim correct that incremental efforts towards a cosmopolitan democracy were 'desirable' per se, or were the communitarians right to emphasise just how restricting the absence of these mechanisms were for cosmopolitan objectives? Before examining what the study of the concept of aggression undertaken here tells us in response to these two questions, it is first necessary to consider developments relevant to aggression which have taken place since 1998.

Developments since 1998

The Working Group on the Crime of Aggression (WGCA)

Since 1998, no further progress has been made on the political divisions at the heart of the controversy surrounding the crime of aggression, despite what recent press releases by the chairman of the Working Group on the Crime of Aggression might claim.[1] Established in 2002 by the Assembly of State Parties to the Rome Statute, the WGCA has been working towards achieving the hurdle requirements for the future prosecution of the crime of aggression under ICC jurisdiction as set down in article 5(2) of the Rome Statute – namely a 'definition' of the crime of aggression and agreement as to the circumstances in which the ICC can exercise such jurisdiction. The first opportunity to amend the Rome Statute to incorporate such proposals will be at the initial review conference, currently scheduled for 2010. Thus, efforts are underway to ensure that the WGCA has some proposed amendments to be tabled in time for the review conference.

Instead of progress, WGCA discussions about a 'definition' of the crime of aggression seem to have taken a backward step. The relationship between state aggression and individual aggression has once again emerged to confound and distract work on this issue. Just as attempts to bring the General Assembly Definition of Aggression within the parameters of international criminal law had unnecessarily preoccupied ILC efforts from the early 1980s up until 1996, the list of state acts comprising aggression under the Definition has been included in the draft definition of aggression featuring in the WGCA chairman's discussion paper of June 2008. In addition, the chairman suggests that the Definition be reproduced as an annex to the Rome Statute, 'given the central role of GA Res 3314 for the definition of aggression', though he concedes that this suggestion 'requires further discussion'.[2] By including a list of conduct comprising aggression in the definition, the same old, legal debates from the General Assembly's series of special committees about whether such a list should be exhaustive or non-exhaustive have been resurrected, with a predictable lack of agreement. The incorporation of the General Assembly Definition of Aggression into the chairman's draft definition of aggression has gone ahead, despite the objections of certain delegations since at least 2005. Some of these delegations have argued that the Definition 'was a political instrument negotiated in a different context and not related to issues of individual criminal responsibility'.[3] Unfortunately, however, their appeal seems to have fallen on deaf ears.

The extent to which the relationship between state aggression and individual criminal responsibility has overtaken the WGCA's work is also confirmed by the draft definition's reference to '*acts* of aggression' – a departure from the '*war* of aggression' formula used at Nuremberg. The Report of the 2006 WGCA meeting explained that 'the predominant view was that the inclusion of a reference to a "war of aggression" in the definition would be too restrictive, in particular in light of the acts specified in article 3 of General Assembly Resolution 3314'.[4] Curiously, the chairman's 2008 draft definition then goes on to define an 'act of aggression' by reference to the use of armed force by a state. Given this limitation, the only reason for shifting from 'war of aggression' to 'act of aggression' would seem to be the wish to repeat deliberately the turn of phrase used in both the General Assembly Definition of Aggression and article 39 of the UN Charter – in other words, to link together individual criminal responsibility for aggression, the types of state conduct which comprise aggression according to the General Assembly, and the Security Council's power to rule that a state's conduct comprises aggression. It is precisely this type of linkage between the (criminal) role of the individual and the (criminal? illegal? morally reprehensible?) role of the state in committing aggression, with the resultant controversy it provokes, which left in limbo efforts generally towards an international criminal jurisdiction for more than twenty years.

Attempts to reconcile an international crime of aggression giving rise to individual responsibility with state-based mechanisms for maintaining international peace and security also pose a challenge in relation to the second hurdle requirement – that is, agreed conditions under which the ICC would exercise jurisdiction. The fundamental issue here is whether or not the Security Council should hold the exclusive right to authorise ICC prosecutions of aggression – a first-order political question. Clearly, each state's response to such a question is going to reflect very closely their preferred vision of international organisation – the proper location of authority in international affairs, sources of rule-making, enforcement mechanisms, and so on. While broad coalitions bringing together states of relatively similar preferences are identifiable, to a large extent these contrasting visions have co-existed without much in the way of comprehensive reconciliation; it is this feature which characterises the mitigated anarchy of the international system. In light of this, it is perhaps unsurprising that the WGCA has come nowhere near to compromise on this issue, something it admitted indirectly in a 2005 discussion paper on this topic when it claimed 'the Working Group still has some work to do before it gets close to consensus'.[5] Hence, in 2008, the options for triggering ICC jurisdiction over the crime of aggression included Security Council authorisation; or, where Security Council authorisation is not forthcoming, then Pre-trial Chamber authorisation or a determination of aggression by the General Assembly or the ICJ. All of these options – as well as whether or not such decisions would be of a substantive or procedural nature – remain subject to debate among states, and are likely to remain so for some time to come. No wonder then, when commenting on the issue of a triggering mechanism for the crime of aggression, the chairman of the WGCA commented that it was 'all very legal and very complex and very fascinating, but in the end it's a political question'.[6]

Criminal prosecutions of individual leaders

Another recent trend which points to the declining relevance of the crime of aggression is the further development of other modes of criminal liability for catching top political and military leaders. Reflecting the internal nature of the armed conflicts which arose in the Former Yugoslavia and Rwanda in the 1990s, the jurisdiction of the resulting two international criminal tribunals was limited to genocide, war crimes and crimes against humanity. Whereas at Nuremberg and Tokyo, high-ranking officials faced charges of war crimes, crimes against humanity and aggression – the latter crime clearly forming the 'leadership' link – the fate of leaders in the Former Yugoslavia and Rwanda depended essentially on the extent to which the prosecution could prove command responsibility for the former two categories of crime only. It was not long before ICTY judges themselves elaborated another mode of liability of particular relevance to leaders: joint criminal enterprise (JCE). Although earlier authority exists for this notion,[7] the three types of collective responsibility recognised by JCE were set down in the ICTY's 1999 *Tadic* decision on appeal:

> In the first category cases the co-defendants voluntarily participate in one aspect of the common design and intend its result. In the second category, in actuality really a variant of the first, the accused actively participates in the enforcement of a system of repression with the knowledge of the nature of that system and the intent to further the common concerted design. Cases in the third category ... are categorised by 'a common design to pursue one course of conduct where one of the perpetrators commits an act which,

while outside the common design, was nevertheless a natural and foreseeable consequence of the effecting of that common purpose.'[8]

The ICTY indictments in relation to the Bosnian and Croatian aspects of the Yugoslav conflict both relied on command responsibility and JCE in support of the charges of crimes against humanity laid against Slobodan Milosevic. The purpose of the JCEs of which Milosevic was alleged to be a part were described as

> the forcible removal of the majority of the Croat and other non-Serb population from the approximately one-third of the territory of the Republic of Croatia that he planned to become part of a new Serb-dominated state through the commission of crimes in violation of Articles 2, 3, and 5 of the Statute of the Tribunal.[9]

A similar statement of JCE purpose was alleged in relation to the Bosnian Muslims and Bosnian Croats in the Republic of Bosnia and Herzegovina. While Milosevic died before the end of his trial, it may be expected that prosecutors will also seek to establish command responsibility and/or JCE in the case against Radovan Karadzic. As one of Milosevic's close colleagues during the relevant period and a former president of the Serb Republic of Bosnia, he is now before the ICTY facing charges of genocide, violations of the laws of war and crimes against humanity.

JCE is also at the centre of the charges against Charles Taylor, the former President of Liberia who is currently being tried by the Special Court of Sierra Leone for his involvement in alleged crimes against humanity and violations of international humanitarian law. Initially, the 2003 indictment against Taylor alleged the existence of a JCE 'to take any actions necessary to gain and exercise political power and control over the territory of Sierra Leone, in particular the diamond mining areas'.[10] This JCE 'included gaining and exercising control over the population of Sierra Leone in order to prevent or minimise resistance to their geographic control, and to use members of the population to provide support to the members of the joint criminal enterprise'.[11] Whereas the JCE alleged against Milosevic was clearly expressed in terms of international criminal law – forcible transfer of populations falling squarely within the scope of the definition of crimes against humanity – how the JCE allegedly including Taylor was an international crime was less clear. At best, the political control at the heart of the JCE allegation against Taylor resembled the conspiracy element of the crime of aggression prosecuted at Tokyo, where virtually all Japanese defendants were convicted of participating in a common plan 'to secure for Japan the military, naval, political and economic domination' of parts of the Asia-Pacific region. Given the serious flaws associated with the Tokyo Trial, this is an association the Special Court of Sierra Leone would do well to avoid. It is therefore not surprising that in the second amended indictment against Taylor, lodged in May 2007, Taylor is alleged simply to have participated in a JCE comprising the substantive crimes listed in the indictment, or a JCE involving such crimes, or a JCE in relation to which such crimes 'were a reasonably foreseeable consequence', without any further detail.[12]

While prosecuting high-ranking leaders in this way has the legal advantage of helping to avoid litigation of the merits or otherwise of political decisions leading to armed conflict, care must be taken not to stretch these modes of liability – and/or relax the rules of evidence or standard of proof – to the degree that they undermine the legal validity of the trial process altogether. Such an outcome would fan the flames of those already predisposed to consider the criminal prosecution of belligerent leaders as nothing more than exercises in victors' justice. In addition, considering that such prosecutions usually follow in the wake of large-scale armed conflict, there is a question here about whether the top-level criminal trial *should* be the appropriate forum for considering and accounting for the political events that led up to the war in the first place. While in the post-Cold War era other mechanisms, such as truth and reconciliation commissions, have emerged to address these facets of 'transitional justice', on the other hand, the criminal prosecution of a leader which assiduously avoids a key issue such as responsibility for an armed conflict, and instead concentrates on 'lesser' crimes, is unlikely to inspire the sentiment that 'justice has been served' either.

The trial of Saddam Hussein provides an important case in point. The Coalition Provisional Authority authorised the establishment of the Iraqi Special Tribunal. Under its statute, the IST was empowered to prosecute genocide, war crimes, crimes against humanity, and breaches of Iraqi law allegedly committed during the period July 1968 to May 2003 inclusive, whether in Iraq or elsewhere, 'including crimes committed in connection with Iraq's wars against the Islamic Republic of Iran and the State of Kuwait'.[13] Under article 14(c) of the Statute, recognised as an IST crime was 'the abuse of position and the pursuit of policies that may lead to the threat of war or the use of the armed forces of Iraq against an Arab country'. Accordingly, the arrest warrant for Hussein included seven charges – mainly to do with killing, displacing and suppressing various groups of individuals – but also included one charge concerning the 1990 invasion of Kuwait. After Hussein's capture, his first appearance at the IST was to face these preliminary charges in July 2004. In response to this latter charge, it has been reported that in court Hussein attempted to justify his actions on the basis that Kuwait was trying to reduce the price of oil, and that the invasion was 'for the Iraqi people'.[14] The crime outlined in article 14(c) fell broadly within the parameters set at Nuremberg for the crime of aggression, and yet no reference to aggression was made in the IST Statute.

By the time the trial formally began in October 2005, prosecutors had changed tack, choosing to focus their efforts in relation to the charge of crime against humanity for Hussein's alleged order of the killing of approximately 150 Shias in Dujail in 1982. Hussein was tried with seven co-defendants, was found guilty in November 2006 and sentenced to death by hanging. In August 2006, a second trial commenced against Hussein and six co-defendants, who had held top political and military leadership positions in Iraq, including Minister of Defence, head of the Republican Guard and an intelligence chief. This second trial related to the Anfal Campaign of 1987 to 1988, in which it is estimated that over 100,000 Kurds died.[15] After Hussein's execution in December 2006 he was dropped as a co-defendant in the Anfal trial. In June 2007, five of the remaining co-defendants were found guilty of war crimes and crimes against humanity, with three – including Hussein's infamous cousin 'Chemical Ali' – sentenced to death by hanging and the other two receiving life imprisonment. One co-defendant was acquitted for lack of evidence.

By pursuing convictions against Hussein on these two charges as a matter of priority, and leaving out of the trial process altogether the issues of Hussein's role in both the Iran–Iraq War and the 1990 invasion of Kuwait, the trials of Hussein by the IST have attracted significant legal and political criticism. This prosecutorial reluctance to examine and establish the greater political and historical context in which Hussein's alleged conduct took place negatively affected the legal workings of the Dujail trial itself. Human Rights Watch (HRW) claims that 'important gaps'[16] in evidence with regard to some of the basic elements establishing liability under international criminal law – namely knowledge, intent and responsibility of the particular defendant – were present at this trial. To establish these, it was necessary to investigate and prove, for instance, the legal and actual authority of the various security and political entities implicated in the Dujail killings; the command structures both within and among these entities; and the relationship between political and legal institutions implicated in these killings. Very little evidence on these issues was presented, and thus the conclusion that Hussein did in fact have the requisite knowledge and intent in the absence of such contextual evidence is undermined. Another important legal criticism is that for a conviction to be made, the IST judges did not have to apply the conventional, criminal standard of proof 'beyond reasonable doubt', but merely had to be 'satisfied of guilt'.[17] Combined, these two criticisms on their own suggest that the verdict of Hussein's guilt is unsafe; in conjunction with the many other legal flaws identified, real questions are raised as to whether the legal process has been so eroded that political damage is done – perhaps even more so than if the prosecutors had proactively sought to prosecute Hussein's conduct as aggressions in the first place.

Politically, the requirement that the death penalty be carried out within thirty days from the final decision has also come under attack for depriving victims and witnesses of the chance to establish properly which leaders were responsible in legal terms for the atrocities to which they were subjected. As HRW points out, 'the execution of convicted individuals while other charges are pending against them means that there may never be a public accounting of the evidence for and against them in relation to these events'.[18] Thus, with Hussein already dead, the execution of 'Chemical Ali' for his role in the Anfal Campaign was the 'second-best'[19] justice outcome for Iraqi Kurds, most of whom would have preferred to see Hussein executed for his role in this crime, where victim numbers were 1,000 times more than those at Dujail. Nevertheless, at least Iraqi Kurds had some form of redress – it appears that the Kuwaiti and Iranian victims of Hussein's wars will now never have their own 'day in court'.

From this example, it may be demonstrated that even where the politics of an international use of armed force are deftly avoided by prosecutors in a criminal trial of high-ranking leaders, political issues will surface anyway when considering the individual defendant's responsibility under more traditional categories such as war crimes and crimes against humanity. The shift towards using these latter categories on their own to establish the criminal liability of top political and military leaders has led to the emergence of new modes of responsibility, such as joint criminal enterprise, to link these leaders to events on the ground. However, as the Dujail trial shows, unless prosecutors are willing to grasp and establish as part of the trial process the greater political context in which the alleged crimes occurred, the legal validity of the trial is likely to be significantly undermined. This in turn threatens to endanger the legitimacy of the prosecuting authority and the government of which it is a part. There are other good reasons for seeking to establish the political circumstances surrounding the alleged crimes, such as the importance for victims and others of accounting for the events that took place and the creation of a historical record. To the extent that evidence about the prevailing political, legal and social context is crucial to proving criminal knowledge and/or intent on the part of the defendant, a good case can be made for attempting to establish the wider picture as part of the criminal trial process itself, rather than siphoning off this task to other transitional justice mechanisms. While the crime of aggression may be currently on the wane,[20] the twin themes of international order and justice it raises remain of acute significance today.

Aggression, Walzer's 'universal moment' and cosmopolitan democracy

In relation to the first key question iterated above, the study of the concept of aggression presented in these pages lends greater support to the communitarian thesis. The scale of the horror and outrage generated by World War I was sufficient to provoke initially the creation of a new international security organisation with the moral notion of aggression as its triggering mechanism. The effectiveness of this approach rested on the assumption that all members of the new organisation – states and their nationals alike – would know an aggression when they saw one, based on moral principles, and would agree on what action to take in response. This tallies with Walzer's idea of a 'universal moment' where a 'thin' understanding of aggression is widely acknowledged and endorsed. However, we also saw that this moment of collective moral unity – where outside concerns take priority over community concerns – was very brief, with significant resistance to this new approach arising from European Allies that preferred more traditional security arrangements, as well as from the US Senate. It was also more conventional ideas about punishment and retribution at the end of war which resulted in the concept of aggression being used as justification for the imposition of reparations on Germany in the Treaty of

Versailles. Later, negative reactions to the reparations provisions from Germany and elsewhere demonstrated just how superficial, short-lived and less than universal (though more than localised) the 'thin' understanding of aggression had been. If the attempt to secure international order by relying on the moral concept of aggression represented a step towards global democracy, then clearly it was considered by many as a step too far.

This was also confirmed in the early days of the League, when concerns about the nature of the obligation in article 10 resurfaced, and certain states – with an eye on their own, particular self-interest in avoiding being brought into another world conflict – pushed for greater clarification. Although the duty of League members to preserve each other against aggression was invoked successfully – and in the case of Ethiopia quite creatively – on a couple of occasions, these were more the exception than the rule. Generally, where hostilities broke out involving at least one major regional power, the League proved powerless to act – particularly in relation to those disputes which belligerents chose to settle outside the League.

World War II brought on another 'universal moment' with regard to aggression – this time at Nuremberg. While it was clear from the start of the negotiations for yet another international security organisation that neither reference to, nor a definition of, aggression in the UN Charter attracted broad-based support, the magnitude and industrialisation of the atrocities committed by the German leadership eventually led to agreement of the Allied Powers to prosecute the high-ranking Nazis for the crime of aggression. However, what this actually meant remained subject to debate. Having agreed to empower the judges to exercise jurisdiction over the crime of aggression, the Nuremberg bench produced a well-reasoned, cautious judgment, reflecting both the opportunities and constraints presented by the political circumstances forming the subject of the trial. Nuremberg thus represents what *can* be achieved by legal procedures built on strong political foundations in international affairs.

However, it is important not to overstate this. While Nuremberg is often cited by cosmopolitans as one of the sources of the modern international human rights regime – the evolution of which, it is argued, itself demonstrates progress towards a global democracy – the status of the crime of aggression since Nuremberg actually reveals the extent to which it was a unique, 'universal moment' in time. The subsequent Tokyo trial showed how the different political circumstances of Japanese involvement in World War II posed a significant challenge to the crime of aggression developed at Nuremberg. Nevertheless, the vast majority of Japanese defendants were convicted under this head, showing scant regard for either these political differences or the available evidence. This dubious decision was implicitly acknowledged in the 1950s, when most of the Japanese war criminals sentenced to life imprisonment were freed. In contrast to Nuremberg, Tokyo demonstrated what can result when overenthusiasm for international law leaps ahead of political realities. The damage of Tokyo continues to be felt today: at least ten of the Tokyo defendants convicted of the crime of aggression remain on the list of 'divine spirits' revered at Yasukuni Shrine by five million Japanese visitors a year, a matter which intermittently causes diplomatic tensions between Japan and regional neighbours such as China and Australia. By comparison, most Germans today regard the Nuremberg Trial as fair.[21]

In addition, the fact that, sixty years on from Nuremberg and Tokyo, no prosecutions for the crime of aggression have taken place, the crime's status under the Rome Statute remains uncertain, and recent WGCA discussions suggest that the basic Nuremberg position itself may no longer attract consensus, all serve to highlight just how little progress towards global democracy has been achieved. Although multiple prosecutions for other international crimes, such as genocide, war crimes and crimes against humanity have taken place, it must be remembered that aggression cuts to the very heart of the issue of what types of political or military decisions can and cannot be taken by individuals *against states*. Discussions concerning aggression therefore invoke the fundamental rules of co-existence among states, and from the debates analysed in this study – as well as the emergence of other related topics including humanitarian intervention, the responsibility to protect and the limits of self-defence – it is evident that many outstanding controversies in this area remain. Without widespread consensus on the rules of co-existence – and in the absence of any other non-state mechanism for aggregating and reconciling authoritatively the preferences of individual 'stakeholders' worldwide – the achievement of global democracy seems a long way off indeed.

Aggression, progress and peaceful change

This study also provides positive proof that steps towards cosmopolitan democracy are not necessarily of themselves a good thing. The key example here is the lengthy efforts by the General Assembly to define aggression, culminating in GA Res 3314. In theory, a definition of aggression sounds like a desirable cosmopolitan goal, for all the reasons mentioned previously, such as guiding those bodies with the power to determine the existence of aggression, thereby expediting decision-making and law enforcement; deterring potential aggressors; and mobilising international public opinion. However, in practice, it was shown that states were so divided on the consequences of a definition of aggression – never mind which types of conduct to prohibit – that international consensus was impossible. Despite this fatal political constraint, with work towards an international criminal code and court postponed until a definition of aggression was accomplished, the aim of revisiting the former topics pushed forward efforts to define aggression, and the General Assembly Definition of Aggression was passed in order to clear the way for these other topics to be revived, rather than as a result of a new climate of widespread political agreement. Thus, the Definition preserved within its terms all the outstanding political controversies that existed prior to its passage. Although referred to as a 'definition' of aggression, it was anything but; yet with its passage, it was elevated to a status well beyond what its modest terms could contribute.

This false move – namely pursuing a definition of aggression at any cost, regardless of both prevailing political conditions and the minimal value of the final document – not only delayed further consideration of an international criminal code and court for more than twenty years; it continues to haunt the concept of aggression unnecessarily to this day. It was only once the General Assembly Definition of Aggression was jettisoned from work concerning the international criminal code and court in the mid-1990s that real progress on these topics was made; in 2008, the Definition is back in the WGCA chairman's discussion paper on the 'definition' of the crime of aggression for Rome Statute purposes. Moreover, Chapter 8 demonstrated that the passage of GA Res 3314 in 1974 has not encouraged or compelled the Security Council to determine even *once* the existence of aggression. From this, it may be concluded that far from being a positive development per se, the preoccupation with 'defining' aggression – resulting in the General Assembly Definition of Aggression – at best has contributed little, and at worst has been a distraction and a nuisance. Those working on individual criminal responsibility for aggression seem to feel morally obliged to somehow bring the General Assembly Definition of Aggression into the scope of their task, simply because of its status as the international 'Definition' of Aggression, despite its obvious flaws and uselessness where *individual, criminal* responsibility is concerned. Those critics who currently argue in favour of dropping GA Res 3314 from the WGCA's definition of the crime of aggression, if heeded, are likely to end up saving the WGCA many years' worth of fruitless effort.

The current stalemate concerning the triggering mechanism for the ICC's jurisdiction over the crime of aggression is just one manifestation of a much wider debate about mechanisms for peaceful change in international relations. The European Union, and the work of particular organs such as the European Parliament and European Court of Justice, are often cited as successful examples of international peaceful change mechanisms. While this may be true on a regional level, on a worldwide scale, the proliferation of international fora for the resolution of various types of conflict remains stymied by a lack of centralised and agreed enforcement authority which can *compel* states to pursue the resolution of disputes by peaceful means only. Under the UN Charter, the Security Council can encourage peaceful dispute resolution or even 'recommend appropriate procedures or methods of adjustment',[22] but only when the dispute is judged to endanger international peace and security.[23] This suggests that the Security Council is intended to act as a body of last resort; the disputing parties are left to sort out their differences as they see fit up until such time as the dispute threatens to spill into all-out war. With no compulsory mechanism for upholding – with force if necessary – an agreed, peaceful resolution between the parties, self-help remains one of the only methods of enforcement. It is for this reason that cosmopolitans like Held correctly identify the institutional requirements of cosmopolitan democracy, including 'the entrenchment of cosmopolitan democratic law'[24] and an international military force to defend this law. The range of non-Security Council options for triggering the ICC's jurisdiction over the crime of aggression that are currently tabled – such as by reference to the General Assembly, International Court of Justice, or the ICC's own Pre-trial Chamber – may be interpreted as an effort towards making cosmopolitan democratic law a reality.

The problem for cosmopolitans is that they underestimate how vital the institutional requirements to support international peaceful change are to their project, and seem not to recognise how the pursuit of their goals, without accompanying progress towards creating such mechanisms, can actually undermine their democratic principles. The recent evolution of JCE as a mode of individual criminal responsibility is a clear example. Holding leaders and others criminally responsible for their contribution to the commission of genocide, war crimes and crimes against humanity – in circumstances where they may not have committed the named crimes by their own hands – appears to further the cosmopolitan aim of legal equality and accountability for all persons. For all its faults, at least the crime of aggression was subjected to rigorous political debate among the major Allied powers before they decided to empower both the Nuremberg and Tokyo Tribunals to prosecute this crime. The same cannot be said of JCE, which does not feature in any of the international criminal statutes as a mode of liability – instead, it is a product of judicial innovation, initially by the ICTY.

While JCE has been revised and clarified in various international criminal cases, and it is accepted that a degree of innovation is a necessary part of the proper exercise of judicial functions, weak international legislative mechanisms mean that the *political* debate and decision as to the appropriateness of JCE as a mode of individual criminal liability has not taken place. Whereas at the domestic level such a judicial innovation might be scrutinised by Parliament, debated and addressed in subsequent legislation, on the international stage it is not even clear which body *should* perform this role. Would the appropriate forum for a debate on the political merits of JCE be the Security Council, which established the ICTY in the first place? Or perhaps the General Assembly, where those convicted on the basis of JCE are guaranteed at least to have their state of nationality represented? What about part-international, part-domestic 'hybrid' bodies like the Special Court for Sierra Leone where JCE is presently being relied upon by prosecutors in relation to various defendants – does this give the people of Sierra Leone a particular 'stakeholder' interest in this issue above, say, the people of Guatemala? Do the 'new social movements' to which cosmopolitans refer have a role to play? There are no clear answers to any of these questions, with the effect that formal, international political oversight of judicial innovations such as JCE simply does not happen. This suggests that without agreement on international mechanisms for peaceful change, the pursuit of limited cosmopolitan goals may fall far short of being positive developments in and of themselves – in fact, their cumulative effect may be ultimately to undermine the overall goal of global democracy.

Thus, the concept of aggression in international relations has highlighted the significant limitations of cosmopolitan thinking; while international mechanisms for peaceful change remain undeveloped, 'universal moments' remain possible, though over the longer term they are unlikely to result in the progress towards global democracy that many cosmopolitans favour. Instead, it is more probable that in global debates concerning international morality, law and politics, states will continue to compete and promote as internationally authoritative their own particular understanding of the substance and significance of notions such as aggression.

Appendix 1

Results of the Nuremberg judgment, 1946

Appendix 1 Results of the Nuremberg judgement, 1946

Name	Count				Sentence
	C1	*C2*	*C3*	*C4*	*Sentence*
Goering	G	G	G	G	Death
Hess	G	G	I	I	Life
Bormann	I	–	G	G	Death
Von Ribbentrop	G	G	G	G	Death
Keitel	G	G	G	G	Death
Kaltenbrunner	I	–	G	G	Death
Rosenberg	G	G	G	G	Death
Frank	I	–	G	G	Death
Frick	I	G	G	G	Death
Streicher	I	–	–	G	Death
Funk	I	G	G	G	Life
Schacht	I	I	–	–	Not guilty
Doenitz	I	G	G	–	Ten years
Raeder	G	G	G	–	Life
Von Schirach	I	–	–	G	Twenty years
Sauckel	I	I	G	G	Death
Jodl	G	G	G	G	Death
Von Papen	I	I	–	–	Not guilty
Seyss-Inquart	I	G	G	G	Death
Speer	I	I	G	G	Twenty years
Von Neurath	G	G	G	G	Fifteen years
Fritzsche	I	–	I	I	Not guilty

Source: Compiled from *Trial of the Major War Criminals* (Nuremberg: Germany, 1947).

Notes
G = guilty; I = acquitted; – = not charged with this count.
Count one: Participation in the formulation or execution of a common plan or conspiracy to commit crimes against peace, war crimes and crimes against humanity.
Count two: Participation in the planning, preparation, initiation and waging of wars of aggression, which were also wars in violation of international treaties, agreements and assurances.
Count three: Commission of war crimes.
Count four: Commission of crimes against humanity.

Appendix 2

Results of the Tokyo judgment, 1948

Count 1:   All defendants participated in the formulation or execution of a common plan or conspiracy between 1 January 1928 and 2 September 1945 to secure for Japan the military, naval, political and economic domination of the Asia-Pacific, and for that purpose they conspired that Japan should wage wars of aggression, and wars in violation of international law, treaties, agreements, and assurances, against any country which might oppose that purpose.

Count 54:   Some or all of the accused ordered, authorized and permitted the commission of Conventional War Crimes.

Count 55:   Some or all of the accused failed to take adequate steps to secure the observance, and prevent breaches, of conventions and laws of war in respect of prisoners of war and civilian internees.

Some or all of the accused participated in waging wars of aggression and wars in violation of international law, treaties, agreements, and assurances against:

Count 27:   China between 18 September 1931 and 2 September 1945;

Count 29:   US between 7 December 1941 and 2 September 1945;

Count 31:   British Commonwealth between 7 December 1941 and 2 September 1945;

Count 32:   Netherlands between 7 December 1941 and 2 September 1945;

Count 33:   Araki, Dohihara, Hiranuma, Hirota, Hoshino, Itagaki, Kido, Matsuoka, Muto, Nagano, Shigemitsu and Tojo waged such a war against France on or after 22 September 1940;

Count 35:   Araki, Dohihara, Hata, Hiranuma, Hirota, Hoshino, Itagaki, Kido, Matsuoka, Matsui, Shigemitsu, Suzuki and Togo waged such a war against the Soviet Union during the summer of 1938;

Count 36:   Araki, Dohihara, Hata, Hiranuma, Itagaki, Kido, Koiso, Matsui, Matsuoka, Muto, Suzuki, Togo, Tojo and Umezu waged such a war against Mongolia and the Soviet Union during the summer of 1939.

Appendix 2 Results of the Tokyo judgment, 1948

Names	Counts										Sentence
	C1	*C 27*	*C 29*	*C 31*	*C 32*	*C 33*	*C 35*	*C 36*	*C 54*	*C 55*	
Araki	G	G	I	I	I	I	I	I	I	I	Life: Paroled 1955
Doihara	G	G	G	G	G	I	G	G	G	O	Death
Hashimoto	G	G	I	I	I	–	–	–	I	I	Life: Paroled 1954
Hata	G	G	G	G	G	–	I	I	I	G	Life: Paroled 1954
Hiranuma	G	G	G	G	G	I	I	G	I	I	Life: Paroled 1951
Hirota	G	G	I	I	I	I	I	–	I	G	Death
Hoshino	G	G	G	G	G	I	I	–	I	I	Life: Paroled 1955
Itagaki	G	G	G	G	G	I	G	G	G	O	Death
Kaya	G	G	G	G	G	–	–	–	I	I	Life: Paroled 1955
Kido	G	G	G	G	G	I	I	I	I	I	Life: Paroled 1955
Kimura	G	G	G	G	G	–	–	–	G	G	Death
Koiso	G	G	G	G	G	–	–	I	I	G	Life
Matsui	I	I	I	I	I	–	I	I	I	G	Death
Matsuoka											Died of tuberculosis early in the trial
Minami	G	G	I	I	I	–	–	–	I	I	Life: Paroled 1954
Muto	G	G	G	G	G	I	–	I	G	G	Death
Nagano											Died of natural causes during the trial
Oka	G	G	G	G	G	–	–	–	I	I	Life: Paroled 1954
Okawa											Sent to psychiatric ward on the first day of the trial; freed 1948
Oshima	G	I	I	I	I	–	–	–	I	I	Life: Paroled 1955
Sato	G	G	G	G	G	–	–	–	I	I	Life: Paroled 1956
Shigemitsu	I	G	G	G	G	G	I		I	G	Seven years: Paroled 1950; appointed foreign minister 1954

Shimada	G	G	G	G	G	–	–	–	I	I	Life: Paroled 1955
Shiratori	G	I	I	I	I	–	–	–	–	–	Life
Suzuki	G	G	G	G	G	–	I	I	I	I	Life: Paroled 1955
Togo	G	G	G	G	G	–	–	I	I	I	Twenty years; died 1949
Tojo	G	G	G	G	G	G	–	I	G	O	Death
Umezu	G	G	G	G	G	–	–	I	I	I	Life

Source: Compiled from Brackman (1987) and Horwitz (1950).

Notes
G = guilty; I = acquitted; – = not charged with this count; O = charged but no finding made by the Tribunal on this count.

Appendix 3

General Assembly Resolution 3314: Definition of Aggression, 1974

The General Assembly,

Having considered the report of the Special Committee on the Question of Defining Aggression, established pursuant to its resolution 2330(XXII) of 18 December 1967, covering the work of its seventh session held from 11 March to 12 April 1974, including the draft Definition of Aggression adopted by the Special Committee by consensus and recommended for adoption by the General Assembly, [FN1]

Deeply convinced that the adoption of the Definition of Aggression would contribute to the strengthening of international peace and security,

1   Approves the Definition of Aggression, the text of which is annexed to the present resolution;
2   Expresses its appreciation to the Special Committee on the Question of Defining Aggression for its work which resulted in the elaboration of the Definition of Aggression;
3   Calls upon all States to refrain from all acts of aggression and other uses of force contrary to the Charter of the United Nations and the Declaration on Principles of International Law concerning Friendly Relations and Cooperation among States in accordance with the Charter of the United Nations; [FN2]
4   Calls the attention of the Security Council to the Definition of Aggression, as set out below, and recommends that it should, as appropriate, take account of that Definition as guidance in determining, in accordance with the Charter, the existence of an act of aggression.

2319th plenary meeting
14 December 1974

Annex

Definition of Aggression

The General Assembly,

Basing itself on the fact that one of the fundamental purposes of the United Nations is to maintain international peace and security and to take effective collective measures for the prevention and removal of threats to the peace, and for the suppression of acts of aggression or other breaches of the peace,

Recalling that the Security Council, in accordance with Article 39 of the Charter of the United Nations, shall determine the existence of any threat to the peace, breach of the peace or act of aggression and shall make recommendations, or decide what measures shall be taken in accordance with Articles 41 and 42, to maintain or restore international peace and security,

Recalling also the duty of States under the Charter to settle their international disputes by peaceful means in order not to endanger international peace, security and justice,

Bearing in mind that nothing in this Definition shall be interpreted as in any way affecting the scope of the provisions of the Charter with respect to the functions and powers of the organs of the United Nations,

Considering also that, since aggression is the most serious and dangerous form of the illegal use of force, being fraught, in the conditions created by the existence of all types of weapons of mass destruction, with the possible threat of a world conflict and all its catastrophic consequences, aggression should be defined at the present stage,

Reaffirming the duty of States not to use armed force to deprive peoples of their right to self-determination, freedom and independence, or to disrupt territorial integrity,

Reaffirming also that the territory of a State shall not be violated by being the object, even temporarily, of military occupation or of other measures of force taken by another State in contravention of the Charter, and that it shall not be the object of acquisition by another State resulting from such measures or the threat thereof,

Reaffirming also the provisions of the Declaration on Principles of International Law concerning Friendly Relations and Cooperation among States in accordance with the Charter of the United Nations,

Convinced that the adoption of a definition of aggression ought to have the effect of deterring a potential aggressor, would simplify the determination of acts of aggression and the implementation of measures to suppress them and would also facilitate the protection of the rights and lawful interests of, and the rendering of assistance to, the victim,

Believing that, although the question whether an act of aggression has been committed must be considered in the light of all the circumstances of each particular case, it is nevertheless desirable to formulate basic principles as guidance for such determination,

Adopts the following Definition of Aggression: [FN3]

Article I

Aggression is the use of armed force by a State against the sovereignty, territorial integrity or political independence of another State, or in any other manner inconsistent with the Charter of the United Nations, as set out in this Definition.

Explanatory note: In this Definition the term 'State':

a   Is used without prejudice to questions of recognition or to whether a State is a member of the United Nations;
b   Includes the concept of a 'group of States' where appropriate.

Article 2

The first use of armed force by a State in contravention of the Charter shall constitute *prima facie* evidence of an act of aggression although the Security Council may, in conformity with the Charter, conclude that a determination that an act of aggression has been committed would not be justified in the light of other relevant circumstances, including the fact that the acts concerned or their consequences are not of sufficient gravity.

Article 3

Any of the following acts, regardless of a declaration of war, shall, subject to and in accordance with the provisions of article 2, qualify as an act of aggression:

a   The invasion or attack by the armed forces of a State of the territory of another State, or any military occupation, however temporary, resulting from such invasion or attack, or any annexation by the use of force of the territory of another State or part thereof;
b   Bombardment by the armed forces of a State against the territory of another State or the use of any weapons by a State against the territory of another State;
c   The blockade of the ports or coasts of a State by the armed forces of another State;
d   An attack by the armed forces of a State on the land, sea or air forces, or marine and air fleets of another State;
e   The use of armed forces of one State which are within the territory of another State with the agreement of the receiving State, in contravention of the conditions provided for in the agreement or any extension of their presence in such territory beyond the termination of the agreement;

f   The action of a State in allowing its territory, which it has placed at the disposal of another State, to be used by that other State for perpetrating an act of aggression against a third State;

g   The sending by or on behalf of a State of armed bands, groups, irregulars or mercenaries, which carry out acts of armed force against another State of such gravity as to amount to the acts listed above, or its substantial involvement therein.

Article 4

The acts enumerated above are not exhaustive and the Security Council may determine that other acts constitute aggression under the provisions of the Charter.

Article 5

1   No consideration of whatever nature, whether political, economic, military or otherwise, may serve as a justification for aggression.
2   A war of aggression is a crime against international peace. Aggression gives rise to international responsibility.
3   No territorial acquisition or special advantage resulting from aggression is or shall be recognized as lawful.

Article 6

Nothing in this Definition shall be construed as in any way enlarging or diminishing the scope of the Charter, including its provisions concerning cases in which the use of force is lawful.

Article 7

Nothing in this Definition, and in particular article 3, could in any way prejudice the right to self-determination, freedom and independence, as derived from the Charter, of peoples forcibly deprived of that right and referred to in the Declaration on Principles of International Law concerning Friendly Relations and Cooperation among States in accordance with the Charter of the United Nations, particularly peoples under colonial and racist regimes or other forms of alien domination; nor the right of these peoples to struggle to that end and to seek and receive support, in accordance with the principles of the Charter and in conformity with the above-mentioned Declaration.

Article 8

In their interpretation and application the above provisions are interrelated and each provision should be construed in the context of the other provisions.

Notes

1 Official Records of the General Assembly, Twenty-ninth Session, Supplement No. 19 (A/9619 and Corr. 1).
2 Resolution 2625 (XXV), annex.
3 Explanatory notes on articles 3 and 5 are to be found in paragraph 20 of the Report of the Special Committee on the Question of Defining Aggression (Official Records of the General Assembly, Twenty-ninth Session, Supplement No. 19 (A/9619 and Corr. 1). Statements on the Definition are contained in paragraphs 9 and 10 of the report of the Sixth Committee (A/9890).

Notes

1 The concept of aggression in international relations

1 Rome Statute of the International Criminal Court (UN Doc. A/CONF.183/9*), article 17.
2 *R* v. *Bartle and the Commissioner of Police for the Metropolis and Others, Ex Parte Pinochet; R* v. *Evans and Another and the Commissioner of Police for the Metropolice and Others, Ex Parte Pinochet* [1999] UKHL17.
3 The work of both the International Accounting Standards Board (IASB) and the International Labour Organisation (ILO) in these areas are two examples.
4 Rome Statute, article 5(2).
5 S. Farrell, 'Interview with Hamas leader Dr Mahmoud al-Zahar', *London Times*, 27 January 2006. Available at www.timesonline.co.uk/article/0,,251–2012808,00.html.
6 S. Knight, 'Asia Alert After North Korean Threat to Test Nuclear Weapon', *London Times*, 3 October 2006. Available at www.timesonline.co.uk/article/0,,3–2385992,00.html.
7 D. Miliband, 'Russia Will Not Benefit From Its Aggression', *London Times*, 19 August 2008. Available at www.timesonline.co.uk/tol/comment/columnists/guest_contributors/article4560698.ece.
8 Article 25(1) of the Rome Statute limits the ICC's jurisdiction to 'natural persons'.
9 For example, see SC Res 496 of 15 December 1981 and SC Res 507 of 28 May 1982 condemning 'mercenary aggression' against the Seychelles: also Chapter 8, n. 16.
10 On the demise of the acceptability of wars of conquest in the modern era, see S. Korman, *Right of Conquest: The Forcible Acquisition of Territory in International Law and Practice*, Oxford: Clarendon Press, 1996.
11 D. Held, 'Law of States, Law of Peoples: Three Models of Sovereignty', *Legal Theory* (2002) 8: 1–44, p. 25.
12 D. Morrice, 'The Liberal–Communitarian Debate in Contemporary Political Philosophy and its Significance for International Relations', *Review of International Studies* (2000) 26: 233–251, p. 239.
13 See A. Pagden and J. Lawrence (eds), *Francisco de Vitoria: Political Writings*, Cambridge: Cambridge University Press, 1991, and F. Suarez, 'Tractatus de Legibus ac Deo Legislatore', in J. B. Scott (ed.) *Selections from Three Works*, Oxford: Clarendon Press, 1944. Concerning the role of cosmopolitanism in international relations, see Brown, who has argued that international history over the past 200 years may be understood by reference to the cosmopolitan–communitarian debate: C. Brown, *International Relations Theory: New Normative Approaches*, Hemel Hempstead: Harvester, 1992. Indeed, the current revival in cosmopolitan thinking and the possibility of progress in international affairs has led at least one prominent commentator to announce the eventual advent of global government: see A. Wendt, 'Why a World State is Inevitable', *European Journal of International Relations* (2003) 9(4): 491–542. In response to this,

see V. Shannon, 'Wendt's Violation of the Constructivist Project: Agency and Why a World State is *Not* Inevitable', *European Journal of International Relations* (2005) 11(4): 581–587.

14 D. Archibugi, 'Cosmopolitan Democracy and Its Critics: A Review', *European Journal of International Relations* (2004) 10(3): 437–473, p. 465.

15 Archibugi, 'Cosmopolitan Democracy and Its Critics', p. 439.

16 Ibid.

17 Ibid., p. 443.

18 Ibid., p. 439.

19 Ibid., pp. 451–452.

20 Ibid., p. 465. Archibugi also sees cosmopolitan democracy theory benefiting from: (1) reconsideration of the concept of democracy from the local/state/interstate/regional/global levels, and (2) more direct research into 'the importance of norms and rules in international affairs': also at p. 465.

21 Archibugi, 'Cosmopolitan Democracy and Its Critics', pp. 465–466.

22 Ibid. Emphasis added.

23 Held, 'Law of States', p. 39.

24 Ibid., pp. 23–24. 'Circumstances of cosmopolitanism' is quoted in Held from J. Waldron, 'What is Cosmopolitan?', *The Journal of Political Philosophy* (2000) 8: 227–243, pp. 236–239.

25 Held, 'Law of States', p. 17.

26 Ibid., p. 24. Subsequently, Held has added an eighth principle: sustainability. see D. Held and H. Patomaki, 'Problems of Global Democracy', *Theory, Culture and Society* (2006) 23(5): p. 116.

27 Held, 'Law of States', p. 31.

28 Ibid.

29 Ibid.

30 Ibid., p. 32.

31 Ibid., p. 34.

32 Ibid., p. 35. This requirement is not easily reconciled with Archibugi's dual claim that Held and others 'have never argued in favour of the global concentration of coercive power' (Archibugi, 'Cosmopolitan Democracy and Its Critics', p. 454), and that 'cosmopolitan democracy is not to be identified with the project of global government' (also at p. 454). Despite this latter claim, Archibugi himself clearly recognises the significance of a world parliament for cosmopolitan democracy, as noted earlier. For this reason it is assumed here that cosmopolitanism extends, at least for some theorists, to the theme of world government.

33 Held, 'Law of States', p. 38.

34 Q. Wright, 'The Prevention of Aggression', *American Journal of International Law* (1956) 50(3): 514–532, p. 519.

35 Q. Wright, *The Role of International Law in the Elimination of War*, Manchester: Manchester University Press, 1961, p. 59. In an earlier work, Wright similarly claimed that 'a suitable definition of aggression seems central in the entire work of the United Nations': 'The Prevention of Aggression', p. 519.

36 Q. Wright, 'The Concept of Aggression in International Law', *American Journal of International Law* (1935) 29(3): 373–395, p. 381.

37 Wright, 'The Concept of Aggression in International Law', p. 393.

38 Ibid.

39 Ibid., p. 395. Text in inverted commas quoted from H. Lauterpacht, *The Function of Law in the International Community*, Oxford: Clarendon Press, 1933, p. 82.

40 Wright, *The Role of International Law*, p. 65. By the 1950s, however, Wright acknowledged three circumstances in which use or threat of international armed force would not be aggression: (1) when justified by individual or collective self-defence; (2) when justified by authority of the UN; and (3) when justified by consent of the

state within whose territory armed force is being used (Wright, 'The Prevention of Aggression', pp. 524–526). Subsequently, Dinstein has also argued that there is no room for the resurrection of 'just war' considerations in relation to the UN Charter or its notion of aggression, a view which he points out has been endorsed by Judge Schwebel in his dissenting opinion in the *Nicaragua (Merits)* case: Y. Dinstein, *War, Aggression and Self-defence*, Cambridge: Cambridge University Press, 2005, pp. 89–90.

41 B. Broms, *The Definition of Aggression in the United Nations*, Turku: Turun Yliopisto, 1968.

42 Ibid., p. 157.

43 Ibid., p. 156. It is perhaps due to this steadfast commitment in the face of great political obstacles that Broms was later appointed as chair of UN efforts to define aggression in 1973 to 1974, immediately prior to the adoption of the General Assembly's Resolution 3314, the Definition of Aggression.

44 B. Ferencz, *Defining International Aggression: The Search for World Peace*, New York: Dobbs Ferry, 1975, vol. 2, p. 52.

45 Ibid.

46 GA Res 3314 of 14 December 1974.

47 Ferencz, *Defining International Aggression*, vol. 2, p. 53.

48 See Chapter 7 (this volume).

49 The ILC also recommended that any prosecution of aggression would be contingent upon a prior Security Council determination that aggression had occurred, a similarly contentious conclusion: see B. Ferencz, 'Can Aggression Be Deterred By Law?', *Pace International Law Review* (1999) 11(2): 341–360, pp. 349–350.

50 Dinstein, *War, Aggression and Self-defence*, p. 113.

51 Ibid., p. 120.

52 *USA* v. *Von Leeb* et al. Nuremberg, 1948. 11 *NMT* 462, 486. Quoted in Dinstein, *War, Aggression and Self-defence*, p. 133.

53 Dinstein, *War, Aggression and Self-defence*, p. 134. However, as Dinstein notes, at the Subsequent Proceedings at Nuremberg, certain accuseds falling into this latter category were not convicted of crimes against peace.

54 Dinstein argues that the issue of superior orders should be considered as a relevant factor under one of the listed admissible defences, such as duress or mistake based on lack of intention (p. 131).

55 N. Rengger, 'A City Which Sustains All Things? Communitarianism and International Society', *Millennium* (1992) 21: 353–369, p. 354.

56 T. Erskine, 'Qualifying Cosmopolitanism? Solidarity, Criticism, and Michael Walzer's "View from the Cave"', *International Politics* (2007) 44: 125–149, p. 129.

57 Rengger, 'Communitarianism and International Society', p. 361.

58 Walzer's critics on this point include R. Wasserstrom, 'Review of Michael Walzer's *Just and Unjust Wars*', *Harvard Law Review* (December 1978) 92: 536–545, and G. Doppelt, 'Walzer's Theory of Morality in International Relations', *Philosophy and Public Affairs* (1978) 8(1): 3–27. See M. Walzer, 'The Moral Standing of States: A Response to Four Critics', *Philosophy and Public Affairs* (1980) 9(3): 209–229, p. 210, where he says, 'the state is presumptively, *though by no means always in practice*, the arena within which self-determination is worked out and from which, therefore, foreign armies have to be excluded' (emphasis added).

59 See Erskine, 'Qualifying Cosmopolitanism?', pp. 143–144. Erskine also notes the problems inherent with the communitarian classification in Walzer's case (pp. 129–130).

60 M. Walzer, *Just and Unjust Wars*, New York: Basic Books, 1977, pp. 61–63.

61 Ibid., p. 61.

62 Ibid.

63 M. Walzer, *Thick and Thin: Moral Argument at Home and Abroad*, Notre Dame, IN: University of Notre Dame Press, 1994.

64 Ibid., p. 3.
65 Ibid., p. 18.
66 Erskine, 'Qualifying Cosmopolitanism?', p. 142. For further discussions of Walzer's moral minimalism and maximalism, see M. Cochran, *Normative Theory and International Relations*, Cambridge: Cambridge University Press, 1999.
67 H. Morgenthau, *Politics Among Nations*, New York: Knopf, 1955 (2nd edn), pp. 224–226.
68 Morgenthau, *Politics Among Nations*, p. 228.
69 Ibid., pp. 10–11.
70 Ibid.
71 J. Stone, *Conflict Through Consensus*, Baltimore, MD: The Johns Hopkins University Press, 1977, pp. 123–152.
72 J. Stone, *Aggression and World Order*, London: Stevens & Sons Ltd, 1958, pp. 106–107.
73 Stone did not deny the emotional, symbolic appeal of the concept of aggression, but doubted that this appeal on its own could compel the operation of an effective collective security system with 'aggression' as the trigger: Stone, *Conflict Through Consensus*, p. 14.
74 Ibid., p. 19.
75 Stone, *Aggression and World Order*, p. 53.
76 Stone, *Conflict Through Consensus*, pp. 157–158.
77 Ibid., pp. 161–164.
78 J. Babic, 'War Crimes: Moral, Legal, or Simply Political?', in A. Jokic (ed.) *War Crimes and Collective Wrongdoing*, Oxford: Blackwell, 2001, p. 63.
79 Babic, 'War Crimes: Moral, Legal, or Simply Political?', p. 64.
80 Ibid., p. 63.
81 However, this conclusion about the non-legal nature of the crime of aggression sits uncomfortably with Babic's acknowledgement that 'starting a war is, from the perspective of the *status quo ante*, a violation of the established state and therefore a violation of international contract' (p. 63).
82 Constantine Antonopoulos, 'Whatever Happened to Crimes Against Peace?', *Journal of Conflict and Security Law* (2001) 6: 47. By contrast, Pompe has argued that it is wrong to claim the non-existence of the concept of aggression, 'For the concept of aggression was transferred from the field of particular conventions to that of general international law at the moment an international organ was given the power to designate a State as aggressor, with legal consequences for the whole society of States' (C. A. Pompe, *Aggressive War an International Crime*, The Hague: Martinus Nijhoff, 1953, p. 71).
83 Antonopoulos, 'Whatever Happened to Crimes Against Peace?', p. 62.
84 The main difficulty with Antonopoulos' argument is that it does not actually advance very far the literature on aggression. Even if we accept his contention that aggression is best considered as a category term for unlawful uses of force, the vital decision about the legality or otherwise of a particular use of armed force raises all the same controversial assumptions as when aggression is approached as a concept – for instance, the existence of universal legal standards of state conduct, international authorities with binding power to develop and enforce these standards, and the moral value of peace. When Antonopoulos refers to 'fact and legal evaluation', he overlooks the extent to which, at the international level, these are themselves influenced by political considerations. Antonopoulos' perspective is important, however, in terms of the overall argument of the book: it demonstrates how transforming an unresolved international political debate into a question of international law contributes little, if anything, to the resolution of that debate.

2 Aggression in the post-World War I settlement

1 C. Seymour, *Intimate Papers of Colonel House*, London: Ernest Benn Ltd, 1926, vol. 1, p. 216.
2 Address to the American League to Enforce Peace of 27 May 1916, quoted in B. Williams, *State Security and the League of Nations*, Baltimore, MD: Johns Hopkins University Press, 1927, p. 70.
3 M. Griffiths, *Fifty Key Thinkers in International Relations*, London: Routledge, 2000, p. 97.
4 D. H. Miller, *The Drafting of the Covenant*, New York: GP Putnam's Sons, 1928, vol. 2, p. 70.
5 Miller, *The Drafting of the Covenant*, vol. 1, p. 30.
6 Ibid., vol. 1, pp. 30–33. In his account, Miller claims to have had an equivocal attitude to article 10 at the time of the events. Miller's apparent equivocation may be contrasted with the position taken by Lansing, who was increasingly left out as his opposition to Wilson's objectives and methods became more frequent and rabid: see Lansing's account for a scathing attack on Wilson and the record of the deterioration of their relationship: R. Lansing, *The Peace Negotiations: A Personal Narrative*, Boston, MA: Houghton Mifflin, 1921. However, certain of Lansing's claims have been subject to challenge on the basis that many of the memoranda supposedly comprising his diary may in fact have been written later in time: see A. S. Link (ed.), *The Papers of Woodrow Wilson*, Princeton, NJ: Princeton University Press, 1966, vol. 54, p. 4.
7 Link, *The Papers of Woodrow Wilson*, vol. 55, p. 319. This interpretation – namely that League assistance could not be sought by a member to 'suppress a national movement within its boundaries' – is supported by F. Whelen, *The Covenant Explained, For Speakers and Study Circles*, London: League of Nations Union, 1935, p. 62.
8 Lansing claimed that Wilson announced during a meeting of the American delegation to the Peace Conference: 'I don't want lawyers drafting this treaty' (Link, *The Papers of Woodrow Wilson*, vol. 54, p. 4); however, this claim is dubious for the reasons detailed in n. 6 above. Nevertheless, Lamont's observation of Wilson's intolerance of technicalities in the context of reparations lends support to this view: see T. W. Lamont, 'Reparations', in E. M. House and C. S. Seymour (eds) *What Really Happened at Paris*, London: Hodder & Stoughton, 1921, pp. 259–290.
9 Remarks to Working Women in Paris of 15 January 1919, quoted in Link, *The Papers of Woodrow Wilson*, vol. 54, p. 273. Indeed, Herbert Hoover observed that 'when Mr Wilson arrived in Europe, he was almost believed in as the Second Messiah by the common people of every nation': H. Hoover, *America's First Crusade*, New York: Charles Scribner's Sons, 1942, p. 9. Wilson's tremendous popularity with ordinary folk may be compared with his lack of rapport with their leaders, which has been described thus: 'his presumption of superior knowledge and divine guidance often outraged those who had to do business with him' (G. Scott, *The Rise and Fall of the League of Nations*, London: Hutchinson, 1973, p. 39). This view is supported by the writing of Harold Nicolson – at the time a junior member of the British delegation to the Paris Peace Conference – who wrote, in relation to Wilson's negotiations with Italy concerning the peace settlement, 'It was his early shambling over the Italian question that convinced us that Woodrow Wilson was not a great or potent man (H. Nicolson, *Peacemaking 1919*, London: Constable, 1934, p. 184).
10 Wilson explicitly acknowledged in the lead-up to the Covenant that 'we are depending primarily and chiefly upon one great force, and that is the moral force of the public opinion of the world' (Miller, *The Drafting of the Covenant*, vol. 2, p. 562).
11 Reproduced in Miller, *The Drafting of the Covenant*, vol. 2, pp. 3–6. The Right Hon. Sir Walter G. F. Phillimore served as a Lord Justice of Appeal from 1913 to 1916.

12 Reproduced in Miller, *The Drafting of the Covenant*, vol. 2, pp. 23–60. General Jan Christiaan Smuts served on the British War Cabinet from 1917 to 1919.
13 Reproduced in Miller, *The Drafting of the Covenant*, vol. 2, pp. 61–64. Lord Robert Cecil served as the chief British negotiator for a League of Nations at the Paris Peace Conference.
14 Miller, *The Drafting of the Covenant*, vol. 2, p. 106.
15 Ibid., vol. 1, p. 71.
16 The rest of the provision of the Cecil-Miller draft had read:

> If at any time it should appear that any feature of the settlement made by this covenant and by the present treaties of peace no longer conforms to the requirements of the situation, the League shall take the matter under consideration and may recommend to the parties any modification which it may think necessary. If such recommendation is not accepted by the parties affected, the States, members of the League, shall cease to be under any obligation in respect of the subject matter of such recommendation. In considering any such modification the League shall take into account changes in the present conditions and aspirations of peoples or present social and political relations, pursuant to the principle, which the High Contracting Powers accept without reservation, that Governments derive their just powers from the consent of the governed.
>
> (Miller, *The Drafting of the Covenant*, vol. 2, p. 134)

17 Cecil Hurst was a British legal adviser at the Paris Peace Conference.
18 See the Minutes of the first meeting of the Commission in Miller, *The Drafting of the Covenant*, vol. 2, pp. 231–255. The League of Nations Commission was established on 25 January 1919 by plenary session of the Paris Peace Conference. The Commission comprised two representatives from each of the five great powers – that is, the USA, British Empire, France, Italy and Japan – and five representatives chosen by the lesser Allies – namely Belgium, Brazil, China, Portugal and Serbia (G. W. Egerton, *Great Britain and the Creation of the League of Nations*, London: Scholar Press, 1979, p. 111).
19 Miller, *The Drafting of the Covenant*, vol. 1, pp. 168–169.
20 Ibid., vol. 1, p. 169.
21 Ibid., vol. 1, p. 281; text of the Borden memorandum and Hughes critique, pp. 354–368. This was the beginning of Canada's campaign to demolish article 10 entirely: see below. The high number of casualties lost by Canada and Australia in World War I explained to a great extent their reluctance to commit to an international guarantee against aggression: according to one source, each country lost just under 50 per cent and 65 per cent respectively of the total number of soldiers they mobilised (Lt. the Hon. S. Smith, *Australian Campaigns in the Great War*, Melbourne: Macmillan, 1919). For further details of Canadian and Australian objections, see Egerton, *Great Britain and the Creation of the League of Nations*, pp. 145–147. The UK remained staunchly opposed in principle to the notion of general guarantees throughout the League negotiations (F. S. Northedge, *The League of Nations Its Life and Times 1920–1946*, Leicester: Leicester University Press, 1986, p. 20).
22 Article 19 very generally provided that 'The Assembly may from time to time advise the reconsideration by Members of the League of Treaties which have become inapplicable and the consideration of international conditions whose continuance might endanger the peace of the world'. Available at www.yale.edu/lawweb/avalon/leagcov.htm#art19.
23 In fact, the traditional approach to security based on alliance building remained privately the preference of some French negotiators, such as Clemenceau, the French Premier, who announced on 29 December 1918 that 'there is an old system which appears to be discredited today, but to which ... I am still faithful. Here in this system of alliance ... is the thought which will guide me at the conference' (T. J. Knock, *To*

End All Wars: Woodrow Wilson and the Quest for a New World Order, New York: Oxford University Press, 1992, p. 198).

24 Miller, *The Drafting of the Covenant*, vol. 1, p. 168.
25 Williams, *State Security and the League of Nations*, p. 76.
26 On the French desire for a strong provision see A. E. Zimmern, *The League of Nations and the Rule of Law 1918–1935*, London: Macmillan, 1939, p. 247.
27 Miller, *The Drafting of the Covenant*, vol. 2, p. 330.
28 In article 21 of the Covenant, the effect of 'regional understandings' such as the Monroe Doctrine was expressly preserved. Text available at www.yale.edu/lawweb/avalon/leagcov.htm#art21.
29 Knock, *To End All Wars*, p. 251.
30 Ibid., p. 261. In Wilson's view, the USA was a participant 'whether we would or not, in the life of the world. The interests of all the nations are our own also. We are partners with the rest. What affects mankind is inevitably our affair' (J. Walker, *State Morality and A League of Nations*, London: TF Unwin Ltd, 1919, p. 42).
31 Williams, *State Security and the League of Nations*, p. 76.
32 Williams, *State Security and the League of Nations*, p. 77.
33 Ibid.
34 Ibid. Contrary to Wilson, Williams argues that article 10 did create a legal obligation despite a lack of specified sanction in the Covenant; if the presence or absence of a sanction determined the issue, this would 'set up a criterion of legality which would deny the quality of law to practically the whole body of customary and conventional rules which govern the relations of states' (pp. 85–86).
35 Williams, *State Security and the League of Nations*, pp. 78–79.
36 Lodge described article 10 as a 'very perilous promise' (Link, *The Papers of Woodrow Wilson*, vol. 55, p. 312).
37 Knock, *To End All Wars*, pp. 253–254. Thus, a journalist for *Dial*, the left-wing liberal fortnightly publication, wrote that article 10 was dangerous because it appeared 'in effect to validate existing empires' (p. 253).
38 See the comments of Oswald Garrison Villard, editor of *Nation*, ibid.
39 Knock, *To End All Wars*, pp. 261–262.
40 The Covenant was defeated in the Senate by thirty-eight votes to fifty-three: see H. C. Lodge, *The Senate and the League of Nations*, New York: C. Scribner's Sons, 1925.
41 G. Schwarzenberger, *The League of Nations and World Order*, London: Constable & Co, 1936, p. 46.
42 House and Seymour, *What Really Happened at Paris*, p. 270. For a view of the general approach of the American Delegation to the issue of reparations, see P. M. Burnett, *Reparation at the Paris Peace Conference From the Standpoint of the American Delegation*, New York: Columbia University Press, 1940, 2 vols.
43 H. Elcock, *Portrait of a Decision: the Council of Four and the Treaty of Versailles*, London: Eyre Methuen, 1972, p. 34.
44 These claims were partly made out of necessity: the USA insisted that its Allies repay the loans they obtained from the USA to finance their war efforts, and without some substantial contribution from Germany on top of its repayments for material damage, these debts would have crippled the economies of Britain and France while leaving the German economy relatively unburdened: see M. F. Boemeke (ed.), *The Treaty of Versailles: A Reassessment After 75 Years*, New York: Cambridge University Press, 1998, p. 224.
45 In one of his election speeches, Lloyd George had declared: 'we shall go through these Germans' pockets' (K. F. Nowak (trans. N. Thomas and E. W. Dickes), *Versailles*, London: Victor Gollancz, 1928, p. 145).
46 M. O. Macmillan, *Peacemakers*, London: John Murray, 2003, p. 202.
47 Ibid., p. 192.

48 Ibid., p. 194. Later, in an effort to reduce the UK's share of German payments, and in response to the need for US support to ensure that French security priorities were achieved, France argued that costs resulting from direct damage only should be paid (pp. 202–203). For the role of various French newspapers in pushing for maximum reparations from Germany, see G. B. Noble, *Policies and Options at Paris, 1919*, New York: Macmillan, 1935, pp. 188–192.
49 Macmillan, *Peacemakers*, p. 195.
50 Indeed, Temperley claims that the question of Germany's capacity to pay reparations attracted possibly the widest range of views of any subject discussed at the Conference (H. W. V. Temperley, *A History of the Peace Conference of Paris*, London: Henry Fraude, 1920, vol. 2, p. 49).
51 Allied and Associated Powers (1914–1920), *The Treaties of Peace 1919–1923*, New York: Carnegie Endowment for International Peace, 1924, vol. 1, p. 123.
52 In the end, it was agreed that Germany would pay £1 billion to the inter-Allied Reparation Commission by May 1921, and that this Commission would then determine how much, when, and at what interest levels Germany would pay, up to a maximum of thirty years.
53 Boemeke, *Treaty of Versailles*, p. 226.
54 Macmillan, *Peacemakers*, p. 192.
55 Boemeke, *Treaty of Versailles*, p. 242.
56 Macmillan, *Peacemakers*, p. 490.
57 A. J. Toynbee, 'The Main Features in the Landscape', in Lord Riddell (ed.) *The Treaty of Versailles and After*, London: George Allen & Unwin, 1935, p. 55.
58 J. M. Keynes, *The Economic Consequences of the Peace*, London: Macmillan, 1919.
59 Macmillan, *Peacemakers*, p. 489.
60 On the impact of the Bolshevik revolution in Wilson's thinking at the time of the peace settlement, see N. G. Levin, *Woodrow Wilson and World Politics*, Oxford: Oxford University Press, 1968, pp. 129–153.
61 Article 227 Allied and Associated Powers (1914–1920), *The Treaties of Peace, 1919–1923*, vol. 1, p. 121.
62 Ibid.
63 See articles 228 and 229 in Allied and Associated Powers (1914–1920), *The Treaties of Peace, 1919–1923*, vol. 1, pp. 121–122.
64 See second paragraph of article 228, ibid.
65 Article 230 in *The Treaties of Peace, 1919–1923*, vol. 1, p. 122. Although not specifically referring to aggression, these provisions were the precursor to efforts in the aftermath of World War II to prosecute Japanese and German leaders for the *crime* of aggression; by its terms, article 227 essentially acknowledged that Kaiser Wilhelm's offence was of a moral nature, and not recognised in either international law or criminal law.
66 J. B. Scott, 'The Trial of the Kaiser', in House and Seymour, *What Really Happened at Paris*, pp. 235–236.
67 To support his view that Kaiser Wilhelm should not be pursued for his 'crimes', Wilson was reported to claim: 'Charles I was a contemptible character and the greatest liar in history; he was celebrated by poetry and transformed into a martyr by his execution' (Macmillan, *Peacemakers*, p. 174).
68 Scott, 'The Trial of the Kaiser', p. 237.
69 Ibid., p. 243.
70 Ibid., p. 244.
71 Kaiser Wilhelm died in 1941.
72 G. G. Battle, 'The Trials Before the Leipsic Supreme Court of Germans Accused of War Crimes', *Virginia Law Review* (1921) 8: p. 5.
73 C. Mullins, *The Leipzig Trials*, London: H.F. and G. Witherby, 1922.

3 State aggression at the League, 1920 to 1940

1 D. H. Miller, *The Drafting of the Covenant*, New York: G.P. Putnam's Sons, 1928, vol. 1, p. 358. It is unlikely that article 19 of the Covenant – vaguely permitting the Assembly 'from time to time' to advise League members to consider 'international conditions whose continuance might endanger the peace of the world' – inspired much confidence in Canada that a just and peaceful change of international borders would be achieved by resort to this provision.

2 World Peace Foundation, *Second Yearbook of the League of Nations: Record of 1921*, Boston, 1922, p. 195.

3 Ibid., p. 196.

4 For details of the high proportion of Canadian World War I casualties, see Lt. the Hon. S. Smith, *Australian Campaigns in the Great War*, Melbourne: Macmillan, 1919.

5 World Peace Foundation, *Fourth Yearbook of the League of Nations: Record of 1923*, Boston, 1924, p. 86.

6 F. P. Walters, *History of the League of Nations*, Oxford: Oxford University Press, 1952, p. 259.

7 By the end of 1923 there were fifty-four League member states.

8 Article 11 of the League Covenant read as follows:

> Any war or threat of war, whether immediately affecting any of the Members of the League or not, is hereby declared a matter of concern to the whole League, and the League shall take any action that may be deemed wise and effectual to safeguard the peace of nations. In case any such emergency should arise the Secretary-General shall on the request of any Member of the League forthwith summon a meeting of the Council. It is also declared to be the friendly right of each Member of the League to bring to the attention of the Assembly or of the Council any circumstance whatever affecting international relations which threatens to disturb international peace or the good understanding between nations upon which peace depends.

Article 12 provided that

> The Members of the League agree that if there should arise between them any dispute likely to lead to a rupture, they will submit the matter either to arbitration or to inquiry by the Council, and they agree in no case to resort to war until three months after the award by the arbitrators or the report by the Council. In any case under this Article the award of the arbitrators shall be made within a reasonable time, and the report of the Council shall be made within six months after the submission of the dispute.
>
> (Allied and Associated Powers (1914–1920), *The Treaties of Peace 1919–1923*, New York: Carnegie Endowment for International Peace, 1924, both p. 14)

The text of articles 13 to 16 is available online at www.yale.edu/lawweb/avalon/leagcov.htm. War would still be legal in the event of no award or report being agreed; see, for instance, F. S. Northedge, *The League of Nations Its Life and Times 1920–1946*, Leicester: Leicester University Press, 1986, p. 28.

9 The 1923 Treaty of Mutual Guarantee, which pledged immediate and effective aid to any attacked signatory from all other signatories of the same region, was condemned by the Soviet Union, the USA, Germany, the European neutrals, and Britain and its Dominions. France, Poland, Czechoslovakia, Belgium, the Baltic States and Finland all supported the Treaty. The 1924 Geneva Protocol, which created a rebuttable presumption that in the event of hostilities any state is an aggressor (article 10), was opposed by the League's most important member, Britain.

10 *League of Nations Official Journal* (1928) 9: 671. The year before, Sir Austen Chamberlain, British Foreign Secretary, had expressed in the House of Commons concern that any listed criteria of aggression would create 'a trap for the innocent and a signpost to the guilty': (quoted in J. Stone, *Aggression and World Order*, London: Steven and Sons Ltd, 1958, p. 36).

11 These were: '1) The invasion of the territory of one State by the troops of another State; (2) An attack on a considerable scale launched by one State on the frontiers of another State; and (3) A surprise attack carried out by one State over the territory of another State, with the aid of poisonous gases' (*League of Nations Official Journal* (1928) 9: 671).

12 The Locarno Treaty is discussed in further detail below.

13 *League of Nations Official Journal* (1928) 9: 666. This committee was also responsible for the drafting of the Treaty to Improve the Means of Preventing War (1931) and the Convention on Financial Assistance to a Victim of Aggression (1930), both of which were approved by the Assembly, but which did not enter into force.

14 Miller, *The Drafting of the Covenant*, vol. 1, p. 168.

15 These acts were:

> (1) declaration of war against another State; (2) the invasion by its armed forces of the territory of another State without declaration of war; (3) bombarding the territory of another State by its land, naval or air forces or knowingly attacking the naval or air forces of another State; (4) the landing in, or introduction within the frontiers of, another State of land, naval or air forces without the permission of the Government of such a State, or the infringement of the conditions of such permission, particularly as regards the duration of sojourn or extension of area; (5) the establishment of a naval blockade of the coast or ports of another State.
>
> (Reproduced in B. Ferencz, *Defining International Aggression: The Search for World Peace*, New York: Dobbs Ferry, 1975 vol. 1, pp. 202–203)

16 While, on the one hand, the Soviet draft was supported by France and China, on the other, Britain, Germany, Hungary, Italy, Spain and Switzerland preferred a more flexible definition which would allow all the relevant circumstances in a particular incident to be considered.

17 This theme is explored in greater detail in the following section.

18 Walters, *History of the League of Nations*, p. 579. Although the Soviet Union had already instigated pacts of non-aggression with all her neighbours, none of these obliged the parties to help each other fight aggression from a third party. See the text of these treaties of non-aggression between the Soviet Union and Afghanistan, Finland, Poland, and Estonia, as well as similar security agreements with other states, in M. M. Litvinov, *Against Aggression*, London, 1939, p. 144.

19 B. Williams, *State Security and the League of Nations*, Baltimore: Johns Hopkins Press, 1927, p. 39.

20 Walters, *History of the League of Nations*, p. 341.

21 World Peace Foundation, *Sixth Yearbook of the League of Nations: Record of 1925*, Boston, 1926, p. 1708.

22 W. R. Sharp, *Contemporary International Politics*, New York: Rinehart & Co, 1940, p. 619.

23 The details of this episode can be found in the *League of Nations Official Journal* (1926): 1517–1527.

24 The signatories of the 1928 Kellogg–Briand Pact, which included the USA, agreed in article 1 to renounce war as an instrument of national policy in their relations with one another. John Lewis Gaddis has described the American public of the interwar period as suffering from 'a kind of moral anaesthesia in international affairs' ('Order versus Justice: An American Foreign Policy Dilemma', in R. Foot, J. L. Gaddis

and A. Hurrell (eds) *Order and Justice in International Relations*, Oxford: Oxford University Press, 2002, p. 158).

25 Sharp, *Contemporary International Politics*, p. 576.
26 For instance, at this time, the UK was struggling with the effects of the global eco-nomic depression – on 20 September, two days after the Manchurian affair erupted, the UK went off the gold standard (Northedge, *League of Nations Its Life and Times 1920–1946*, p. 140). Similar economic shocks were experienced in Germany and France (Northedge, *League of Nations Its Life and Times 1920–1946*, p. 141).
27 In its application, China also referred to Covenant article 15.
28 World Peace Foundation, *League of Nations Official Journal* (1932) 13: 344.
29 German and Italian assistance to the Spanish rebels during the Spanish War – which commenced in July 1936 – was the substance of an appeal by Spain to the League. Although Spain put forward the case that this amounted to a new kind of aggression which needed to be dealt with under the Covenant accordingly, the ongoing concern of Britain and France not to provoke an open conflict with the Axis powers compelled the former to use their positions of power to discourage League action on the Spanish question. When the issue was finally examined by the Assembly, the response to Spain's wish to be declared a victim of foreign aggression was a proposed resolution that unless all foreign combatants were withdrawn from the conflict immediately and completely, League members would consider abandoning their policy of non-intervention. However, this resolution was defeated; no further League action was able to be taken and the Axis powers were free to continue their activities in Spain.
30 Despite this failure to act, the League did continue to provide technical assistance to China, particularly in relation to the prevention of epidemics among refugees fleeing from the dispute (Walters, *History of the League of Nations*, p. 738).
31 Namely the 1928 Treaty of Amity, Conciliation and Arbitration between Italy and Ethiopia (see A. Zimmern, 'The League's Handling of the Italo-Abyssinian Dispute', *International Affairs* (1935) 14: 751–768, p. 752).
32 Walters, *History of the League of Nations*, p. 628.
33 Ibid., p. 632.
34 C. K. Webster, *The League of Nations in Theory and Practice*, London: Allen & Unwin, 1933, p. 165. Other allies also wished not to weaken Poland as a bulwark against Russia.
35 Later, W. L. Westermann, of the American Peace Commission to Paris, seemed to express regret that the US too had refused to accept a mandate over Armenia:

> The history of the Russian advance over Trans-Caucasia in the nineteenth century and the geographic position of Armenia marks it as a legitimate sphere of Russian influence. Turkish Armenia lies in the pathway of Slavic Russian expansion. Soviet Russia now controls Russian Armenia. I hold no brief for Bolshevism, but we might as well be honest and face facts. Bolshevist Russia has done that thing which we have refused to do – gone in and protected the Armenians. It seems obvious to me that the Armenian question must be looked at primarily in connection with the Russian problem.
> ('The Armenian Problem and the Disruption of Turkey', in E. M. House and C. S. Seymour (eds) *What Really Happened at Paris*, London: Hodder & Stoughton, 1921, p. 468)

36 World Peace Foundation, *League of Nations Official Journal* 20 (1939): 540.
37 Walters, *History of the League of Nations*, p. 778.

4 Aggression and individual criminal responsibility at Nuremberg and subsequent trials

1 As Kaiser Wilhelm had done successfully in 1918 (see B. F. Smith, *The Road to Nuremberg*, London: Andre Deutsch, 1981, p. 19).
2 Bradley F Smith (ed.), *The American Road to Nuremberg: The Documentary Record 1944–1945*, Stanford: Hoover Institution Press, 1982, p. 7.
3 Smith, *The Road to Nuremberg*, p. 23.
4 Ibid., pp. 22–23.
5 W. R. Harris, *Tyranny on Trial*, Dallas: Southern Methodist University Press, 1954, p. 8.
6 Smith, *The Road to Nuremberg*, pp. 37–38.
7 P. Maguire, *Law and War: An American Story*, New York: Columbia University Press, 2001, p. 88.
8 Ibid., p. 93.
9 Ibid., p. 89. Indeed, Churchill has been reported to have commented in October 1944 that 'I'd like sixty or seventy of the people around Hitler shot without any trial, but I am against shooting all the German General Staff' (D. A. Sprecher, *Inside the Nuremberg Tribunal*, Lanham: University Press of America Inc, 1999, vol. 1, p. 28).
10 Smith, *The Road to Nuremberg*, p. 186.
11 Ibid., p. 188.
12 A. Tusa and J. Tusa, *The Nuremberg Trial*, London: Macmillan, 1984, p. 63. This tallies with Churchill's opinion of Russian preferences in October 1944: 'Russia [could] do what she likes by force, but she would like sanction at the Peace Conference that her action was just and correct' (Sprecher, *Inside the Nuremberg Tribunal*, vol. 1, p. 28).
13 D. Bloxham, '"The Trial That Never Was": Why There Was No Second International Trial of Major War Criminals at Nuremberg' *History* (2002) 87: 41–60, p. 42.
14 Harris, *Tyranny on Trial*, pp. 10–11. The role of the concept of aggression at the UNCIO is further examined in Chapter 6.
15 The establishment of the UNWCC was suggested by Churchill to Roosevelt in June 1942 in response to demands from the governments-in-exile, and growing British public interest, to take concrete action in relation to war crimes. It ran from January 1944 until March 1948, collecting evidence of war crimes, and comprised seventeen founding Allied nations, excluding the Soviet Union (see A. J. Kochavi, 'Britain and the Establishment of the United Nations War Crimes Commission', *The English Historical Review* (1992) 107: 323–349).
16 Smith, *The Road to Nuremberg*, p. 92.
17 Ibid., pp. 104–105.
18 Maguire, *Law and War*, pp. 95–96.
19 Ibid., p. 96.
20 Smith, *The Road to Nuremberg*, p. 145.
21 Ibid., p. 215.
22 See the comments by Sir David Maxwell-Fyfe in 'Minutes of Conference Session of July 19, 1945', in Department of State Publication 3080, *Report of Robert H. Jackson, United States Representative to the International Conference on Military Trials: London, 1945*, Washington: Government Printing Office, 1949 (available at www.yale.edu/lawweb/avalon/imt/jackson/jack37.htm).
23 See the comments by Professor Gros in 'Minutes of Conference Session of July 19, 1945', *Report of Robert H Jackson*.
24 Tusa, *The Nuremberg Trial*, p. 81.
25 See 1933 Soviet Draft Definition of an Aggressor, reproduced in B. Ferencz, *Defining International Aggression: The Search for World Peace*, New York: Dobbs Ferry, 1975, vol. 1, pp. 202–203.

26 See the comments by Mr Justice Jackson in 'Minutes of Conference Session of July 19, 1945', *Report of Robert H Jackson*.

27 See Jackson's comments in 'Minutes of Conference Session of July 19, 1945', *Report of Robert H Jackson*.

28 See Maxwell-Fyfe's comments in 'Minutes of Conference Session of July 19, 1945', *Report of Robert H Jackson*.

29 Ibid.

30 See the comments of General Nikitchenko in 'Minutes of Conference Session of July 19, 1945', *Report of Robert H Jackson*.

31 The Moscow Declaration was made in November 1943 and the Yalta Declaration in February 1945. Both were published in Senate Committee on Foreign Relations and the Department of State, *A Decade of American Foreign Policy: Basic Documents, 1941–1949*, Washington: GPO, 1950 (available at www.yale.edu/lawweb/avalon/wwii/moscow.htm and www.yale.edu/lawweb/avalon/wwii/yalta.htm respectively).

32 See Nitkichenko's comments in 'Minutes of Conference Session of July 19, 1945', *Report of Robert H. Jackson*.

33 View expressed by Professor Gros in 'Minutes of Conference Session of July 19, 1945', *Report of Robert H. Jackson*.

34 Jackson's comment, in 'Minutes of Conference Session of July 19, 1945', *Report of Robert H. Jackson*.

35 See first paragraph of article 6 of the 'Charter of the International Military Tribunal', in *Trial of The Major War Criminals before the International Military Tribunal*, Nuremberg: International Military Tribunal, 1947, vol. 1, p. 11. The desire to restrict the crime of aggression to the Axis powers can only be explained by reference to Soviet sensitivities in relation to its own World War II conduct, which included the violation of its non-aggression pact with Poland and its invasion of Finland, both in 1939 (see G. A. Finch, 'The Nuremberg Trial and International Law', *American Journal of International Law* (1947) 41: 27–28). Concern over Soviet conduct in relation to Poland and Finland during the war also led the major powers to prohibit the Nuremberg defendants from using the *tu quoque* defence – namely defending one's own conduct on the ground that the accuser is guilty of the same conduct (see J. E. Persico, *Nuremberg: Infamy on Trial*, New York: Viking, 1994, pp. 35–36).

36 Article 6 of the 'Charter of the International Military Tribunal', *Trial of The Major War Criminals*, vol. 1, p. 11.

37 See count 1 of the indictment in *Trial of The Major War Criminals*, vol. 1, p. 29.

38 Hans Ehard described conspiracy as a concept 'not ... familiar to continental law' ('The Nuremberg Trial Against the Major War Criminals and International Law', *American Journal of International Law* (1949) 43: 223–245, p. 226).

39 Sprecher, *Inside the Nuremberg Trial*, vol. 1, p. 97.

40 For further details of charges and convictions, see Appendix 1.

41 Although no separate findings about war in violation of international treaties were made by the IMT, in considering whether aggression had taken place, the IMT took into account various post-World War I treaties such as the Kellogg–Briand Pact, and draft documents such as the 1923 Treaty of Mutual Assistance and the 1924 Geneva Protocol, to establish the status of international law concerning aggression at the relevant time (see 'Judgment', *Trial of The Major War Criminals*, vol. 1, pp. 218–224).

42 The four defendants acquitted of aggression were Schacht, Sauckel, Von Papen and Speer. Both Sauckel and Speer were found guilty of war crimes and crimes against humanity; as Schacht and Von Papen had not been charged with these offences, they went free at the end of the trial, along with Fritzsche.

43 Von Papen retired soon after the Anschluss and Schacht was arrested by the Gestapo and placed in a concentration camp in 1944.

44 'Judgment', *Trial of The Major War Criminals*, vol. 1, p. 330.

45 Ibid., p. 327.
46 Thus, the Tribunal took into consideration the fact that from 1936, Schacht opposed for economic reasons the vigorous arms stockpiling policies pursued by Hitler. Schacht's rejection of the Nazi regime grew, and eventually led him to participate in two plans to remove Hitler from power. The Tribunal accepted Schacht's claim that he wanted to 'build up a strong and independent Germany which would carry out a foreign policy which would command respect on an equal basis with other European countries'. The Tribunal reconfirmed that rearmament itself was not a crime under the Charter, but if shown to have been accomplished in pursuit of the Nazi plan to wage wars of aggression, it would be sufficient to result in a conviction ('Judgment', *Trial of The Major War Criminals*, vol. 1, p. 309). The Tribunal also pointed out Von Papen's opposition to certain of the Nazi regime's policies.
47 These included Goering, Von Ribbentrop, Keitel, Rosenberg, Frick, Jodl, Seyss-Inquart and Bormann. Bormann was tried *in absentia*, presumed dead. A few hours before he was scheduled to be hanged, Goering committed suicide while in custody.
48 Namely Hess, Funk and Raeder.
49 That is, Von Neurath.
50 Namely Doenitz.
51 'Judgment', *Trial of The Major War Criminals*, vol. 1, p. 186.
52 F. B. Schick, 'The Nuremberg Trial and the International Law of the Future', *American Journal of International Law* (1947) 41: 770–794, pp. 778–779.
53 The way in which Nazism had infiltrated all facets of German society, especially all tiers of government, meant that in practice, a trial of Nazi elites by a newly formed German government was a long-term prospect at best.
54 See article 16, 'Charter of the International Military Tribunal', *Trial of The Major War Criminals*, vol. 1, p. 14. Against these extensive protections, defence counsel objected to the IMT's more relaxed rules of evidence, which permitted draft and unsigned documents to be considered by the Tribunal, such as the documents recording the four key secret conferences which weighed heavily in the IMT's judgment. However, the Tribunal overruled these defence objections, pointing out that despite the form of these documents, the defence did not deny their basic authenticity ('Judgment', *Trial of The Major War Criminals*, vol. 1, p. 188).
55 Otherwise known as the *Ministries* case. This trial was held pursuant to Control Council Law #10 which established a common legal basis for the prosecution of lesser alleged war criminals throughout the various occupation zones of Germany (see 'Control Council Law No. 10', in T. Taylor, *Final Report to the Secretary of the Army on the Nuernberg War Crimes Trials under Control Council law No. 10*, Washington: GPO, 1949 (available at www.yale.edu/lawweb/avalon/imt/imt10.htm)).
56 That is, the principle that promises or agreements made will be honoured. This principle is identified by Bull as one of the three aims of all societies (see H. Bull, *The Anarchical Society*, London: Macmillan, 1977).
57 United Nations, *Historical Review of Developments Relating to Aggression*, New York: United Nations, 2003, p. 59.
58 Namely the principle that there is no crime except in accordance with the law.
59 Scharf traces the origins of the *ex post facto* criticism to Ohio Senator Robert Taft in 1946, but claims the criticism gained significant public attention when Taft's speech was reprinted in John F. Kennedy's 1956 book, *Profiles of Courage* (see M. P. Scharf, 'Have We Really Learned the Lessons of Nuremberg?', *Military Law Review* (1995) 149: 65–71, p. 67).
60 Schick, 'The Nuremberg Trial and the International Law of the Future', p. 783.
61 Thus, it is Paul Johann Anselm Ritter von Feuerbach's Bavarian Code of 1813 which is usually credited as the source of the present-day version of these principles (see J. Hall, 'Nulla Poena Sine Lege', *The Yale Law Journal* (1937) 47: 165–193, p. 169;

(anon), 'The Use of Analogy in Criminal Law', *Columbia Law Review* (1947) 47: 613–629, p. 614; and P. Weidenbaum, 'Liberal Thought and Undefined Crimes', *Journal of Comparative Legislation and International Law* (1937) 19: 90–97, p. 91).

62 How this consideration would play out in the context of the Nuremberg trials was of concern within the US administration; in a cable to senior members of his Department of War in April 1945, Secretary Stimson referred to 'the possibility that the defence may assert vigorously the existence of wrongs by other nations against Germany and make reference to historic instances of nations which have used aggressive action as an instrument of national policy' (paraphrased telegram from Henry Stimson to John McCloy, John Weir and R. A. Cutter dated April 1945 (available at www.trumanlibrary.org/ whistlestop/study_collections/nuremberg)).

63 On the importance of prosecuting non-military Nazi leaders, Maxwell-Fyfe remarked:

> What is in my mind is getting a man like Ribbentrop or Ley. It would be a great pity if we failed to get Ribbentrop or Ley or Streicher. Now I want words that will leave no doubt that men who have originated the plan or taken part in the early stages of the plan are going to be within the jurisdiction of the Tribunal. I do not want any argument that Ribbentrop did not direct the preparation because he merely was overborne by Hitler, or any nonsense of that kind.
>
> (See 'Minutes of Conference Session of July 19, 1945', *Report of Robert H. Jackson*)

5 Aggression and individual criminal responsibility at the Tokyo Trial

1 For a recent examination of such criticisms, see N. Boister and R. Cryer, *The Tokyo International Military Tribunal: A Reappraisal*, Oxford: Oxford University Press, 2008.

2 Cairo Declaration of 1 December 1943 (available at www.yale.edu/lawweb/avalon/ wwii/cairo.htm).

3 Potsdam Declaration of 26 July 1945 (available at www.ibiblio.org/hyperwar/PTO/ Dip/Potsdam.html).

4 A. Tusa and J. Tusa, *The Nuremberg Trial*, London: Macmillan, 1984, pp. 33–35.

5 A. C. Brackman, *The Other Nuremberg: The Untold Story of the Tokyo War Crimes Trials*, New York: Quill, 1987, pp. 34–35.

6 B.-A. Shillony, *Politics and Culture in Wartime Japan*, Oxford: Clarendon Press, 1981, p. 174.

7 Japanese Qualified Acceptance of the Potsdam Declaration of 10 August 1945 (available at www.ibiblio.org/hyperwar/PTO/IMTFE/IMTFE-A1.html#A1a). It is important to keep in mind that at this time the fact that the Allies had just exhausted their atomic arsenal was kept secret (Brackman, *The Other Nuremberg*, p. 36).

8 Reply by Secretary of State to Japanese Qualified Acceptance of 11 August 1945 (available at www.ibiblio.org/hyperwar/PTO/IMTFE/IMTFE-A1.html#A1b).

9 Australia and the Soviet Union were particularly keen to indict the Emperor (see Brackman, *The Other Nuremberg*, p. 47).

10 Apart from his royal status, Prince Konoye had twice been Prime Minister of Japan: he first served in this role from 1937 to 1939 and subsequently from July 1940 to October 1941 (see National Diet Library of Japan, *Historical Figures*. 2003–2004 (available at www.ndl.go.jp/constitution/e/etc/figures.html)).

11 Brackman, *The Other Nuremberg*, p. 50.

12 Prince Nashimoto was later released without charge in April 1946.

13 Article 29 of the Nuremberg Charter states: 'In case of guilt, sentences shall be carried out in accordance with the orders of the Control Council for Germany, which may at any time reduce or otherwise alter the sentences, but may not increase the severity

thereof. ('Charter of the International Military Tribunal', *Trial of The Major War Criminals before the International Military Tribunal*, Nuremberg: International Military Tribunal, 1947, vol. 1, p. 16).

14 That is, the nine Allied states which were signatory to the surrender document – namely the USA, UK, China, Soviet Union, Australia, Canada, France, the Netherlands and New Zealand – plus the Philippines and India (see J. A. Appleman, *Military Tribunals and International Crimes*, Indianapolis: The Bobbs-Merrill Company, 1954, p. 239).

15 R. J. Pritchard, 'The International Military Tribunal for the Far East and its Contemporary Resonances', *Military Law Review* (1995) 149: 25–35, pp. 26–27.

16 The official reason for not prosecuting the Emperor was that he was a mere figurehead, and therefore he could not be held responsible for his role in the Pacific War. Piccigallo claims that the decision not to prosecute the Emperor was actually an astute political move, as the plan was to use existing forms of government in Japan to implement US occupation policy. There were also concerns that any attempt, whether real or illusory, to abolish the Emperor could incite chaos, violence and administrative collapse in Japan, which would also hinder occupation policy (see P. R. Piccigallo, *The Japanese on Trial*, Austin: University of Texas Press, 1979, pp. 16–17; and T. P. Maga, *Judgment at Tokyo*, Lexington: University Press of Kentucky, 2001, pp. 35–39).

17 Indeed, the value of evidence about political affairs from imperial titleholders was not entirely excluded by the Tokyo Trial; Henry P'u Yi, the ex-Emperor of China, was a key witness for the prosecution in its case concerning Japanese activities in Manchuria (see Brackman, *The Other Nuremberg*, pp. 155–156).

18 This position was conferred on the Emperor under Japan's 1889 Constitution (see Shillony, *Politics and Culture in Wartime Japan*, p. 36).

19 J. T. C. Liu, 'The Tokyo Trial: Source Materials', *Far Eastern Survey* (1948) 17: 168–170.

20 'The Separate Opinion of the President of the Tribunal (Sir William Flood Webb), the Member for Australia', pp. 18–21, and 'The Dissenting Opinion of the Member for France (Henri Bernard)', p. 22, reproduced in R. J. Pritchard (ed.), *The Tokyo Major War Crimes Trial: The Records of the International Military Tribunal for the Far East*, New York: The Edwin Mellen Press, 1998, vol. 109 and vol. 105 respectively.

21 Why the archives were not obliterated in accordance with official orders is discussed in Tusa, *The Nuremberg Trial*, pp. 96–97.

22 P. Lowe, 'The Tokyo Trial of Japanese Leaders, 1946–1948', in R. A. Melikan (ed.) *Domestic and International Trials 1700–2000*, Manchester: Manchester University Press, 2003, pp. 137–156, p. 142.

23 Brackman, *The Other Nuremberg*, p. 40.

24 Thus, Nobutaka's volume translates notes of various liaison and imperial conferences taken for Army use (see I. Nobutaka, *Japan's Decision For War*, California: Stanford University Press, 1967). Nobutaka indicates that the records used in this volume were discovered in the Military History Archives of the Japanese Defense Agency (p. xiii). It is unclear whether these records were discovered in time for the Tokyo Trial.

25 S. Horwitz, 'The Tokyo Trial', *International Conciliation* (1950) 28: 473–584, p. 494.

26 By contrast, Tokyo prosecutors had ample evidence from survivors and eyewitnesses to sustain charges of conventional war crimes and crimes against humanity against those Japanese who were at the scene of the alleged crime. This is reflected in the prosecution's summation at trial: over one-third of its general discussion of all the charges concerns war crimes and crimes against humanity, though these accounted for only three of the fifty-five charges in total made against the defendants (see R. J. Pritchard and S. M. Zaide, *Tokyo War Crimes Trial Index and Guide*, New York: Garland, 1987, vol. 3, pp. 1025–1057).

27 On the role of the Meiji Constitution in prewar Japan, see T. Nakamura, *A History of Showa Japan 1926–1989*, Tokyo: University of Tokyo Press, 1998, pp. 2–4.

28 Shillony, *Politics and Culture of Wartime Japan*, p. 37.
29 Ibid., pp. 37–38.
30 In accordance with the view expressed in the Nuremberg Charter and judgment, conspiracy is considered here as part of, and not a separate offence from, the crime of aggression ('Judgment', *Trial of the Major War Criminals*, p. 224).
31 The activities of Itagaki, Oshima and Shiratori are instructive on this point. Itagaki was held by the Tokyo Tribunal to have orchestrated the Mukden Incident of 1931 as an excuse for Japanese military response, and to have suppressed efforts to prevent such a response to that incident, though at the time he only held the rank of colonel (see Pritchard, *The Tokyo Major War Crimes Trial*, p. 49796). Similarly, as military attaché in the Japanese Embassy at Berlin, Oshima was convicted on the basis that he used this position to bypass the Japanese ambassador and to negotiate directly with von Ribbentrop in an effort to effect a full military alliance between Japan and Germany (see Pritchard, *The Tokyo Major War Crimes Trial*, p. 49823). Shiratori, who was the Japanese ambassador to Rome from 1938, was convicted on similar grounds to Oshima, except the target of Shiratori's efforts was Italy, not Germany (see Pritchard, *The Tokyo Major War Crimes Trial*, p. 49836). The significant role of middle management as the instigator of policy and in decision-making generally in Japan during this period and today is discussed in Nakamura, *A History of Showa Japan 1926–1989*, pp. 252–253.
32 See article 1 of the Kellogg–Briand Pact of 27 August 1928 (available at www.yale. edu/lawweb/avalon/imt/kbpact.htm). This argument remains the Nuremberg Trial's single most important target of criticism. For a critical view of the Nuremberg Trial generally, see F. B. Schick, 'Crimes Against Peace', *Journal of Criminal Law and Criminology* (1948) 38: 445–465.
33 See p. 52.
34 Article 5(a) of the Tokyo Charter of 19 January 1946 defined crimes against peace as 'namely, the planning, preparation, initiation or waging of a *declared or undeclared* war of aggression, or a war in violation of international law, treaties, agreements or assurances, or participation in a common plan or conspiracy for the accomplishment of any of the foregoing' (emphasis added) (available at www.yale.edu/lawweb/avalon/imtfech.htm).
35 Reproduced in United Nations, *Historical Review of Developments Relating to Aggression*, New York: United Nations, 2003, p. 87.
36 That is, to include East Asia, the Western and Southwestern Pacific Ocean and the Indian Ocean, and certain islands in these oceans only (see 'Tokyo Judgment' (1949), p. 1137 (available at www.ibiblio.org/hyperwar/PTO/IMTFE/IMTFE-9.html)).
37 The issue of whether the conduct alleged falls within the parameters of the crime of aggression (and therefore whether the conduct is criminal at all) has a parallel in more recent discussions concerning Joint Criminal Enterprise (JCE), a legal doctrine similar to conspiracy which has been recognised and developed in jurisprudence emanating particularly from international judicial bodies including the International Criminal Tribunal for the Former Yugoslavia. See the concluding chapter of this volume for more on this point.
38 Whereas at Nuremberg, special importance was assigned to the records of the four secret conferences mentioned above to prove that a conspiracy existed among eight of the defendants, it was Okawa's public statements in favour of the extension of Japanese territory to continental Asia and of Japanese domination of other areas, combined with the support this idea attracted from 'a party of military men' and 'other civilian supporters' which proved the Japanese conspiracy, according to the Tokyo Tribunal (see 'Tokyo Judgment', p. 1138).
39 Although there were originally twenty-eight Tokyo defendants, Matsuoka and Nagano died at trial and Okawa was committed. For further details of the charges and convictions at the Tokyo Trial, see Appendix 2.
40 Namely Matsui. However, Matsui was sentenced to death for his failure to prevent

breaches of the laws of war concerning POWs and civilians (see Horwitz, 'The Tokyo Trial', p. 584).

41 Bormann, Kaltenbrunner, Frank, Streicher, Von Schirach and Fritzsche were acquitted of conspiracy and not charged with waging aggressive war; and Schacht, Sauckel, Von Papen and Speer were acquitted of both conspiracy and waging aggressive war.

42 One of the more worrying differences concerned each Tribunal's powers with respect to jurisdiction. Article 6 of the Nuremberg Charter indicates that its tribunal 'shall have the power *to try and punish persons who ... committed any of the following crimes*' (emphasis added). By contrast, article 5 of the Tokyo Charter states that its tribunal 'shall have the power *to try and punish* Far Eastern war *criminals who ... are charged with offences which include Crimes Against Peace*' (emphasis added). It is possible that the latter provision is simply an example of exceptionally poor drafting, but in light of the Tokyo Trial's other numerous features reflecting an overwhelming political bias, this provision does leave open the conclusion that the Tokyo defendants were already considered criminal and therefore punishable *at the time of being charged* rather than on conviction at the end of a trial process.

43 Aside from the issue that no neutral nations were represented on the Tokyo bench, three judges had prior experiences linked to the issues before the Tokyo Tribunal which made their appointment theoretically challengeable on grounds of partiality. While the Australian judge had previously investigated Japanese atrocities in New Guinea, and the second American judge had advised Roosevelt on responsibility for the Pearl Harbor attack, perhaps the most serious challenge available to the defence was against the Philippine judge, who had survived the Bataan death march – a specific subject of the Tokyo proceedings. After the defence challenged the Australian judge's qualifications, the Tribunal indicated that no objections to any of the judges would be entertained, on the basis that no provision for review existed in the Tokyo Charter (see R. H. Minear, *Victors' Justice: the Tokyo War Crimes Trial*, Princeton: Princeton University Press, 1971, pp. 81–83).

44 For further discussion of these points see Pritchard, 'The International Military Tribunal for the Far East and its Contemporary Resonances', pp. 25–35.

45 That is, Koiso, Shiratori, Togo and Umezu.

46 These included Araki, Hashimoto, Hata, Hiranuma, Hoshino, Kaya, Kido, Minami, Oka, Oshima, Sato, Shigemitsu, Shimada, and Suzuki.

47 Namely Hess, Doenitz, Von Schirach and Speer. Funk, Von Neurath and Raeder were released in the mid-1950s on grounds of ill health (see A. Kochavi, *Prelude to Nuremberg*, Chapel Hill: UNC Press, 1998, p. 245).

48 'Judgment', *The Trial of the Major War Criminals*, p. 186.

49 The Member for India was particularly strident in his opposition, entering a 1200-page opinion which refuted virtually every point made in the majority's judgment (see Pritchard, *The Tokyo Major War Crimes Trial*, vols 106–108).

50 This quotation is attributed to Stimson, describing German aims in World War II (quoted in W. R. Harris, *Tyranny on Trial*, Dallas: Southern Methodist University Press, 1954, p. 8).

6 The UN's 'definition' of state aggression, 1944 to 1974

1 T. Hoopes and D. Brinkley, *FDR and the Creation of the UN*, New Haven: Yale University Press, 1997, p. 44.

2 J. G. Ruggie, 'Third Try at World Order? America and Multilateralism After the Cold War', *Political Science Quarterly* (1994) 109: 553–570, p. 555.

3 R. C. Hilderbrand, *Dumbarton Oaks*, Chapel Hill: University of North Carolina Press, 1990, p. 35. 'Unanimity with abstention' meant that great power unanimity was required for a decision to be validly made, but any of the great powers could choose

to abstain from voting, which would not impact upon the outcome of the vote. Only a negative vote by one or more of the great powers could prevent a decision from being made. For further discussion of the American position in relation to voting procedures, see T. M. Campbell, 'US Motives in the Veto Power', *International Organization* (1974) 28: 557–560; and by the same author, 'Nationalism in America's UN Policy 1944–1945', *International Organization* (1973) 27: pp. 25–44.

4 Hilderbrand, *Dumbarton Oaks*, p. 71. Eagleton claims the early delivery of the US plan to the three other governments in July 1944, its 'constitutional form' and greater detail were the reasons why it became the working document at Dumbarton Oaks (see C. Eagleton, 'The Charter Adopted at San Francisco', *American Political Science Review* (1945) 39: 934–942, pp. 934–935).

5 Hoopes, *FDR and the Creation of the UN*, pp. 69–70.

6 Hilderbrand, *Dumbarton Oaks*, p. 50.

7 Kelsen supported the exclusion of the term 'aggression' from the UN Charter on similar grounds. In his view, aggression was a 'military–technical' term rather than a legal term, which could 'hardly be defined in a way satisfactory for legal purposes' (H. Kelsen, 'The Old and the New League: The Covenant and the Dumbarton Oaks Proposals', *American Journal of International Law* (1945) 39: 45–83, p. 74).

8 Hilderbrand, *Dumbarton Oaks*, p. 50.

9 Ibid., pp. 46–47.

10 Hoopes, *FDR and the Creation of the UN*, pp. 142–143.

11 E. Borchard, 'The Dumbarton Oaks Conference', *American Journal of International Law* (1945) 39: 97–101, p. 98.

12 For instance, see Agreement Between the Governments of the United Kingdom and the United States of America on the Principles Applying to Mutual Aid in the Prosecution of the War Against Aggression (the Lend-Lease Agreement) of 23 February, 1942 (available at www.yale.edu/lawweb/avalon/decade/decade04.htm); the Moscow Declaration of November 1943, signed by the US, UK, Soviet Union and China, where reference is made to the 'menace of aggression': see Senate Committee on Foreign Relations and the Department of State, *A Decade of American Foreign Policy: Basic Documents, 1941–1949*, Washington: GPO, 1950 (available at www.yale.edu/lawweb/avalon/wwii/moscow.htm); and the Cairo Declaration of December 1, 1943, signed by the USA, UK and China, which refers to the 'aggression of Japan' (available at www.yale.edu/lawweb/avalon/wwii/cairo.htm).

13 Hilderbrand, *Dumbarton Oaks*, pp. 137–138.

14 Ibid., p. 138.

15 The US position at this time against including a statement about aggression in the UN Charter is difficult to reconcile with its signing of the Act of Chapultepec only a month prior to the commencement of the San Francisco Conference. This regional treaty declared

> That every attack of a State against the integrity or the inviolability of the territory, or against the sovereignty or political independence of an *American* state, shall … be considered as an act of aggression against the other states which sign this Act. In any case invasion by armed forces of one state into the territory of another trespassing boundaries established by treaty and demarcated in accordance therewith shall constitute an act of aggression' [emphasis added].
>
> (G. A. Finch, 'The United Nations Charter', *American Journal of International Law* (1945) 39: 541–546, p. 543)

16 This formula featured in two different sections of the Proposals. It first appeared in Chapter I, which dealt with the purposes of the organisation, as follows: 'The purposes of the Organisation should be: 1. To maintain international peace and security; and to that end to take effective collective measures for prevention and removal of threats to the peace and the suppression of acts of aggression or other breaches of the

peace....' It also appeared under Chapter VIII, Section B: '2. In general the Security Council should determine the existence of any threat to the peace, breach of the peace or act of aggression and should make recommendations or decide upon the measures to be taken to maintain or restore peace and security' (available at www.ibiblio.org/pha/policy/1944/441007a.html). The San Francisco conference is discussed in more detail in the following section.

17 Hilderbrand, *Dumbarton Oaks*, p. 138.

18 At the second round of meetings at Dumbarton Oaks between the USA, UK and China, the latter delegation reintroduced the suggestion that a definition of aggression be included in the Dumbarton Oaks Proposals. China argued that such definition would expedite Security Council action, promote confidence in the new organisation, enable public opinion to identify an aggressor quickly and act as a deterrent to potential aggressors. China thought that some statement of examples of aggression would suffice as an indicator of that term's meaning; a full definition was not necessary. However, having already addressed this issue with the Soviets, the UK and USA were evidently able to persuade China that it would be better to leave to the Security Council the discretion to decide on an ad hoc basis what conduct amounted to aggression, and no alterations to the Proposals were made.

19 L. M. Goodrich and E. Hambro, *Charter of the United Nations: Commentary and Documents*, Boston: World Peace Foundation, 1949, p. 263.

20 Bolivia's proposed definition read as follows:

> A state shall be designated an aggressor if it has committed any of the following acts to the detriment of another state. (a) Invasion of another state's territory by armed forces. (b) Declaration of war. (c) Attack by land, sea, or air forces, with or without declaration of war, on another state's territory, shipping or aircraft. (d) Support given to armed bands for the purpose of invasion. (e) Intervention in another state's internal or foreign affairs. (f) Refusal to submit the matter which has caused a dispute to the peaceful means provided for its settlement. (g) Refusal to comply with a judicial decision lawfully pronounced by an International Court.

The proposed definition submitted by the Philippines provided:

> Any nation should be considered as threatening the peace or as an aggressor, if it should be the first party to commit any of the following acts: (1) To declare war against another nation; (2) To invade or attack, with or without declaration of war, the territory, public vessel, or public aircraft of another nation; (3) To subject another nation to naval, land or air blockade; and (4) To interfere with the internal affairs of another nation by supplying arms, ammunition, money or other forms of aid to any armed band, faction or group, or by establishing agencies in that nation to conduct propaganda subversive of the institutions of that nation.

Both proposed definitions are reproduced in *United Nations Conference on International Organization Documents*, London: United Nations Information Organisation, 1945, vol. 3, p. 585 and p. 538 respectively.

21 *United Nations Conference on International Organization Documents*, vol. 12, p. 341.

22 Ibid., p. 342.

23 W. T. R. Fox, 'Collective Enforcement of Peace and Security', *American Political Science Review* (1945) 39: 970–981, p. 973.

24 *United Nations Conference on International Organization Documents*, vol. 12, p. 342.

25 Ibid.

26 *United Nations Conference on International Organization Documents*, vol. 12, p. 349.

27 See articles 1(1) and 39 of the UN Charter (available at www.un.org/aboutun/charter).

28 See GA Res 193 (III) of 27 November 1948.

29 See GA Res 292 (IV) of 8 December 1949.

30 See GA Res 509 (VI) of 14 December 1951.

31 see GA Res 378 (V) of 17 November 1950.

32 For instance, pro-definition states argued that a definition was necessary, while anti-definition states claimed it was not; the former further argued that a definition was in any case desirable, whereas the latter provided reasons why it was not.

33 See GA Res 688 (VII) of 20 December 1952. Discussion of the related topic concerning international criminal jurisdiction will be developed in Chapter 7.

34 A/2638, reproduced in B. Ferencz, *Defining International Aggression: The Search for World Peace*, New York: Dobbs Ferry, 1975, vol. 2, pp. 187–201.

35 Art 2(1) of the UN Charter.

36 Art 2(7) of the UN Charter.

37 Art 1(2) of the UN Charter.

38 Ferencz, *Defining International Aggression*, vol. 2, p. 195.

39 Ibid., p. 199.

40 During this time, China was represented at the UN by the Republic of China. The People's Republic of China was recognised by the UN as the legitimate government of China in 1971.

41 The 1953 Report does not identify specifically which states opposed a definition of aggression; however; excluding the supporters of a definition, the remaining committee members represented the following states: Brazil, China, Dominican Republic, Netherlands, Norway, Pakistan, the USA and UK. It may be surmised that these latter two states at least were firmly opposed to a definition.

42 Ferencz, *Defining International Aggression*, vol. 2, p. 197.

43 Ibid., p. 198.

44 Of 31 January 1952. In its preamble, this resolution stated: 'considering that ... it is nevertheless possible and desirable ... to define aggression by reference to the elements which constitute it'.

45 Of 20 December 1952. This resolution referred to 'the *need* for a detailed study of (a) the various forms of aggression ...' (emphasis added).

46 A/3574, reproduced in Ferencz, *Defining International Aggression*, vol. 2, pp. 215–247.

47 Of 4 December 1954.

48 Of 14 December 1954.

49 As a result of the long-standing difficulties each successive special committee had in defining aggression, the impact of GA Res 897(IX) and 898(IX) was to postpone work on these related topics indefinitely. As will be revealed below, the impact of this postponement played an important role in the development of the General Assembly Definition of Aggression.

50 The seventh draft was not the subject of comprehensive discussion.

51 Ferencz, *Defining International Aggression*, vol. 2, p. 231.

52 Other than Yugoslavia, the 1956 Report does not identify opponents of a definition of aggression which extends to economic, ideological or indirect means, merely indicating that their numbers are substantial (see Ferencz, *Defining International Aggression*, vol. 2, p. 222).

53 That is, subversive activities such as fomenting civil strife in foreign nations and assisting armed bands.

54 Ferencz, *Defining International Aggression*, vol. 2, p. 225.

55 Under GA Res 377A (V) of 3 November 1950, also referred to as the Uniting For Peace resolution, the General Assembly conferred upon itself the power to make 'appropriate recommendations to Members for collective measures', in the event that the Security Council fails, as a consequence of P5 division, to perform its functions where 'there appears to be a threat to the peace, breach of the peace, or act of aggression'. Originally passed in order to enable UN action during the Suez Crisis, to which the UK and France were parties, GA Res 377A has subsequently been used as a basis for calling emergency special sessions of the General Assembly in response

to outbreaks of international hostilities: see Chapter 8 (this volume) for further details.

56 This conclusion is left open in the draft definitions forwarded to the 1956 Committee by Paraguay, Iran, Panama and Mexico, which do not specify the Security Council but merely refer to the 'competent organ of the United Nations' (Ferencz, *Defining International Aggression*, vol. 2, pp. 245–246).

57 Indeed, the US representative pointed out 'the artificial and insubstantial character of the impression that a large measure of agreement existed in the United Nations on the possibility of drafting an acceptable definition of aggression', where in his view there was only 'fundamental and irreconcilable differences' (Ferencz, *Defining International Aggression*, vol. 2, p. 1225).

58 Ferencz, *Defining International Aggression*, vol. 2, p. 226.

59 Ibid.

60 Ferencz, *Defining International Aggression*, vol. 2, p. 228.

61 Ibid.

62 Ferencz, *Defining International Aggression*, vol. 2, p. 226.

63 See GA Res 1181 (XII) of 29 November 1957.

64 Ferencz, *Defining International Aggression*, vol. 2, p. 275.

65 The reports of the Special Committee from 1968 to 1973 are reproduced in Ferencz, *Defining International Aggression*, vol. 2, pp. 280–319, 326–364, 372–438, 446–484, 493–509 and 519–539.

66 R. L. Garthodd, *Detente and Confrontation: American–Soviet Relations from Nixon to Reagan*, Washington, DC: Brookings Institute, 1994.

67 Ferencz, *Defining International Aggression*, vol. 2, p. 292.

68 Ibid., pp. 294–295.

69 Ibid., p. 298.

70 Ibid.

71 See paragraphs 2 and 3 of the Soviet draft (Ferencz, *Defining International Aggression*, vol. 2, pp. 330–331) and paragraph 5 of the Thirteen Power draft submitted by Colombia, Cyprus, Ecuador, Ghana, Guyana, Haiti, Iran, Madagascar, Mexico, Spain, Uganda, Uruguay and Yugoslavia (Ferencz, *Defining International Aggression*, vol. 2, p. 332). While these two drafts referred explicitly to the non-binding nature of a definition, the Six Power draft submitted by Australia, Canada, Italy, Japan, the USA and UK simply stated that 'aggression is a term to be applied by the Security Council when appropriate' (Ferencz, *Defining International Aggression*, vol. 2, p. 333).

72 Ferencz, *Defining International Aggression*, vol. 2, p. 545.

73 The text of the General Assembly Definition of Aggression is reproduced in Appendix 3. A further example of the tensions inherent in this resolution is revealed by comparing preambular paragraph 2, which refers to the enforcement provisions in the UN Charter, and article 7, which upholds the right to self-determination.

74 This conclusion was reached by the League's Committee on Arbitration and Security (see Chapter 3 (this volume)).

7 The International Law Commission's attempts to criminalise state aggression, 1946 to 1998

1 See GA Res 177 of 21 November 1947. Hereafter referred to as Draft Code. Although the title of the 1951 Draft Code refers to 'offences' rather than 'crimes', the difference is cosmetic rather than substantive, as the commentaries to the 1951 Draft Code – which refer to crimes – makes clear. The Draft Code was renamed the Draft Code of Crimes Against the Peace and Security of Mankind in 1987.

2 See Chapter 4, pp. 50–51 (this volume).

3 'Report by J. Spiropoulos, Special Rapporteur' (A/CN.4/25), *Yearbook of the International Law Commission*, 1950, vol. 2, p. 262. Emphasis added.

4 'Report of the International Law Commission to the General Assembly' (A/1858), *Yearbook of the International Law Commission*, 1951, vol. 2, p. 135. The threat of aggression was also included in the 1954 draft as a separate offence, but was later dropped: see below.

5 Ibid.

6 Ibid. Note the Security Council's powers under article 39 of the UN Charter, to 'determine the existence of any threat to the peace, breach of the peace, or act of aggression'.

7 In relation to Austria, the judgment simply concluded that 'the methods employed to achieve the object were those of an aggressor' and that 'a calculated design to resort to force' was behind the seizure of Czechoslovakia (see 'Judgment', *Trial of The Major War Criminals before the International Military Tribunal*, Nuremberg: International Military Tribunal, 1947, vol. 1, p. 194 and p. 196 respectively).

8 Of 4 December 1954.

9 See article 34(1) of the Statute of the International Court of Justice (available at www.icj-cij.org/icjwww/ibasicdocuments/ibasictext/ibasicstatute.htm#CHAPTER_II).

10 See Chapter VII of the UN Charter.

11 GA Res 260 B of 9 December 1948.

12 See principle (9), 'Report by Ricardo J. Alfaro, Special Rapporteur' (A/CN.4/15*), *ILC Yearbook*, 1950, p. 17. However, the Special Rapporteur thought that in appropriate circumstances the Security Council might authorise a state to commence proceedings directly. The 1950 Report also outlined ten general principles upon which an international criminal jurisdiction could be established, and many of these principles – such as those on defence protections and judges' qualifications – are now recognisable in the statutes of the ICTY, ICTR and ICC.

13 See 'Report of the 1953 Committee on International Criminal Jurisdiction 27 July– 20 August 1953' (A/2645), *General Assembly Official Records* Ninth Session, Supplement No. 12, p. 23.

14 Thus, on virtually all of these issues, the Report indicated that 'some members' took one view, while 'other members' took another. ILC members of the 1953 Committee came from the following states: Argentina, Australia, Belgium, China, Denmark, Egypt, France, Israel, Netherlands, Panama, Peru, Philippines, UK, USA, Venezuela and Yugoslavia. Officially, ILC members act in their own private capacity, not as representatives of their home states. However, the reluctance of the Report to reveal the views of these individuals demonstrates, in reality, the strongly political nature of these positions.

15 'Report of the 1953 Committee on International Criminal Jurisdiction 27 July– 20 August 1953' (A/2645), *GAOR* (9th Sess.), p. 23.

16 'Report of the 1953 Committee on International Criminal Jurisdiction 27 July– 20 August 1953' (A/2645), *GAOR* (9th Sess.), p. 22.

17 See GA Res 36/106 of 10 December 1981.

18 See A. Bos, 'The Experience of the Preparatory Committee', in M. Politi and G. Nesi (eds) *The Rome Statute of the International Criminal Court*, Aldershot: Ashgate, 2001, p. 21.

19 D. Thiam, 'Second Report on the Draft Code of Offences Against the Peace and Security of Mankind' (A/CN.4/377*), *Yearbook of the International Law Commission*, 1984, vol. 2, p. 100.

20 D. Thiam, 'Fourth Report on the Draft Code of Offences Against the Peace and Security of Mankind' (A/CN.4/398), *Yearbook of the International Law Commission*, 1986, vol. 1, p. 84. Article 5 of the General Assembly Definition of Aggression, which referred to 'international responsibility' and described a war of aggression as a crime, was excluded on the grounds that this was precisely the subject of the present draft.

21 See *Yearbook of the International Law Commission*, 1986, vol. 1, p. 83.

22 Emphasis added. See Thiam, 'Fourth Report on the Draft Code of Offences Against the Peace and Security of Mankind', *ILC Yearbook*, 1986, p. 82.

23 'Summary Records of the Meetings of the Fortieth Session: 2085th Meeting', *Yearbook of the International Law Commission*, 1988, vol. 1, pp. 291–299.
24 'Summary Records of the Meetings of the Forty-third Session: 2237th Meeting', *Yearbook of the International Law Commission*, 1991, vol. 1, p. 200.
25 The Italian ILC member, 'Summary Records of the Meetings of the Forty-seventh Session: 2408th Meeting', *Yearbook of the International Law Commission*, 1995, vol. 1, p. 203.
26 The Sri Lankan ILC member, 'Summary Records of the Meetings of the Forty-seventh Session: 2408th Meeting', *ILC Yearbook*, 1995, p. 210.
27 The Moroccan ILC member, 'Summary Records of the Meetings of the Forty-seventh Session: 2408th Meeting', *ILC Yearbook*, 1995, p. 211.
28 Article 16 of the 1996 Draft Code (available at www.un.org/law/ilc).
29 Conspiracy, which had been such an important part of the prosecution of aggression at Nuremberg and Tokyo, was not expressly mentioned in the final Draft Code with regard to the crime of aggression, though it did apply in relation to the other crimes (see article 2(3)(e) of the 1996 Draft Code).
30 See GA Res 44/39 of 4 December 1989.
31 The five listed crimes were genocide; systematic or mass violations of human rights; apartheid; illicit international trafficking in drugs; and seizure of aircraft and kidnapping of diplomats or internationally protected persons (see 'Draft Code of Crimes Against the Peace and Security of Mankind: Report of the Working Group on the Question of an International Criminal Jurisdiction' (A/CN.4/L.471), *Yearbook of the International Law Commission*, 1992, vol. 2, p. 61).
32 D. Thiam, 'Eleventh Report on the Draft Code of Crimes Against the Peace and Security of Mankind' (A/CN.4/449), *Yearbook of the International Law Commission*, 1993, vol. 2, pp. 115–116.
33 see article 20 of the 1994 Draft Statute for an International Criminal Court (available at untreaty.un.org/ilc/texts/instruments/english/draft%20articles/7_4_1994.pdf).
34 'Report of the International Law Commission on the Work of its Forty-sixth Session, 2 May–22 July 1994' (A/49/10), *Yearbook of the International Law Commission*, 1994, vol. 2, pp. 38–39.
35 'Report of the International Law Commission on the Work of its Forty-sixth Session, 2 May-22 July 1994', *ILC Yearbook*, 1994, p. 39.
36 A provision to this effect was included in article 23(2) of the 1994 Draft Statute.
37 see GA Res 49/53 of 9 December 1995.
38 'Report of the Preparatory Committee on the Establishment of an International Criminal Court' (A/51/22), *General Assembly Official Records*, 51st Sess., 1996, p. 18.
39 For the text of these proposals, see 'Report of the Preparatory Committee on the Establishment of an International Criminal Court' (A/51/22), *GAOR*, 51st Sess., 1996, p. 58.
40 *De minimis* considerations reflect the views held by some that only certain situations of sufficient gravity qualify as aggression. For contrasting views, see 'Report of the Preparatory Committee on the Establishment of an International Criminal Court' (A/51/22), *GAOR* (51st Sess.), 1996, p. 19.
41 M. C. Bassiouni, 'Observations Concerning the 1997–1998 Preparatory Committee's Work', *Nouvelles Etudes Penales*, Chicago: International Human Rights Law Institute,1997, vol. 13, p. 24.
42 'Report of the Preparatory Committee on the Establishment of an International Criminal Court' (A/CONF.183/2/Add.1) of 14 April 1998, p. 12 (available at www.un.org/icc/prepcom.htm).
43 'Report of the Preparatory Committee on the Establishment of an International Criminal Court' (A/CONF.183/2/Add.1), 1998, p. 14.
44 For instance, option 1 read as follows:

[For the purpose of the present Statute, the crime [of aggression] [against peace] means any of the following acts committed by an individual [who is in a position of exercising control or capable of directing political/military action in a State]: (a) planning, (b) preparing, (c) ordering, (d) initiating, or (e) carrying out [an armed attack] [the use of armed force] [a war of aggression] [a war of aggression, or a war in violation of international treaties, agreements or assurances, or participation in a common plan or conspiracy for the accomplishment of any of the foregoing] by a State against the [sovereignty,] territorial integrity [or political independence] of another State [when this] [armed attack] [use of force] [is] [in contravention of the Charter of the United Nations] [[in contravention of the Charter of the United Nations as determined by the Security Council].]

For the text of the other two options, see 'Report of the Preparatory Committee on the Establishment of an International Criminal Court' (A/CONF.183/2/Add.1), 1998, pp. 13–14.

45 These states included: Egypt, Republic of Korea, Slovenia, Czech Republic, Lithuania, Philippines, Albania, Germany, Austria, FYR Macedonia, Namibia, Afghanistan, Italy, Slovakia, Tajikistan, Guinea, Zambia, Azerbaijan, Lebanon, Bulgaria, Greece, Gabon, Madagascar, Qatar, Cape Verde, Niger, Vietnam, Jordan, Georgia, Cyprus, Angola, Uganda (see *United Nations Diplomatic Conference of Plenipotentiaries on the Establishment of an International Criminal Court Official Records (Rome, 15 June–17 July 1998)*, New York: United Nations, 2002, vol. 2, pp. 64–121).

46 These states were: Japan, Sweden, Kazakhstan, Latvia, Armenia, Syria, Portugal, Sierra Leone, Mozambique, Brunei, Hungary, Iran, Cuba, Poland, Estonia, Moldova, Belgium, Ireland, Netherlands, Paraguay, Mexico, Oman, Nigeria, Trinidad and Tobago, Denmark, Malta, Russia, Belarus, Bahrain, and Ecuador (ibid.).

47 These states were: Norway, Venezuela, Lesotho, Holy See, Indonesia, Algeria, Ivory Coast, Tanzania, Peru, Kenya, Costa Rica, Andorra, Singapore, Burkina Faso, Croatia, UK, Finland, Nepal, Sudan, Thailand, Malawi, Bosnia and Herzegovina, Haiti, Iraq, Monaco, Australia, Canada, Romania, Kyrgyzstan, Pakistan, Senegal, Colombia, Ghana, Chile, Luxembourg, France, Argentina, Rwanda, Switzerland, Malaysia, Samoa, Democratic Republic of Congo, Uruguay, and Botswana (ibid.).

48 During the Conference, France and the UK became associated generally with the Like-minded Group of states, though on certain issues they continued to side with other P5 states. Most members of the European Union belonged to the Like-minded Group.

49 See the statements of representatives from India, US, Morocco, Turkey and Israel.

50 See the remarks of the representatives for Trinidad and Tobago, and Italy (*United Nations Diplomatic Conference of Plenipotentiaries on the Establishment of an International Criminal Court Official Records*, vol. 2, p. 175 and p. 178 respectively).

51 Ukraine holds observer status within the Non-aligned Movement.

52 For instance, see the statement of the Norwegian representative that 'he was not persuaded that a consensus on [the question of the Security Council] was possible at the current stage' (p. 172); and of the Mexican representative who 'doubted whether the problems [associated with jurisdiction over the crime of aggression] could be solved' (p. 175).

53 Even at this late stage, the Bureau was still acknowledging that 'discussions are still ongoing as to the inclusion of the crime of aggression and on the definition'. The Bureau also suggested that continuing interest in reviving the 1974 Definition might somehow be accommodated in the 'definition' (see 'Bureau Discussion Paper' (A/CONF.183.C.1/L.53), *United Nations Diplomatic Conference of Plenipotentiaries on the Establishment of an International Criminal Court Official Records*, vol. 2, p. 204).

54 See the statement of the Maltese representative in *United Nations Diplomatic Conference*

of Plenipotentiaries on the Establishment of an International Criminal Court Official Records, vol. 2, p. 290.

55 *United Nations Diplomatic Conference of Plenipotentiaries on the Establishment of an International Criminal Court Official Records*, vol. 2, p. 279. Note that at the end of the Conference India was one of just seven states to vote against the Statute (ww.un.org/law/icc/statute/iccq&a.htm).

56 *United Nations Diplomatic Conference of Plenipotentiaries on the Establishment of an International Criminal Court Official Records*, vol. 2, p. 271 and p. 288 respectively. Denmark also came close to making the same point when it declared that 'to claim that aggression could not be included in the Statute because it had not been defined was unacceptable' (p. 286).

57 Sweden (p. 270), Norway (p. 271) and Australia (p. 273) made this comment.

58 This point was raised by Samoa (p. 279).

59 The UK came to this conclusion, (p. 272).

60 'Bureau Proposal' (A/CONF.183/C.1/L.59), *United Nations Diplomatic Conference of Plenipotentiaries on the Establishment of an International Criminal Court Official Records*, vol. 2, p. 212.

61 'Bureau Proposal' (A/CONF.183/C.1/L.59), article 5.

62 *United Nations Diplomatic Conference of Plenipotentiaries on the Establishment of an International Criminal Court Official Records*, vol. 2, p. 322.

63 Thus, in terms of the Security Council's powers of suspending an investigation or prosecution, a time limit was fixed and it was stipulated that such a request from the Security Council must take the form of a resolution, in accordance with Egypt's wishes. In addition, the crime of aggression was included in the Statute, another key wish of Egypt. However, its other requests – namely that a role for the General Assembly equal to that of the Security Council be conferred, and that the Court be empowered with the right to request the Security Council to examine a situation of aggression if the Security Council had not done so itself – did not feature in the final document.

64 For example, see the comments of Norway (p. 344), Congo (p. 344), Andorra (p. 347) and Slovakia (p. 347).

65 For instance, see the remarks of Mozambique (p. 341), Algeria (p. 337) and Tanzania (p. 339).

66 Article 5(2) of the Rome Statute reads:

> The Court shall exercise jurisdiction over the crime of aggression once a provision is adopted in accordance with articles 121 and 123 defining the crime and setting out the conditions under which the Court shall exercise jurisdiction with respect to this crime. Such a provision shall be consistent with the relevant provisions of the Charter of the United Nations.

In the final vote on the ICC Statute, twenty-one states abstained from voting, while seven voted against the Statute. In the latter category was the USA, China, Israel, Yemen, Qatar, Libya and Iraq.

8 State aggression at the UN, 1945 to 2009

1 SC Res 82 of 25 June 1950 was entitled 'Complaint of Aggression upon the Republic of Korea'.

2 Of 2 August 1990.

3 C. Greenwood, 'New World Order or Old? The Invasion of Kuwait and the Rule of Law', *Modern Law Review* (1992) 55: 153–178, p. 159.

4 See SC Res 387 of 31 March 1976, and SC Res 454 of 2 November 1979.

5 SC Res 574 of 7 October 1985.

6 SC Res 577 of 6 December 1985.

7   SC Res 574 of 7 October 1985.
8   SC Res 455 of 23 November 1979.
9   SC Res 527 of 15 December 1982.
10 SC Res 568 of 21 June 1985.
11 SC Res 602 of 25 November 1987.
12 The embargo's lack of success may be implied from SC Res 574 of 7 October 1985, in which the Security Council reiterated its call to states to 'implement fully' the arms embargo first made mandatory eight years earlier.
13 SC Res 386 of 17 March 1976 and SC Res 411 of 30 June 1977.
14 SC Res 455 of 23 November 1979.
15 SC Res 573 of 4 October 1985.
16 For instance, the Security Council also condemned 'the act of armed aggression' committed against Benin (SC Res 405 of 14 April 1977) and the 'mercenary aggression' against the Seychelles (SC Res 496 of 15 December 1981 and SC Res 507 of 28 May 1982), without explicitly identifying the state from which such conduct originated, let alone making a determination under article 39.
17 This observation is discussed on pp. 80–81.
18 See, for example, SC Res 1088 of 12 December 1996, SC Res 1575 of 22 November 2004, and SC Res 1639 of 21 November 2005 on Bosnia and Herzegovina; SC Res 1079 of 15 November 1996, and SC Res 1120 of 14 July 1997 on Croatia; and SC Res 1244 of 10 June 1999 on Kosovo.
19 SC Res 1132 of 8 October 1997.
20 SC Res 1374 of 19 October 2001.
21 SC Res 788 of 19 November 1992.
22 SC Res 1529 of 29 February 2004.
23 SC Res 1125 of 6 August 1997 and SC Res 1136 of 6 November 1997.
24 SC Res 1464 of 4 February 2003.
25 SC Res 1267 of 15 October 1999 and SC Res 1333 of 19 December 2000.
26 SC Res 794 of 3 December 1992.
27 GA Res 377 of 3 November 1950.
28 In addition, one emergency session, dealing with the Six Day War of 1967, was convened on the basis of a letter from the Soviet Union under rule 20 of the General Assembly's rules of procedure.
29 First Emergency Special Session of the GA held on 7–10 November 1956 (see GA Res 997–1003 (ES-I)).
30 Second Emergency Special Session of the GA held on 4–10 November 1956 (see GA Res 1004–1005 (ES-II)).
31 Fifth Emergency Special Session of the GA held on 17 June–18 September 1967 (see GA Res 2252–2257 (ES-V)).
32 Sixth Emergency Special Session of the GA held on 10–14 January 1980 (see GA Res ES-6/2).
33 The General Assembly's three emergency special sessions referring to aggression were: (1) its seventh session in 1982, in which the General Assembly indicated it was 'deeply alarmed at the explosive situation in the Middle East resulting from the Israeli aggression against the sovereign state of Lebanon and the Palestinian people, which poses a threat to international peace and security' (see GA Res ES-7/7); (2) its eighth session in 1981 on Namibia; and (3) its ninth session in 1982 concerning the Israeli administration and occupation of the Golan Heights. The latter two emergency special sessions are discussed below.
34 SC Res 269 of 12 August 1969.
35 GA Res S-9/2 at paragraphs 10, 11 and 12 respectively. However, it should be noted that the General Assembly generally and somewhat pre-emptively stated that it 'considers that any attempt to annex a part or the whole of the Territory of South West Africa constitutes an act of aggression' (GA Res 1889 of 6 November 1963) and

siders further that any attempt to annex a part or the whole of Territory of South West Africa constitutes an act of aggression' (GA Res 2074 of 17 December 1965).

36 See GA Res 43/26 and SC Res 387 of 1976 respectively.

37 Where the Security Council can agree on what action to take, it is even less clear what value the General Assembly's moral judgments about the existence of aggression hold. Hence, what motivated the General Assembly's finding that 'the Central People's Government of People's Republic of China, by giving direct aid and assistance to those who were already committing aggression in Korea and by engaging in hostilities against United Nations forces there, has itself engaged in aggression in Korea' more than seven months after the Security Council had determined a breach of the peace had occurred, and almost four months after US forces crossed the 38th parallel, is uncertain.

38 Compare SC Res 530 of 19 May 1983 with GA Res 38/10 of 11 November 1983. However, despite the General Assembly's strong language in this resolution, it did not explicitly identify which state or states were the culprit/s.

39 See GA Res 37/233 of 20 December 1982; GA Res 38/36 of 1 December 1983; GA Res 39/50 of 12 December 1984; GA Res 40/97 of 13 December 1985; GA Res 42/14 of 6 November 1987; GA Res 43/26 of 17 November 1988.

40 See GA Res 39/146 of 14 December 1984; GA Res 40/168 of 16 December 1985; GA Res 41/162 of 4 December 1986; GA Res 42/209 of 11 December 1987; GA Res 43/54 of 6 December 1988; GA Res 44/40 of 4 December 1989 and GA Res 45/83 of 13 December 1990.

41 GA Res 46/242 of 25 August 1992. Also note GA Res 47/121 of 18 December 1992 and Res 48/88 of 20 December 1993 which include references to 'aggressive acts' and the 'continuation of aggression' respectively.

42 GA Res 49/10 of 3 November 1994.

43 See GA Res 49/87 and GA Res 49/88, both of 16 December 1994.

44 GA Res 60/40 of 1 December 2005.

45 See, for example, GA Res 50/159 of 28 February 1996, in which the General Assembly 'condemns all those from within and outside [Burundi] who are attacking innocent populations, arming extremists, heedlessly violating human rights and seriously undermining national peace and security'; GA Res 59/32 of 31 January 2005, in which the General Assembly 'reiterates its determination that any actions taken by Israel to impose its laws, jurisdiction and administration on the Holy City of Jerusalem are illegal and therefore null and void and have no validity whatsoever'; and GA Res 53/203A-B of 12 February 1999 in which the General Assembly

> condemns the fact that foreign military support to the Afghan parties continued unabated through 1998 and calls upon all States strictly to refrain from any outside interference [in Afghanistan] and immediately to end ... the presence and involvement of any foreign military, paramilitary or secret service personnel.

46 See, for example, the Questions of Interpretation and Application of the 1971 Montreal Convention arising from the Aerial Incident at Lockerbie (*Libyan Arab Jamahiriya* v. *United Kingdom*), *(Libyan Arab Jamahiriya* v. *United States) (1992–2003)* cases, which were discontinued at the request of Libya, the UK and the USA; and the Aerial Incident of 3 July 1988 (*Islamic Republic of Iran* v. *United States of America*) *(1989–1996)*, which was discontinued at the request of Iran and the USA. Further details are available at www.icj-cij.org/icjwww/idecisions.htm.

47 *Military and Paramilitary Activities in and Against Nicaragua (Nicaragua* v. *United States of America) (1984–1991)* (available at www.icj-cij.org/icjwww/idecisions.htm).

48 As summarised by the ICJ in its judgment on admissibility (hereinafter 'Admissibility Judgment'), p. 431, paragraph 89 (available at www.icj-cij.org/icjwww/icases/inus/inusframe.htm).

49 'Admissibility Judgment', p. 434, paragraph 94 (available at www.icj-cij.org/icjwww/icases/inus/inusframe.htm).

50 *Military and Paramilitary Activities in and Against Nicaragua (Nicaragua v. United States of America) (1984–1991)* (available at www.icj-cij.org/icjwww/idecisions.htm).

51 'Merits Judgment', p. 103, paragraph 195 (available at www.icj-cij.org/icjwww/icases/inus/inusframe.htm). Article 3 states:

> Any of the following acts, regardless of a declaration of war, shall, subject to and in accordance with the provisions of art 2, qualify as an act of aggression.... (g) The sending by or on behalf of a State of armed bands, groups, irregulars, or mercenaries, which carry out acts of armed force against another State of such gravity as to amount to the acts listed above, or its substantial involvement therein.

52 *Democratic Republic of the Congo v. Uganda) (1999–2005)* (available at www.icj-cij.org/icjwww/idecisions.htm).

53 see 'Application Instituting Proceedings' of 23 June 1999, p. 17 (available at www.icj-cij.org/icjwww/idocket/ico/icoapplication/ico_iapplication_19990623.pdf).

54 In his declaration, Judge Koroma points out that the events forming the subject of the case cost three to four million lives ('Declaration of Judge Koroma', paragraph 1), and Judge Simma emphasises that during the events in question, Uganda controlled Congolese territory the size of Germany ('Separate Opinion of Judge Simma', paragraph 2 (available at www.icj-cij.org/icjwww/idocket/ico/icoframe.htm)).

55 'Judgment of 19 December 2005', paragraph 165 (available at www.icj-cij.org/icjwww/idocket/ico/icoframe.htm).

56 'Country Profile: Democratic Republic of Congo', 30 April 2008 (available at news.bbc.co.uk/1/hi/world/africa/country_profiles/1076399.stm).

57 'Separate Opinion of Judge Elaraby', paragraph 17 (available at www.icj-cij.org/icjwww/idocket/ico/icoframe.htm).

58 'Separate Opinion of Judge Elaraby', paragraph 20.

59 'Separate Opinion of Judge Simma', paragraphs 2, 3 and 15 respectively (emphasis in original). The Democratic Republic of the Congo also filed separate applications similarly requesting declarations that Burundi and Rwanda had committed 'acts of armed aggression' against it, but these proceedings were later discontinued (see Press Release 2001/2 of 1 February 2001 (available at www.icj-cij.org/icjwww/idocket/icb/icbframe.htm)). The Congo later sought to make a fresh application against Rwanda on 28 May 2002, but the ICJ ruled on 3 February 2006 that it had no jurisdiction to hear the matter on the basis that Rwanda had not consented to the proceedings (see Press Release 2006/4 (available at www.icj-cij.org/icjwww/idocket/icrw/icrwframe.htm)).

60 The ICJ's reluctance to make rulings which confirm the possibility of state criminality may also be implied from its 2007 judgment that the state of Serbia did not commit genocide during the 1990s Bosnian war, but did violate its obligation to prevent genocide under the Genocide Convention in relation to the Srebrenica genocide of 1995 (see ICJ Press Release of 26 February 2007 (available at www.icj-cij.org/presscom/index.php?pr=1897&pt=1&p1=6&p2=1)).

9 Conclusion

1 UN Press Briefing of 31 January 2007, which opens with 'while progress had been made on the definition of aggression' (available at www.un.org/News/briefings/docs/2007/070131_Wenaweser.doc.htm).

2 'Discussion Paper on the Crime of Aggression Proposed by the Chairman (Revision June 2008)' (available at www.icc-cpi.int/library/asp/ICC-ASP-6-SWGCA-2__English.pdf, paragraph 8).

3 'Report of the Special Working Group on the Crime of Aggression', January 2007 (available at www.icc-cpi.int/library/asp/Report_SWGCA_English.pdf, paragraph 22).

4 'Informal Intersessional Meeting of the Special Working Group on the Crime of Aggression', November–December 2006 (available at www.icc-cpi.int/library/asp/ICC-ASP-5-SWGCA-INF1_English.pdf report, paragraph 23).

5 'Discussion Paper 2 The Conditions for the Exercise of Jurisdiction with respect to the Crime of Aggression', November–December 2005 (available at www.icc-cpi.int/library/asp/Discussion_paper_2-annex_II_C_-_English.pdf, opening paragraph).

6 UN Press Briefing of 31 January 2007 (available at www.un.org/News/briefings/docs/2007/070131_Wenaweser.doc.htm).

7 G. Boas *et al.*, *Forms of Responsibility in International Criminal Law*, Cambridge: Cambridge University Press, 2008, p. 10.

8 *Prosecutor* v. *Tadic*, Case No. IT-94–1-A, Judgment, 15 July 1999, paragraphs 196–204.

9 *Prosecutor* v. *Milosevic*, Case No. IT-01–50-I, Indictment, 2001 (available at www.un.org/icty/indictment/english/mil-ii011008e.htm,paragraph 6).

10 *Prosecutor* v. *Taylor*, Case No. SCSL-03-I, Indictment, 3 March 2003, paragraph 23.

11 *Prosecutor* v. *Taylor*, paragraph 24.

12 *Prosecutor* v. *Taylor*, Prosecution's Second Amended Indictment', 29 May 2007 (available at www.sc-sl.org/Documents/Taylor/SCSL-03–01-PT-263.pdf, paragraph 33).

13 Article 1 (b) of the Statute (available at www.ictj.org/static/MENA/Iraq/iraq.cpaorder48.121003.eng.pdf).

14 'Defiant Saddam Rejects Court, Charges', 1 July 2004 (available at www.cnn.com/2004/WORLD/meast/07/01/iraq.saddam/index.html).

15 'Timeline: Anfal Trial', 24 June 2007 (available at news.bbc.co.uk/1/hi/world/middle_east/5272224.stm).

16 Human Rights Watch, *Judging Dujail: the First Trial Before the Iraqi High Tribunal*, November 2006 (available at www.hrw.org/reports/2006/iraq1106/6.htm#_Toc151270364, p. 83).

17 L. Beehner, 'Iraq: Saddam's Trial', *Background Paper of the Council on Foreign Relations*, 14 March 2006 (available at www.cfr.org/publication/8750/#8).

18 Human Rights Watch, *Judging Dujail*, p. 87.

19 This was the view of BBC reporter Jim Muir, in Baghdad at the time, who claimed 'while many Kurds would have liked to see Saddam himself executed for the crimes, Majid ["Chemical Ali"] personified Anfal for them and was thus a good second-best' ("Chemical Ali" Sentenced to Hang', 24 June 2007, available at news.bbc.co.uk/1/hi/world/middle_east/6233926.stm).

20 Another example drawn from domestic criminal law lending support to this conclusion is the recent House of Lords case of *R* v. *Jones; R* v. *Milling; R* v. *Olditch; R* v. *Pritchard; R* v. *Richards; Ayliffe* v. *Director of Public Prosecutions; Swain* v. *Director of Public Prosecutions* [2006] UKHL 16, in which it was decided that the crime of aggression was not capable of constituting a 'crime' under s3 of the Criminal Law Act 1967 (UK), nor an 'offence' within the meaning of s68(2) of the Criminal Justice and Public Order Act 1994 (UK). The defendants, peace protesters, had sought to defend their actions against British military bases on the eve of the Iraq War on the grounds that they were intended to prevent the crime of unlawfully going to war. For further discussion, see J.-Y. Gilg, 'International Aggression Not a Crime', *Solicitors Journal* (31 March 2006) 150: 374.

21 The results of secret polls conducted by the USA and released in 2002 revealed that the majority of Germans felt this way from the 1970s (see 'Germany Marks Nuremberg Tribunals', 20 November 2005 (available at news.bbc.co.uk/2/hi/europe/4453790.stm)). Strong and vocal German support for the inclusion of the crime of aggression in the Rome Statute also suggests that Germany upholds the validity of the Nuremberg Trial.

22 Article 36, UN Charter (available at www.uncharter.org).

23 Article 33, UN Charter (available at www.uncharter.org).

24 See Chapter 1, p. 9.

Bibliography

Aerial Incident of 3 July 1988 (Islamic Republic of Iran v. United States of America) *(1989–1996)*, available at www.icj-cij.org/icjwww/idecisions.htm.

Agreement Between the Governments of the United Kingdom and the United States of America on the Principles Applying to Mutual Aid in the Prosecution of the War Against Aggression (the Lend–Lease Agreement) of 23 February, 1942, available at www.yale.edu/lawweb/avalon/decade/decade04.htm.

Allied and Associated Powers (1914–1920), *The Treaties of Peace 1919–1923*, New York: Carnegie Endowment for International Peace, 1924.

Anon, 'The Use of Analogy in Criminal Law', *Columbia Law Review* (1947) 47: 613–629.

Appleman, J. A., *Military Tribunals and International Crimes*, Indianapolis: The Bobbs-Merrill Company, 1954.

Archibugi, D., 'Cosmopolitan Democracy and Its Critics: A Review', *European Journal of International Relations* (2004) 10(3): 437–473.

R v. Bartle and the Commissioner of Police for the Metropolis and Others, Ex Parte Pinochet; R v. Evans and Another and the Commissioner of Police for the Metropolice and Others, Ex Parte Pinochet [1999] UKHL 17.

Bassiouni, M. C., 'Observations Concerning the 1997–1998 Preparatory Committee's Work', *Nouvelles Etudes Penales*, Chicago: International Human Rights Law Institute, 1997, vol. 13, no. 5.

Battle, G. G., 'The Trials Before the Leipsic Supreme Court of Germans Accused of War Crimes', *Virginia Law Review* (1921) 8: 1.

Beehner, L., 'Iraq: Saddam's Trial', *Background Paper of the Council on Foreign Relations*, 14 March 2006, available at www.cfr.org/publication/8750/#8.

Bloxham, D., '"The Trial That Never Was": Why There Was No Second International Trial of Major War Criminals at Nuremberg', *History* (2002) 87: 41–60.

Boas, G. *et al.*, *Forms of Responsibility in International Criminal Law*, Cambridge: Cambridge University Press, 2008.

Boemeke, M. F. (ed.), *The Treaty of Versailles: A Reassessment After 75 Years*, New York: Cambridge University Press, 1998.

Boister, N. and R. Cryer, *The Tokyo International Military Tribunal: A Reappraisal*, Oxford: Oxford University Press, 2008.

Borchard, E., 'The Dumbarton Oaks Conference', *American Journal of International Law* (1945) 39: 97–101.

Bos, A., 'The Experience of the Preparatory Committee', in M. Politi and G. Nesi (eds) *The Rome Statute of the International Criminal Court*, Aldershot: Ashgate, 2001, pp. 17–28.

Brackman, A. C., *The Other Nuremberg: The Untold Story of the Tokyo War Crimes Trials*, New York: Quill, 1987.

Broms, B., *The Definition of Aggression in the United Nations*, Turku: Turun Yliopisto, 1968.

Brown, C., *International Relations Theory: New Normative Approaches*, Hemel Hempstead: Harvester, 1992.

Bull, H., *The Anarchical Society*, London: Macmillan, 1977.

Cairo Declaration of December 1, 1943, available at www.yale.edu/lawweb/avalon/wwii/cairo.htm.

Campbell, T. M., 'US Motives in the Veto Power', *International Organization* (1974) 28: 557–560.

Campbell, T. M., 'Nationalism in America's UN Policy 1944–1945', *International Organization* (1973) 27: 25–44.

'"Chemical Ali" Sentenced to Hang', 24 June 2007, available at news.bbc.co.uk/1/hi/world/middle_east/6233926.stm.

'Country Profile: Democratic Republic of Congo', 30 April 2008, available at news.bbc.co.uk/1/hi/world/africa/country_profiles/1076399.stm.

Covenant of the League of Nations, 28 June 1919, available at avalon.law.yale.edu/20th_century/leagcov.asp.

'Defiant Saddam Rejects Court, Charges', 1 July 2004, available at www.cnn.com/2004/WORLD/meast/07/01/iraq.saddam/index.html.

Democratic Republic of the Congo v. Uganda (1999–2005), available at www.icj-cij.org/icjwww/idecisions.htm.

Department of State Publication 3080, *Report of Robert H. Jackson, United States Representative to the International Conference on Military Trials: London, 1945*, Washington: Government Printing Office, 1949, available at www.yale.edu/lawweb/avalon/imt/jackson/jack37.htm.

Dinstein, Y., *War, Aggression and Self-defence*, Cambridge: Cambridge University Press, 2005.

'Discussion Paper 2 The Conditions for the Exercise of Jurisdiction with respect to the Crime of Aggression', November–December 2005, available at www.icc-cpi.int/library/asp/Discussion_paper_2-annex_II_C_-_English.pdf.

'Discussion Paper on the Crime of Aggression Proposed by the Chairman (Revision June 2008)', available at www.icc-cpi.int/library/asp/ICC-ASP-6-SWGCA-2__English.pdf.

Doppelt, G., 'Walzer's Theory of Morality in International Relations', *Philosophy and Public Affairs* (1978) 8(1): 3–27.

Draft Code of Crimes Against the Peace and Security of Mankind, 1996, available at untreaty.un.org/ilc/texts/instruments/English/draft%20articles/7_4_1996.pdf.

'Draft Code of Crimes Against the Peace and Security of Mankind: Report of the Working Group on the Question of an International Criminal Jurisdiction' (A/CN.4/L.471), *Yearbook of the International Law Commission*, 1992.

Draft Statute for an International Criminal Court, 1994, available at untreaty.un.org/ilc/texts/instruments/english/draft%20articles/7_4_1994.pdf.

Eagleton, C., 'The Charter Adopted at San Francisco', *American Political Science Review* (1945) 39: 934–942.

Egerton, G. W., *Great Britain and the Creation of the League of Nations*, London: Scholar Press, 1979.

Ehard, H., 'The Nuremberg Trial Against the Major War Criminals and International Law', *American Journal of International Law* (1949) 43: 223–245.

Elcock, H., *Portrait of a Decision: the Council of Four and the Treaty of Versailles*, London: Eyre Methuen, 1972.

Erskine, T., 'Qualifying Cosmopolitanism? Solidarity, Criticism, and Michael Walzer's "View from the Cave"', *International Politics* (2007) 44: 125–149.

Farrell, S., 'Interview with Hamas leader Dr Mahmoud al-Zahar', *London Times*, 27 January 2006, available at www.timesonline.co.uk/article/0,,251-2012808,00.html.

Ferencz, B., *Defining International Aggression: The Search for World Peace*, New York: Dobbs Ferry, 1975, 2 vols.

Ferencz, B., 'Can Aggression Be Deterred By Law?', *Pace International Law Review* (1999) 11(2): 341–360.

Finch, G. A., 'The United Nations Charter', *American Journal of International Law* (1945) 39: 541–546.

Finch, G. A., 'The Nuremberg Trial and International Law', *American Journal of International Law* (1947) 41: 20–37.

Fox, W. T. R. 'Collective Enforcement of Peace and Security', *American Political Science Review* (1945) 39: 970–981.

Gaddis, J. L., 'Order versus Justice: An American Foreign Policy Dilemma', in R. Foot, J. L. Gaddis and A. Hurrell (eds) *Order and Justice in International Relations*, Oxford: Oxford University Press, 2002, pp. 155–175.

Garthodd, R. L., *Detente and Confrontation: American-Soviet Relations from Nixon to Reagan*, Washington DC: Brookings Institute, 1994.

'Germany Marks Nuremberg Tribunals', 20 November 2005, available at news.bbc.co.uk/2/hi/europe/4453790.stm.

Gilg, J.-Y., 'International Aggression Not a Crime', *Solicitors Journal* (31 March 2006) 150: 374.

Goodrich L. M. and E. Hambro, *Charter of the United Nations: Commentary and Documents*, Boston: World Peace Foundation, 1949.

Greenwood, C., 'New World Order or Old? The Invasion of Kuwait and the Rule of Law', *Modern Law Review* (1992) 55: 153–178.

Griffiths, M., *Fifty Key Thinkers in International Relations*, London: Routledge, 2000.

Hall, J., 'Nulla Poena Sine Lege', *The Yale Law Journal* (1937) 47: 165–193.

Harris, W. R., *Tyranny on Trial*, Dallas: Southern Methodist University Press, 1954.

Held, D., 'Law of States, Law of Peoples: Three Models of Sovereignty', *Legal Theory* (2002) 8: 1–44.

Held, D. and H. Patomaki, 'Problems of Global Democracy', *Theory, Culture and Society* (2006) 23(5): 115–133.

Hilderbrand, R. C., *Dumbarton Oaks*, Chapel Hill: University of North Carolina Press, 1990.

Hoopes, T. and D. Brinkley, *FDR and the Creation of the UN*, New Haven: Yale University Press, 1997.

Hoover, H., *America's First Crusade*, New York: Charles Scribner's Sons, 1942.

Horwitz, S., 'The Tokyo Trial', *International Conciliation* (1950) 28: 473–584.

Human Rights Watch, *Judging Dujail: the First Trial Before the Iraqi High Tribunal*, November 2006, available at www.hrw.org/reports/2006/iraq1106/6.htm#_Toc151270364.

ICJ Press Release 2001/2 of 1 February 2001, available at www.icj-cij.org/icjwww/idocket/icb/icbframe.htm.

ICJ Press Release 2006/4, available at www.icj-cij.org/icjwww/idocket/icrw/icrwframe.htm.

ICJ Press Release of 26 February 2007, available at www.icj-cij.org/presscom/index. php?pr=1897&pt=1&p1=6&p2=1.

'Informal Intersessional Meeting of the Special Working Group on the Crime of Aggression', November–December 2006, available at www.icc-cpi.int/library/asp/ICC-ASP-5-SWGCA-INF1_English.pdf.

Japanese Qualified Acceptance of the Potsdam Declaration of 10 August 1945, available at www.ibiblio.org/hyperwar/PTO/IMTFE/IMTFE-A1.html#A1a.

R v. *Jones; R* v. *Milling; R* v. *Olditch; R* v. *Pritchard; R* v. *Richards; Ayliffe* v. *Director of Public Prosecutions; Swain* v. *Director of Public Prosecutions* [2006] UKHL 16.

'Judgment of 19 December 2005', Democrative Republic of Congo v Uganda, available at www.icj-cij.org/docket/files/116/10455.pdf.

Kelsen, H., 'The Old and the New League: The Covenant and the Dumbarton Oaks Proposals', *American Journal of International Law* (1945) 39: 45–83.

Keynes, J. M., *The Economic Consequences of the Peace*, London: Macmillan, 1919.

Knight, S., 'Asia Alert After North Korean Threat to Test Nuclear Weapon', *London Times*, 3 October 2006, available at www.timesonline.co.uk/article/0,,3–2385992,00. html.

Knock, T. J., *To End All Wars: Woodrow Wilson and the Quest for a New World Order*, New York: Oxford University Press, 1992.

Kochavi, A. J., 'Britain and the Establishment of the United Nations War Crimes Commission', *The English Historical Review* (1992) 107: 323–349.

Kochavi, A., *Prelude to Nuremberg*, Chapel Hill: UNC Press, 1998.

Korman, S., *Right of Conquest: The Forcible Acquisition of Territory in International Law and Practice*, Oxford: Clarendon Press, 1996.

Lamont, T. W., 'Reparations', in E. M. House and C. S. Seymour (eds), *What Really Happened at Paris*, London: Hodder & Stoughton, 1921, pp. 259–290.

Lansing, R., *The Peace Negotiations: A Personal Narrative*, Boston: Houghton Mifflin, 1921.

Lauterpacht, H., *The Function of Law in the International Community*, Oxford: Clarendon Press, 1933.

Lawrence, J. (ed.), *Francisco de Vitoria: Political Writings*, Cambridge: Cambridge University Press, 1991.

Levin, N. G., *Woodrow Wilson and World Politics*, Oxford: Oxford University Press, 1968.

Link, A. S. (ed.), *The Papers of Woodrow Wilson*, Princeton: Princeton University Press, 1966, vol. 54.

Litvinov, M. M., *Against Aggression*, London, 1939.

Liu, J. T. C., 'The Tokyo Trial: Source Materials', *Far Eastern Survey* (1948) 17: 168–170.

Lodge, H. C., *The Senate and the League of Nations*, New York: C Scribner's Sons, 1925.

Lowe, P., 'The Tokyo Trial of Japanese Leaders, 1946–1948', in R. A. Melikan (ed.), *Domestic and International Trials 1700–2000*, Manchester: Manchester University Press, 2003, pp. 137–156.

Macmillan, M. O., *Peacemakers*, London: John Murray, 2003.

Maga, T. P., *Judgment at Tokyo*, Lexington: University Press of Kentucky, 2001.

Maguire, P., *Law and War: An American Story*, New York: Columbia University Press, 2001.

'Merits Judgment', *Military and Paramilitary Activities in and against Nicaragua, (Nicaragua* v. *United States of America)*, ICJ Reports 1986.

Miliband, D., 'Russia Will Not Benefit From Its Aggression', *London Times*, 19 August

2008, available at www.timesonline.co.uk/tol/comment/columnists/guest_contributors/ article4560698.ece.

Military and Paramilitary Activities in and Against Nicaragua (Nicaragua v. *United States of America) (1984–1991)*, available at www.icj-cij.org/icjwww/idecisions.htm.

Miller, D. H., *The Drafting of the Covenant*, New York: GP Putnam's Sons, 1928, 2 vols.

Minear, R. H., *Victors' Justice: the Tokyo War Crimes Trial*, Princeton: Princeton University Press, 1971.

Morgenthau, H., *Politics Among Nations*, New York: Knopf, 1955 (2nd edn).

Morrice, D., 'The Liberal–Communitarian Debate in Contemporary Political Philosophy and its Significance for International Relations', *Review of International Studies* (2000) 26: 233–251.

Mullins, C., *The Leipzig Trials*, London: H.F. and G. Witherby, 1922.

Nakamura, T., *A History of Showa Japan 1926–1989*, Tokyo: University of Tokyo Press, 1998.

National Diet Library of Japan, *Historical Figures*. 2003–2004, available at www.ndl.go.jp/ constitution/e/etc/figures.html.

Nicolson, H., *Peacemaking 1919*, London: Constable, 1934.

Noble, G. B., *Policies and Options at Paris, 1919*, New York: Macmillan, 1935.

Nobutaka, I., *Japan's Decision For War*, California: Stanford University Press, 1967.

Northedge, F. S., *The League of Nations its Life and Times 1920–1946*, Leicester: Leicester University Press, 1986.

Nowak, K. F. (trans. by N. Thomas and E. W. Dickes), *Versailles*, London: Victor Gollancz, 1928.

Persico, J. E., *Nuremberg: Infamy on Trial*, New York: Viking, 1994.

Piccigallo, P. R., *The Japanese on Trial*, Austin: University of Texas Press, 1979.

Pompe, C. A., *Aggressive War an International Crime*, The Hague: Martinus Nijhoff, 1953.

Potsdam Declaration of 26 July 1945, available at www.ibiblio.org/hyperwar/PTO/Dip/ Potsdam.html.

Pritchard, R. J., 'The International Military Tribunal for the Far East and its Contemporary Resonances', *Military Law Review* (1995) 149: 25–36.

Pritchard, R. J. (ed.), *The Tokyo Major War Crimes Trial: The Records of the International Military Tribunal for the Far East*, New York: The Edwin Mellen Press, 1998.

Pritchard, R. J. and S. M. Zaide, *Tokyo War Crimes Trial Index and Guide*, New York: Garland, 1987.

'Proposals for the Establishment of a General International Organization', 7 October 1944, available at www.ibiblio.org/pha/policy/1944/441007a.html.

Prosecutor v. *Milosevic*, Case No. IT-01–50-I, Indictment, 2001, available at www.un.org/ icty/indictment/english/mil-ii011008e.htm.

Prosecutor v. *Tadic*, Case No. IT-94–1-A, Judgment, 15 July 1999, available at www. specialcourt.org/documents/WhatHappening/Indictments.html.

Prosecutor v. *Taylor*, Case No. SCSL-03-I, Indictment, 3 March 2003, available at www. icty.org/x/cases/tadic/acjug/en/tad-aj990715e.pdf.

Prosecutor v. *Taylor*, Prosecution's Second Amended Indictment', 29 May 2007, available at www.sc-sl.org/Documents/Taylor/SCSL-03–01-PT-263.pdf.

Questions of Interpretation and Application of the 1971 Montreal Convention arising from the Aerial Incident at Lockerbie (Libyan Arab Jamahiriya v. United Kingdom), *(Libyan Arab Jamahiriya* v. *United States) (1992–2003)*, available at www.icj-cij.org/ icjwww/idecisions.htm.

Rengger, N., 'A City Which Sustains All Things? Communitarianism and International Society', *Millennium* (1992) 21: 353–369.

Reply by Secretary of State to Japanese Qualified Acceptance of 11 August 1945, available at www.ibiblio.org/hyperwar/PTO/IMTFE/IMTFE-A1.html#A1b.

'Report by Ricardo J. Alfaro, Special Rapporteur' (A/CN.4/15*), *ILC Yearbook*, 1950.

'Report by J. Spiropoulos, Special Rapporteur' (A/CN.4/25), *Yearbook of the International Law Commission*, 1950.

'Report of the 1953 Committee on International Criminal Jurisdiction 27 July–20 August 1953' (A/2645), *General Assembly Official Records* Ninth Session, Supplement No. 12.

'Report of the International Law Commission to the General Assembly' (A/1858), *Yearbook of the International Law Commission*, 1951.

'Report of the International Law Commission on the Work of its Forty-sixth Session, 2 May–22 July 1994' (A/49/10), *Yearbook of the International Law Commission*, 1994.

'Report of the Preparatory Committee on the Establishment of an International Criminal Court' (A/51/22), *General Assembly Official Records*, 51st Sess., 1996.

'Report of the Preparatory Committee on the Establishment of an International Criminal Court' (A/CONF.183/2/Add.1) of 14 April 1998, p. 12, available at www.un.org/icc/prepcom.htm.

'Report of the Special Working Group on the Crime of Aggression', January 2007, available at www.icc-cpi.int/library/asp/Report_SWGCA_English.pdf.

Rome Statute of the International Criminal Court (UN Doc. A/CONF.183/9*), 17 June 1998, available at untreaty.un.org/cod/icc/statute/romefra.htm.

Ruggie, J. G., 'Third Try at World Order? America and Multilateralism After the Cold War', *Political Science Quarterly* (1994) 109: 553–570.

Scharf, M. P., 'Have We Really Learned the Lessons of Nuremberg?', *Military Law Review* (1995) 149: 65–71.

Schick, F. B., 'The Nuremberg Trial and the International Law of the Future', *American Journal of International Law* (1947) 41: 770–794.

Schick, F. B., 'Crimes Against Peace', *Journal of Criminal Law and Criminology* (1948) 38: 445–465.

Schwarzenberger, G., *The League of Nations and World Order*, London: Constable & Co, 1936.

Scott, G., *The Rise and Fall of the League of Nations*, London: Hutchinson, 1973.

Scott, J. B., 'The Trial of the Kaiser', in E. M. House and C. S. Seymour, *What Really Happened at Paris*, London: Hodder & Stoughton, 1921, pp. 231–258.

Scott, J. B. (ed.), *Selections from Three Works*, Oxford: Clarendon Press, 1944.

Senate Committee on Foreign Relations and the Department of State, *A Decade of American Foreign Policy: Basic Documents, 1941–1949*, Washington: GPO, 1950.

'Separate Opinion of Judge Elaraby', *Democratic Republic of Congo* v. *Uganda*, 19 December 2005, available at www.icj-cij.org/docket/files/116/10465.pdf.

'Separate Opinion of Judge Simma', *Democratic Republic of Congo* v. *Uganda*, 19 December 2005, available at www.icj-cij.org/docket/files/116/10467.pdf.

Seymour, C., *Intimate Papers of Colonel House*, London: Ernest Benn, 1926.

Shannon, V., 'Wendt's Violation of the Constructivist Project: Agency and Why a World State is *Not* Inevitable', *European Journal of International Relations* (2005) 11(4): 581–587.

Sharp, W. R., *Contemporary International Politics*, New York: Rinehart and Co, 1940.

Shillony, B-A., *Politics and Culture in Wartime Japan*, Oxford: Clarendon Press, 1981.

Smith, B. F., *The Road to Nuremberg*, London: André Deutsch, 1981.

Smith, B. F. (ed.), *The American Road to Nuremberg: the Documentary Record 1944–1945*, Stanford: Hoover Institution Press, 1982.

Smith, S., Lt the Honourable, *Australian Campaigns in the Great War*, Melbourne: Macmillan, 1919.

Sprecher, D. A., *Inside the Nuremberg Tribunal*, Lanham: University Press of America Inc, 1999.

Statute of the International Court of Justice, 26 June 1945, available at un.by/en/documents/statut/.

Statute of the Iraqi Special Tribunal, 12 October 2003, available at www.ictj.org/static/MENA/Iraq/iraq.cpaorder48.121003.eng.pdf.

Stone, J., *Aggression and World Order*, London: Stevens & Sons, 1958.

Stone, J., *Conflict Through Consensus*, Baltimore: The Johns Hopkins University Press, 1977.

'Summary Records of the Meetings of the Fortieth Session: 2085th Meeting', *Yearbook of the International Law Commission*, 1988.

'Summary Records of the Meetings of the Forty-third Session: 2237th Meeting', *Yearbook of the International Law Commission*, 1991.

'Summary Records of the Meetings of the Forty-seventh Session: 2408th Meeting', *Yearbook of the International Law Commission*, 1995.

Taylor, T., *Final Report to the Secretary of the Army on the Nuremberg War Crimes Trials under Control Council law No. 10*, Washington: GPO, 1949, available at www.yale.edu/lawweb/avalon/imt/imt10.htm.

Telegram from Henry Stimson to John McCloy, John Weir and R. A. Cutter, April 1945, available at www.trumanlibrary.org/whistlestop/study_collections/nuremberg.

Temperley, H. W. V., *A History of the Peace Conference of Paris*, London: Henry Fraude, 1920.

Thiam, D., 'Second Report on the Draft Code of Offences Against the Peace and Security of Mankind' (A/CN.4/377*), *Yearbook of the International Law Commission*, 1984.

Thiam, D., 'Fourth Report on the Draft Code of Offences Against the Peace and Security of Mankind' (A/CN.4/398), *Yearbook of the International Law Commission*, 1986.

Thiam, D., 'Eleventh Report on the Draft Code of Crimes Against the Peace and Security of Mankind' (A/CN.4/449), *Yearbook of the International Law Commission*, 1993.

'Timeline: Anfal Trial', 24 June 2007, available at news.bbc.co.uk/1/hi/world/middle_east/5272224.stm.

Tokyo Charter, 19 January 1946, available at www.yale.edu/lawweb/avalon/imtfech.htm.

'Tokyo Judgment', 1949, available at www.ibiblio.org/hyperwar/PTO/IMTFE/IMTFE-9.html.

Toynbee, A. J., 'The Main Features in the Landscape', in Lord Riddell (ed.) *The Treaty of Versailles and After*, London: George Allen & Unwin, 1935.

Tusa, A., and J. Tusa, *The Nuremberg Trial*, London: Macmillan, 1984.

United Nations Conference on International Organization Documents, London: United Nations Information Organisation, 1945.

United Nations Diplomatic Conference of Plenipotentiaries on the Establishment of an International Criminal Court Official Records (Rome, 15 June–17 July 1998), New York: United Nations, 2002.

United Nations, *Historical Review of Developments Relating to Aggression*, New York: United Nations, 2003.

UN Press Briefing of 31 January 2007, available at www.un.org/News/briefings/docs/2007/070131_Wenaweser.doc.htm.

USA v. *Von Leeb et al.*, Nuremberg, 1948, 11 *NMT* 462, 486.

Waldron, J., 'What is Cosmopolitan?', *The Journal of Political Philosophy* (2000) 8: 227–243.

Walker, J., *State Morality and A League of Nations*, London: TF Unwin, 1919.

Walters, F. P., *History of the League of Nations*, Oxford: Oxford University Press, 1952.

Walzer, M., *Just and Unjust Wars*, New York: Basic Books, 1977.

Walzer, M., 'The Moral Standing of States: A Response to Four Critics', *Philosophy and Public Affairs* (1980) 9(3): 209–229.

Walzer, M., *Thick and Thin: Moral Argument at Home and Abroad*, Notre Dame, IN: University of Notre Dame Press, 1994.

Wasserstrom, R., 'Review of Michael Walzer's *Just and Unjust Wars*', *Harvard Law Review* (December 1978) 92: 536–545.

Webster, C. K., *The League of Nations in Theory and Practice*, London: Allen & Unwin, 1933.

Weidenbaum, P., 'Liberal Thought and Undefined Crimes', *Journal of Comparative Legislation and International Law* (1937) 19: 90–97.

Wendt, A., 'Why a World State is Inevitable', *European Journal of International Relations* (2003) 9(4): 491–542.

Westermann, W. L., 'The Armenian Problem and the Disruption of Turkey', in E. M. House and C. S. Seymour (eds) *What Really Happened at Paris*, London: Hodder & Stoughton, 1921.

Whelen, F., *The Covenant Explained, For Speakers and Study Circles*, London: League of Nations Union, 1935.

Williams, B., *State Security and the League of Nations*, Baltimore: Johns Hopkins Press, 1927.

World Peace Foundation, *Second Yearbook of the League of Nations: Record of 1921*, Boston, 1922.

World Peace Foundation, *Fourth Yearbook of the League of Nations: Record of 1923*, Boston, 1924.

World Peace Foundation, *Sixth Yearbook of the League of Nations: Record of 1925*, Boston, 1926.

World Peace Foundation, *League of Nations Official Journal* 1926.

World Peace Foundation, *League of Nations Official Journal* 1928.

World Peace Foundation, *League of Nations Official Journal* 1932.

World Peace Foundation, *League of Nations Official Journal* 1939.

Wright, Q., 'The Concept of Aggression in International Law', *American Journal of International Law* (1935) 29(3): 373–395.

Wright, Q., 'The Prevention of Aggression', *American Journal of International Law* (1956) 50(3): 514–532.

Wright, Q., *The Role of International Law in the Elimination of War*, Manchester: Manchester University Press, 1961.

Zimmern, A., 'The League's Handling of the Italo-Abyssinian Dispute', *International Affairs* (1935) 14: 751–768.

Zimmern, A. E., *The League of Nations and the Rule of Law 1918–1935*, London: Macmillan, 1939.

Index

References to notes are prefixed by *n*.

For Product Safety Concerns and Information please contact our EU
representative GPSR@taylorandfrancis.com
Taylor & Francis Verlag GmbH, Kaufingerstraße 24, 80331 München, Germany

www.ingramcontent.com/pod-product-compliance
Lightning Source LLC
Chambersburg PA
CBHW050712280326
41926CB00088B/3004

9780415691567